MARXISM AFTER MARX
REVOLUTIONARY POLITICS & PROSPECTS

Marxism After Marx:
Revolutionary Politics & Prospects
Text © 2016 Herb Gamberg,
Tony Thomson, and Zhanbin Ma
Design © 2016 Inkflight

ink/light

All rights reserved. No part of this book may be stored in a retrieval system, reproduced or transmitted in any form or by any other means without written permission from the publisher or a licence from the Canadian Copyright Licensing Agency. Critics and reviewers may quote brief passages in connection with a review or critical article in any media.

www.inkflight.com

Text set in Sabon.

Every reasonable effort has been made to contact the copyright holders of all material reproduced in this book.

FIRST EDITION / FIRST PRINTING

LIBRARY AND ARCHIVES CANADA CATALOGUING IN PUBLICATION

Gamberg, Herbert, 1933– author
  Marxism after Marx : revolutionary politics and prospects / Herb Gamberg, Tony Thomson, Zhanbin Ma.

Includes bibliographical references.
ISBN 978-1-77226-257-5 (paperback)

1. Communism.
2. Socialism.
3. Marx, Karl, 1818–1883.
I. Thomson, Anthony, 1949–, author
II. Ma, Zhanbin, 1963–, author
III. Title.

HX73.G34 2016   335.4   C2015-908408-3

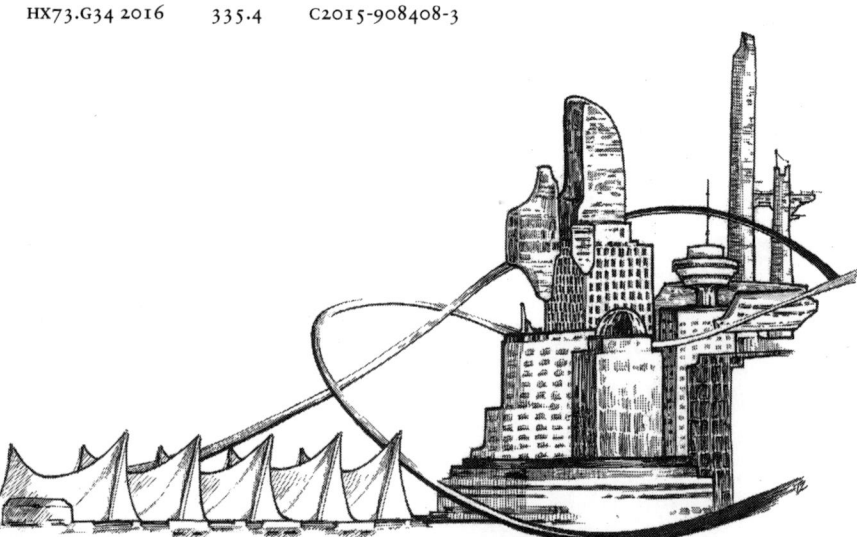

MARXISM AFTER MARX

REVOLUTIONARY POLITICS & PROSPECTS

HERB GAMBERG
TONY THOMSON
ZHANBIN MA

VANCOUVER:
INKFLIGHT
2016

CONTENTS

1 Introduction 7
2 Anarchism 15
3 Social Democracy and Reformism 73
4 Lenin and Leninism 117
5 Trotsky, Trotskyism, and Stalin 148
6 Mao and Marxism 206
7 Rural Revolution in China – Problems and Prospects 235
8 Feminism and Marxism 277
9 Conclusion 304
  Appendix 347
  Endnotes 350
  References 354

CHAPTER ONE

Introduction

It is extraordinary how prescient were the nineteenth century economic ideas of Karl Marx and Frederick Engels. The ideas of these thinkers, unlike virtually all others at the time, have demonstrated amazing power to explain and predict many of the contours of modern capitalist society. Capitalism has moved irrevocably from a system of small competitive enterprises to one of huge integrated corporations, still competitive but in different ways from the past. The orthodox ideas that defended the initiation of capitalism did not expect these results, and the ideas that continue to defend capitalism have great difficulty in defending the consequences reaped by gigantic enterprise. Only Marxism has clearly predicted and understood the meaning of oligopolistic capitalism. Marxism also predicted that in the process of this great change, the vast majority of workers, those who do the producing, selling, and information shuffling, would become propertyless leaving them with nothing to sell but their labour.

Even more important in the Marxist approach to capitalism has been its understanding of the inherently irrational nature of the system. Marxism pinpoints the factors that lead capitalism into inevitable and insoluble crises. While recognizing the unprecedentedly explosive powers of capitalism, only Marxism perceives and understands how the mode of this production produces misery, war, and perpetual instability. Fundamentally, capitalism at its beginnings and in its modern guise remains an exploitative system where the inherent drive to accumulate profit by paying workers as little as possible and selling the products of labour for as much as possible generates contradictions not solvable by any means as long as capitalism exists. Even in its present monopoly phase where prices of products are now more easily controlled and where the return on investment assumes more predictability, crises must continue to occur resulting from the more or less permanent stagnation of glutted corporations, which cannot find profitable investment and cannot sell all their produce to an inherently underpaid workforce. The famous epigram of Fourier in the nineteenth century that capitalism is the first system that suffers not from scarcity, but from a "crisis of plethora" has come to haunt the system with a vengeance. At the same time, the global spread of capitalism, especially to China and Russia, the insidious nature of speculative capital that was revealed in 2008, and the conundrum of climate change have introduced new dynamics to the crisis potential of the system.

The crises developing from these contradictions, said Marx, can only be resolved by doing away with capitalist production itself and introducing a system of democratic, cooperative control of property and its fruits. In short, there is no solution to the crises generated by capitalism except its transformation into socialism. In spite of the many contemporary factors that were, in the main, unforeseen by the originators of Marxism – the triumph of monopoly without an accession to socialism, the changes in the composition of the working class, the present quiescence of working-class consciousness in advanced capitalism, the rise of revolution in the technically backward parts of the world, the threats to the very viability of our species on the planet – it is still extraordinary how vital the Marxist economic analysis remains, especially when compared with the bankrupt and apologetic nature of other traditions.

Marxism is too often discussed by its adherents in economic terms alone where one can usually find a good deal of unanimity. But Marxism is also a political theory about the ideas and strategy that are meant to transform capitalism into socialism. Not only is this aspect less discussed, but in those unusual arenas where Marxist politics are the primary interest, there is often more conflict than unanimity. In fact, the world of Marxist politics is often so suffused with storm and stress that it has generated movements so at odds with each other that battles within Marxism appear more significant than battles with capitalism.

The writers of this book accept the view that only Marxist theory holds out hope not only for understanding capitalism, but for superseding the problems and depredations of capitalist societies. Having had some experience in the minefield of Marxist politics, we also realize that political Marxism is, in many ways, an area where even progressive people can get bogged down. The first questions a person facing the world of Marxist politics might ask are: "What are they all fighting about? Don't we all have the same enemy, and can't we easily get together to fight it?"

These are legitimate questions and they are often difficult to answer, especially in the realm of ideas alone. Often direct experience with the application of ideas is the best teacher in this political arena. We will try in this book, however, to articulate the similarities and differences in the major strands of political Marxism that have arisen since the death of its founders. In this way, we hope to present some sense of the contours of the problem. At the present moment in history when Marxist politics in the advanced capitalist world is at a particularly low point in popular militancy, a lack of understanding will only lead to a recapitulation of many older problems, especially when progressive militancy is re-aroused (as we are sure it will be).

Looking at the issue of Marxist politics in a broader historical sweep, the divisions within it appear unexpected and anomalous. Part of the reason for this lies in the specific vision of science and history shared by virtually all thinkers (including Marx and Engels) in the nineteenth century. That century already witnessed the great disjuncture between the promise of capitalism and the actuality of urban poverty and squalor, as well as predictable periods of boom and bust. In scientific circles, however, the nineteenth century was roseate with optimism. Problems when recognized were seen as temporary. The physical sciences of chemistry and biology as well as their application in engineering, mining, and medicine were proceeding at such a rapid pace that there seemed no limits to the possibilities of scientific progress. Full human understanding and mastery over the natural environment was seen to be just over the horizon. Moreover, the realm of human history was also conceived as within the purview of scientific comprehension. The thinkers dealing with human affairs, whether in the liberal tradition stemming from August Comte or the radical tradition beginning with St. Simon, all believed that just as laws of nature could be comprehended, so could the laws of history. It was no accident that Marx wished to dedicate his greatest work, *Capital* to Charles Darwin, a dedication implicitly declaring a connection between the human and biological sciences for scientific progress.

The idea of scientific progress in the nineteenth century was firmly linked to the idea of natural law. While natural law in the earlier medieval tradition referred to the laws of a deity and was supported and defended by a clergy intent on maintaining popular ignorance (as is still the case in much of fundamentalist religion today), the scientific idea of natural law refers to the rules of the natural world external to any conscious transcendental intention. These rules are amenable to human intelligence; that is, to all humans who approach the world objectively. As such, the scientific approach to knowledge, as opposed to the religious traditional outlook, is both democratic and progressive, particularly when science is seen in its non-positivistic, more probabilistic sense.

In the eighteenth and early nineteenth century variant, the idea of scientific law was mechanistic, deterministic, and changeless. It was mechanistic in that its image of the natural world was that of a machine with moving parts, yes, but always moving in the same way. The image often used for this view of the universe was a clock where rotation occurs in endlessly repetitive and uniform cycles. The determinism in this outlook is obvious since the causes of events always lead in definite and inexorable directions. In the science of biology, for example, the earth's stock of animals was seen to have all been here from the beginning until Darwin's evolutionary theory exploded this comfortable illusion. Thus, Darwin's great contribution to knowledge recognized that natural processes were subject to inevitable change. But even with Darwinian evolution, where for the first time change enters the biological world, the tree of life appears in a unilinear form, perhaps with a few branches, but with an apparently sturdy trunk leading relentlessly from single-celled organisms at the bottom to humans at the top.

Marx and Engels working with human history could not but embrace the idea of change and movement since this is what history is all about. But they still were steeped in other aspects of nineteenth century science. They meant to do for history what Darwin and others had done for nature: to discover, as Marx once said, its "laws of motion." This motion is real motion, an advance over the recurrent and cyclical idea found in earlier science, but it still involved 'laws.' And laws in this context took on a deterministic hue since laws in Newtonian-inspired science usually refer to unerring fixed notions about the way things always work, a final truth about phenomena. Thus, when Marx at one time wrote about stages of history moving from primitive communism to slave society, then to feudalism, capitalism, and ultimately to socialism, it was all too easy in nineteenth century context to see these stages as an inevitable progression. To be completely clear about this question of Marx's view of stages, it is not that he ever formally presented them as some *philosophy* of history (in fact Marx was explicitly against the idea that such a philosophy was possible). It is that the nineteenth century intellectual atmosphere all too easily saw scientific theory in this way and it seems impossible, at least in hindsight, for anyone writing at that time not to be affected by it. In any event, this atmosphere, as we shall attempt to show, strongly affected the development of Marxism.

This development, in the first instance, took on a specifically scientistic cast, and this scientistic cast has coloured much of the debate and conflict within Marxism. While of course always touching upon economic issues, the debate was much more vitriolic in what may be properly called political Marxism. It has spawned what might be considered the major debate in modern Marxism, that between its apparently more scientific side and its more revolutionary side. More than a debate, this difference has actually led to the development of two worlds of analysis, worlds that often do little talking to each other. On the seemingly more scientific side we see the development (often positive and progressive) of Marxist political economy usually rooted and even respectable in the university context. This analysis charts the course of capitalist development, the changes in it, and the situation of the major contending classes within it. Its academic context gives it little connection to active political engagement, which leads it implicitly and explicitly to a more evolutionary view of Marxist politics. There, Marxism appears as a fairly uniform and agreeable outlook since its basic validity makes it easily superior in analytic power, especially when compared to everything else that goes under the rubric of social science or history in the modern university. Yet, there has developed another and almost separate Marxism, more manifestly political dealing with the more difficult problem of applying the lessons learned from Marxist engagement with changing the world. In this context, there is little unanimity and much storm and stress. Facing consequences inevitably unforeseen by its founders and needing to interpret errors, mistakes, revisions, and unanticipated, even aborted revolutions, fissures and conflicts have occurred such that instead of one political Marxism, we now apparently find many. It is the purpose of this book to outline the contours of the various political Marxisms that have developed in the last century – their conflicts and consequences, their weaknesses and their strengths as we see them.

During Marx's life, there were continual attacks on his politics from those who considered themselves even more revolutionary, especially from Bakunin. This is the anarchist critique of Marxism, which has had amazing staying power right up to the contemporary period. Although it is not within the purview of Marxism proper, it is so inextricably linked to it, if only negatively, that we begin our discussion of Marxist politics with this ongoing anarchist critique 'from the left.'

Introduction

While Marxist politics present an apparent unanimity from the end of the nineteenth century until early in the next one, a great split occurred with the First World War beginning in 1914. At that time, Marxism as reform within capitalism and Marxism as the demand for revolutionary transformation of capitalism became opposing and clashing outlooks. Our chapter on social democracy attempts to outline the origins and contours of this great division within the Marxist camp.

After that, we will explore the first great recognition of this fissure in Marxism itself in the ideas and actions of V. I. Lenin. Before Lenin, there was relative harmony in the Marxist camp; after him, things would never be the same.

Trying to give some chronological sense to a problem, which does not often follow a neat chronology, we will then try to deal with the knotty problem of the Stalin question. It is conventional to refer to 'Stalinism' when discussing this issue, but we are calling this a question since we are not sure that Stalin really added anything significant enough in either theory or practice to warrant an 'ism.' Stalin, as a particularly Marxist problem, did not arise until after Lenin's death. 'Stalinism' is introduced to history as an 'ism' by Leon Trotsky and has had its staying power initially in Trotsky's articulation and interpretation of Stalin's historical legacy. Trotsky's significance arose in opposition to Stalin, and while it has demonstrated staying power well beyond Stalin's period, we think that Trotskyism can only be understood by examining the earlier context. Thus we will introduce the Stalin problem as part of the great Stalin/Trotsky conflict arising in the 1920s and continuing on the ideological and political front up to this day.

Following this chapter is an analysis of the more recent development of political Marxism, the work of Mao Zedong in the Chinese Revolution. We also in this case are not calling this Maoism, a name that is usually used in the West where an 'ism' seems to be applied to any apparently reprehensible ideology while the Chinese, with some apparent modesty, referred to Mao Zedong Thought. While recognizing that Mao made significant contributions to revolutionary Marxism, we also recognize that the Chinese Revolution has all too easily been transformed into something different from socialism, and this result must also be understood as a product of profound mistakes and limitations within Mao and the Party he led. Accordingly, we present both a general chapter on the politics of the Chinese Revolution and a detailed chapter, done with first-hand research by our Chinese author, on the strengths and weaknesses of Party policy in one Chinese village.

Finally, we have a short chapter on feminism, not because it is part of Marxism, but because it has become a major progressive movement, which sometimes contends with Marxism, but more often, it seems to us, adds an important dimension to the problem of socialist transformation.

Our concluding chapter is a summation of what we consider problems and prospects for Marxism. While much of contemporary thought is celebrating its demise, we are fairly sure of a rejuvenation of Marxism since the predictable crises in capitalism happening now before our eyes will most certainly spawn this most fundamental opposition. We hope this book will highlight what is most positive in Marxism, critique what is most negative in its development, and help to identify if not resolve its most recalcitrant problems.

CHAPTER TWO

Anarchism

IN THE HISTORY of the Left, anarchism has always played a strange and more or less underground part. It was there at the beginning; it has been a permanent, if small, force throughout the major events and crises of the contemporary period; and it continues today as a more or less significant body of thought and action. Yet in spite of its historical continuity, anarchism appears to have little historical development. While taking on the coloration of local events, the theory of anarchism propounded in the nineteenth century remains almost the same in our own times. In fact, it is often asserted even by strong sympathizers that anarchism possesses no really developed theory in the first place; that whatever else it may be, anarchism is not a well-worked out doctrine of theoretical principles. David Apter in his introductory essay to a series of articles surveying the anarchist movement throughout the world goes so far as to say that anarchism "gives little sense of consistent accumulation of ideas and theories." With its emphasis on action rather than ideas, it often "makes happenings into a substitute solution for programs."

The response to anarchism from the Marxist left, from Marx onward and including all of its varieties, has been clear and categorical. It not only rejects anarchism, it denies that anarchism plays a progressive role in historical development. For conventional and conservative thought on the other hand, anarchism conjures up images of pathological violence and arbitrary terrorism. In the West in the early twenty-first century, it sometimes appears that only anarchists are willing to oppose global capitalism and its institutions with direct action and sometimes violence, which reflects the disarray among Marxists but makes confronting anarchism even more important.

What then is this thing, which has difficulty defining itself yet which others have little difficulty denouncing? Since anarchism lacks any unifying body of principles, perhaps it is best summed up as a particular mood or temperamental predisposition. In his conclusion to the book of articles on the subject, James Joll actually says the same thing in suggesting that "if there is a living anarchist tradition, it should be sought in psychological and temperamental attitudes to society as much as in sociological analysis of the societies in which anarchism has flourished." We have little quarrel with this definition except to add that psychological predispositions like this one have social roots and definite socio-political consequences. It is these latter consequences that must be addressed in any attempts to locate where anarchism may lie (if it lies clearly at all) on the political spectrum.

The psychological state that seems to come closest to grasping anarchism is one of permanent rebellion. Relentless disobedience to any and all authority seems to be the rallying call for anarchism regardless of the creeds and tactics within which such a call is made. And while anarchism often at times appeals to disobedience as a collective endeavor, whether in the name of classes, nations, age groups, or other form of social identity, its first attention is to each individual's rejection of authority wherever it may be. In this sense, Rousseau's famous outcry that man (sic) is born free yet everywhere he is in chains would strike a responsive chord among anarchists. For Rousseau, one of the founders of modern liberalism, is here postulating the existence of the individual rebel pitted against overwhelming forces of orthodoxy and tyranny, a position so much at the root of anarchist thought that it might be suggested that anarchism originates with the bourgeois revolution.

Origins of Anarchism

YET ANARCHISM is as ambiguous about its historical roots as it is about basic principles, which is not surprising since uncertainty about doctrinal coherence is probably connected to uncertainty about origins. How can one know where one comes from if one doesn't know where one is? For example, Atindranath Bose's *A History of Anarchism* sees its origins in almost all recorded civilizations. From the Garden of Eden on, most peoples have had images of a golden age of peace and plenty, with no private property, no state, and no laws. This image appears in Chinese, Indian, and Greek thought. In all of these civilizations where states already existed, forms of thought arose, which considered that government rested upon base human instincts, which can be purified only if humans lose their quest for power. Thus, for example, Taoism called for the destruction of established political institutions and a demand for a return to natural harmony rooted in the family and small production. In India, Bose says, "The anarchist tradition centres on the myth of the krita age ... [the] stateless society without the divisions of property, caste, and class." And in ancient Greece, especially in stoical thought, is the idea of humankind united together in "an empire of reason without force and authority." Often, in practice, the result of the outlook was a rendering unto Caesar what was Caesar's and a retreat into a situation of presumed peace and tranquility. The Taoist, for example, "leads mankind by his inaction." Bose sees the revolutionary character of the Christian gospel in its connection to Greek stoicism, "when Christ demands a quest for an inner spiritual egalitarianism leaving the world of external authority intact."

When we come closer to the modern period, as Bose points out, anarchist-type tendencies are seen in the views and activities of numerous Protestant sects in their attempts to return to the fundamentals of the Gospel. Peasant revolts in Germany in the sixteenth century, such as those of the Anabaptists, share ideas often associated with anarchism. And many subsequent Christian rejections of established churches, such as those of the Mennonites, Dukhobors, Quakers, and Methodists were similar to the Anabaptist initiators. They all were extremely individualist in matters of faith and accepted the state as at best a necessary evil. This engagement with freedom of conscience was connected with an antipathy to any established churchly organization having rights to set down rules and regulations for religious believers. The compromise with secular authority required only the unfettered freedom of religion. For individualistic forms of Protestantism, resistance against the state is reserved for intrusions into matters defined as specifically religious. In its spiritual and religious forms, early tendencies towards anarchism proposed only an individual and moral route to a better world. Mao, in a more clearly secular Marxist tradition, claimed only that socialism would resolve the problems stemming from a class society and indicated that the great harmony of socialism would not be without conflict.

Since anarchism in its most coherent form is a modern phenomenon and therefore partakes of that commitment to secularism and rationalism so unique to the contemporary era, perhaps it is unfair to pinpoint the outlook's vagueness by reference to viewpoints found in more non-rational and theological ages. However, we think the connection to ancient history is a significant one in the case of anarchism, for of all the revolts against older tradition so symptomatic of the post-French Revolutionary period, anarchism maintains the closest connection to earlier forms of rebellion. If we look at the two greatest bodies of revolutionary activities defining our era, those of liberalism and socialism, they are unceasing in their devotion to rationalism, science, and secular progress. And they clearly distinguish themselves from a pre-revolutionary past considered irrational, non-scientific, and theological. With modern anarchism, the connection to the past is less clear cut, less defined, and manifestly hazy. This is another reason that anarchism so lacks a coherent theory to define it. It maintains in principal that social change arises from individual actions that are guided by moral principles. Insofar as anarchist thought partakes of a belief in a golden age of complete harmony and conflictless serenity, then it is quite contradictory to the idea of human perfectibility through progressive enlightenment. In fact the idea of a golden age is much closer to theological conceptions of heaven than it is to the historical progress promised by the modern era.

What we mean by social theory is so inextricably linked to modern assumptions about rationalism and science that the absence of anarchist theory is partly accounted for by its non-acceptance of these assumptions (and here too, depending upon the anarchist, there will be inconsistencies on this point as well). Insofar as anarchism postulates the idea of total human freedom facing neither authority nor even limits to actions and desires, then such freedom approaches a mystique since even modern liberalism situates the free individual within the possibilities of human rationalities. Yet, as we have said above, anarchism has always been vague enough in its initial premises and assumptions that to castigate it for its potential mysticism and irrationality can easily be countered by pointing to more modern anarchists more clearly devoted to humanism and rationality. To be fair to a doctrine that is all too often treated unfairly by critics from every side, we must look at anarchism in its more contemporary, secular forms, which Marx confronted directly.

For there is a modern, humanistic anarchism, one committed to human betterment through human activities and devoid of much of the millennial utopianism of earlier types of rebellion. Bose identifies its father as William Godwin, a thinker spawned, as with all that begins our age, by "the expectations and disillusionments of the French Revolution. ... [He is the] first architect of a rational anarchist system of thought ... [which] discards the dreams of the classical age and the dogma of Christian theology." Unlike earlier thought, which rejected existing social institutions in the name of a transworldly millennium that harked back to a presumed state of perfect human innocence (much like, for example, the myth of the Garden of Eden), Godwin squarely faces what he considers the falsity and tyranny of his own society as something to be understood and changed through the application of human intelligence: "With him, virtuous conduct is rational conduct of which only a thinking and civilized man is capable." Godwin had faith in human perfectibility through the application of individual reason, which was guided by a moral compass that was open to rational proofs. Similar to later anarchism, Godwin believed that one's moral principles must be lived immediately and daily; that one's own conduct could be a microcosm and example for others who wished to live freely and independently. Like many others of this creed, he failed to do more than inspire a few like-minded people to lead, for a time, a standard of reason and morality that he believed would characterize human relations in the better world of the future.

For Godwin, social criticism and social programme begin and end with the individual. It is in this sense, as well, that modern anarchism and liberalism "stemmed from the same utilitarian root: the principle of the greatest happiness and the greatest freedom of the individual" (Bose). Another significant strand of Godwin's thought places it squarely within the liberal tradition and continues to weave through modern anarchism as well. It is a fundamental axiom of the liberal ethos that security of property is an unquestioned principle and that the existence of government is accepted reluctantly as the safeguard of that property. The best government, according to classical liberalism, is that which governs least. Moreover, what has always been implied here is that least government means local government putatively close to the people as opposed to faraway, centralized national government. The utopian views of liberalism as well as much subsequent anarchism appear to flow from these premises. In Godwin, Bose says, they are fused into an image of a world of simple, agricultural life, "which rejects property and government and secures liberty and equality ... based on a decentralized confederacy of small independent local groups." The slight difference between liberalism and anarchism appears to be the greater antipathy to government found in anarchism, but otherwise there is a striking similarity between the anarchism of Proudhon, Kropotkin, Tolstoy, and even Gandhi and the liberalism of Jeffersonian democracy. It might be noted that what they oppose is not only government per se, but bigness in government as well as bigness in everything else. Both seem to be involved with the romance of the small producer against the encroachments of government and economic monopoly.

Marxism is against the glorification of smallness, but it does not oppose bigness in principal (as does most of anarchism). Smallness must be evaluated in its tactical context, especially now when much of the organized progress, for example, with regard to climate change is occurring in smaller jurisdictions. Universalizing small-production is not a revolutionary strategy in itself and has its limitations and in-built class contradictions. It reflects the key problem of inflating a tactical necessity into a principle and a putative strategy for deep-rooted social change.

Pierre-Joseph Proudhon

THIS INTERCONNECTION between anarchism and liberalism is continued in the person even more closely associated with the origins of modern anarchism – Pierre-Joseph Proudhon. It is here, in Proudhon, that we also see why modern anarchism, while often claiming itself to be socialist, is also often quite contradictory to the socialist tradition. Socialism, whatever its form, has always been fully committed to the advantages of larger, technically proficient enterprise and cognizant of the class nature of small production. Proudhon, on the other hand, was in the main against the introduction of machine production, which he saw as the destroyer of the small independent producer. Thus Proudhon was not against property per se, but against what he considered the abuses of property involved in big industrialized units. He also had a singular distrust of majority rule by parliamentary democratic process since he conceived individual men (sic) as the thinkers and collectivities as mobs. The very common perceptions of society broken into an elite of thinkers and a mass of sheep, which still resonates through much scholarly and popular thought, owes much to Proudhon. Implicit to this conception has always been one of the major dilemmas of anarchism. Since rebellion against political elites appears to be perhaps the one consistent plank in an uncertain anarchist platform and since the untrustworthy masses are the agents of rebellion, what are the means by which the masses become virtuous and knowledgeable? Does this not demand the intervention of some training mechanism, some leadership to forge rebellion into progressive directions? And since, to anarchism, any leadership is ultimately as untrustworthy as the masses themselves, how is the conundrum to be resolved? Proudhon's rejection of all conventional politics, constitutions, and states in the name of a free confederation of individual producers contains the kernel of all later anarchist thought. Along with this kernel remains a profound distrust of all political entities (except perhaps oneself) to act as the stimulus for social transformation.

Proudhon is the true initiator of modern anarchism not only for his writings since, in many ways, he went little beyond Godwin who predated him; his paternity resides in the fact that he led a large popular movement in nineteenth century France representing his ideas. And this paternity was fully recognized by perhaps the best known and greatest representative of modern anarchism, the Russian Mikhail Bakunin. Bakunin's life and the thought that suffused his life are so fully enlivened with an anarchist animus that it is important to pay more attention to biographical detail in this case, a task undertaken by E. H. Carr in his book *Michael Bakunin*.

Mikhail Bakunin

BAKUNIN WAS BORN to a liberal family of landed nobility in 1814, and like many more liberal families of this class, members were deeply involved in the Decembrist plot to overthrow the Tsar in the late 1820. In fact a second cousin of his brother was one of those hanged in the repression that followed. And Bakunin was quite aware of this background, also demonstrating a lively interest in the normal intrigue of large feudal families. His early life was passed in an era of intense romanticism in the 1830s, a romanticism of revolt against older fixed conventions. Thus, when Bakunin's sister was promised in marriage to a man she did not love, it was her brother who fought most strongly against the proposed marriage (at this time, women did not easily fight for themselves). For Bakunin, Carr says, "To love was man's highest mission on earth." Here, the automatic acceptance of parental authority, that hallowed core of feudal acquiescence to all authority, was early judged, condemned, and attacked by Bakunin.

In his biography of Bakunin, Carr quite perceptively sees the romantic revolt of the nineteenth century as a revolt against the idea of reason and order ushered in by the eighteenth century French Revolution. One of the major anarchist antagonisms has been its hostility to science, and since the legacy of the French Revolution saw science as the unfolding of human reason, so both science and reason have often been condemned by the anarchist spirit. On this point turns perhaps a major difference between Marxism and anarchism. Whereas Marx and Marxism have always seen themselves as a continuation of the bourgeois revolutionary engagement with reason (that is, only rejecting that revolution because it was not reasonable enough), anarchism has often rejected reason in the name and spirit of instinct and raw passion. Bakunin is the prototype of this type of rebellion.

For Bakunin, all conventions, all laws are simply limits to the instinctive human desire for freedom from all limits. The ideal of freedom is to be realized by continual rebellion against all established order. To be human and free is to be undefined, unpredictable, and against all authority. His own life in its continual, restless, and often arbitrary defiance of the powers that be is clearly reflective of the outlook. In fixing upon Bakunin as a most complete embodiment of anarchism, it is best to focus upon his more mature and fully-developed years since Bakunin like anyone else must be expected to be inconsistent, inchoate, and often silly in his formative years. This point would not be important if it were not the case that great progenitors of ideas are often seen as fully developed in their doctrines from the first moment of intellectual conception. Or, in contrast, all of their later behavior is judged by the yardstick of earlier, still youthful folly. In Bakunin's case, for example, the presence of a confession written for the Tsar after his imprisonment in Russia early in his life is often used by those opposed to anarchism as a proof of not only Bakunin's, but of anarchism's bankruptcy, as well.

To be more specific for the moment, as a young rebel during the revolutions sweeping Europe in 1848, Bakunin became a cause célèbre as an immediate agitator in whatever revolutionary situation had developed in whatever city in Europe. As a Russian subject when Tsarist Russia was the counterrevolutionary bastion of the continent, Bakunin's active engagement with insurrectionary activities led, after the defeats suffered in these revolutions, to extradition and imprisonment in Russia. And during this imprisonment as a young man, Bakunin wrote and signed a confession to the Russian Tsar, an extraordinary document for a progressive at that or any other time. In it he literally grovels before the Tsar while expressing the most backward opinions. Not only does he confess that his democratic "projects and actions were to the highest degree laughable, senseless, insolent, and criminal," he also asserts that "even in the most recent times, in defiance of all democratic concepts and as though against my will, I deeply, deeply respected you!" and again to the Tsar: "I shall speak before you as though I were speaking before God himself, whom it is impossible to deceive by either flattery or lies."

In his submissive actions, his rejection of democracy, his primitive Slavophilism, and his suggestion that the Tsar would be the saviour of Europe, Bakunin is quite obviously worthy of the highest condemnation. But, and this is the important 'but,' his more mature thought fundamentally rejects all this, and it is inappropriate to tarnish all of anarchism, as is too often done, because of Bakunin's early confessions (written obviously under great duress). Anarchism should stand and be understood with reference to the later and more adult Bakunin, and should not be condemned on purely personalistic grounds.

That the adult Bakunin was the almost complete anarchist, there can be little doubt. Apparently burning with revolutionary fervour at every moment, he spent a lifetime in political activity never once becoming involved in work of a usual kind. He wrote little and did not develop a system of integrated principles, but this in itself is symptomatic of the anarchist animus since one of its major postulates is the rejection of too fixed a doctrine. This tendency often makes anarchism much more at one with the personality of the anarchist than with the exposition of a doctrinal system. Carr is getting at this point when he says that:

> The personality of Bakunin is one of those phenomena which cannot be explained in rational terms. His ambitions were ill-defined and chimerical. His writings, though rigorous, were incoherent; and, both in his writings and his actions, he seldom finished what he had begun. His chequered career was void of any concrete attainment. Yet he produced on his contemporaries an impression of overwhelming vitality and power.

Yet there must be some at least minimal strains of thought, which allow us to call acts and thoughts by the name of anarchism, and these can be found in Bakunin. The emphasis on strains of thought is important here since it is not only the case that Bakunin lacked theoretical coherence; it is that his type of thought makes a virtue out of such incoherence. The whole thrust of his theorizing is to be anti-theory; he expresses the anarchist credo as an aggregate of spontaneous passions. Again to quote Carr, "Few men whose life and thought have exercised so powerful an influence on the world as those of Mikhail Bakunin have left so confused and imperfect a record of their opinions. Bakunin was a prolific, but incoherent, writer." If Carr is suggesting that this confusion and incoherence is simply a matter of personality or circumstance, we would claim that this is not the case. These characteristics appear intrinsic to the outlook for which Bakunin so clearly stands. And, to repeat, we think this outlook is defined by this most representative practitioner by a particular spirit and emotional texture rather than anything else. This texture, then, is undergirded by specific ideological components by which anarchism may be defined.

At the centre of Bakunin's anarchism is the hostility to all authority and sympathy for those who are actually or potentially hostile to authority. While suspicion and mistrust of authority is not specific to anarchism – in fact, as was suggested above, it is connected to liberalism and to other creeds – the engagement with underdogs against their more powerful oppressors is more characteristic of anarchism. Whenever there was a cause or an issue of oppression of one group by others with power, then Bakunin felt it incumbent to leap into the fray. Moreover, since at any time the variety of oppressed groups is usually very great, so Bakunin's life is wondrous in the degree to which it flits about from place to place, and sometimes issue to issue. The picture of Bakunin that emerges is that of a mobile revolutionary who, for example, in 1848 when rebellion was breaking out everywhere, would leave Paris to make revolution in Posen and then on to Dresden, having no plans and no connections, with just the spirit of revolution to guide him. At that time immersed in Pan Slav nationalism, he jumps from a moderate Pan Slav congress where he represents Russia virtually alone (since there is no organization that authorizes his presence) to the barricades of a student/worker insurrection in Prague. When this is put down, he simply slips away. From Bakunin we confirm this image of anarchism as not so much a doctrine as an individual spirit of restless rebellion which, with the anarchist, is more significant than the principles that he/she may be espousing.

Yet again, it would be unfair to Bakunin and to anarchism to claim that it lacks all coherence. While he, like most humans, changed during his lifetime, certain enduring issues animate definite stages of his life. So during the bourgeois revolution of 1845, Bakunin's revolution was more purely liberal in its demands of the social order. These included the abolition of serfdom, aristocracy, and inherited privilege, all demands which were the core of the French Revolution in the eighteenth century; and with the defeat of these revolutions, Bakunin, along with all those who were radicalized by the meekness and cowardice shown by the bourgeoisie in its own revolution, changed from a more narrowly political revolutionary to a more totally social one. With Marx, Bakunin saw the need for a total transformation of society rather than reform of its political institutions. And again with Marx, he sometimes emphasized the centrality of class conflict as the motor force in this transformation. That the bottom of society is exploited and oppressed, and that this bottom has the right, indeed the duty, to overthrow the ruling elite in order to usher in a new world of equity and justice is a position upon which there is solid agreement between Bakunin and Marx. And on this basis, there evolved many points of alliance and common political work in the lives of these great protagonists.

Yet Bakunin had fundamental differences with Marx, differences which in the end made mortal enemies of them and often the viewpoints for which they stood. In the first instance, Bakunin differed not only in the substance of his social analysis, but in his approach to it as well. In almost all his statements about the significance of science and its relevance to revolutionary change, Bakunin revealed a marked ambivalence. Insofar as his thought is modern, he is positive about the significance of rational processes in approaching nature and, with limitations, society. Never did he engage in any appeals to deities or spiritual entities representing supposedly fixed truths. Even in his early adulation of the Russian Tsar in the aforementioned confessions, Bakunin does not allude to the accepted theological justifications for Tsarist rule, and his appeal to the Russian ruler is couched in secular terms. Moreover, throughout his adult life, Bakunin was steadfast in his rejection of all religious thought and never wavered from vehement atheism. All this points in the direction of a conjured rationalism, a rationalism which, in fact, does lead to some positive stance towards modern rationality and science.

Another strain of Bakunin's anarchism also elevates the scientific spirit. This is his acceptance of the need for technical development as the precondition for overall social development. Unlike the anarchist tendencies of Thoreau or Gandhi or some modern communalists, Bakunin is no exponent of a pristine return to a more natural, simpler life. Thus, for him, as with most of modern anarchism, natural science as the handmaiden of technical advancement is both necessary and right. On the other hand, Bakunin demonstrates a particular revulsion against science when applied to society and history. This revulsion, moreover, is connected to aspects of nineteenth century thought, which are quite contrary to progressive ideas in our time

The early nineteenth century is set off from other times by its reaction to the harbinger of the modern era, the French Revolution. Ushering in liberal capitalism and bourgeois rule to France with its great promise of prosperity, peace, and cooperation for all, it fell short in its actualization. Early capitalist industrialization in Europe was ghastly in its exploitation of labour. Its creation of brutalizing, slum-ridden cities set in motion rebellion everywhere. Marx represents the most optimistic prognostications to flow from the hiatus between liberal promise and capitalist reality. By applying the tools of a rationalist science to human history, he uncovered the agents of progress in the very disasters produced by industrial capitalist development. For Marx, science and technology were positive, but were limited by their bourgeois nature. Therefore what must be done was to deepen our understanding of social reality by applying new scientific method and different political action to that reality. In fundamental ways, Marxism is a progressive development of the thought and actions activated by bourgeois society itself (which indeed is something for which it is accused by Bakunin).

Another rebellion was generated by this early crisis in industrial capitalism – the romantic rebellion. While accepting the tremendous advances produced by natural science in its application to technology (to reject these would be foolhardy and only occurred amongst a hardy minority of medievalists), this rebellion occurred mainly in the realm of history, the arts, and social thought. In it swells up the great divide between nature and society, between the objectivity of science and the alleged freedom of human action. Bakunin's thought on these matters appears rooted in this particular nineteenth century rebellion. The romantic rebellion against science and technical progress could not frontally attack the obvious advances made in natural science since the Newtonian revolution in physics and later the Darwinian in biology became too firmly rooted in popular and intellectual consciousness (and these advances contributed mightily to the everyday comforts of these rebels of privileged origins). Thus public life, which capitalist society, with its emphasis on far flung markets and work outside the home, had so clearly demarcated from private life of intimacy and emotion, became to the romantics, the institutionalized focus of objectivity and science. For them science and industrial work took on the coloration of dullness, order, obedience, and emotionless routine. In short, science and its concomitant, industrial development, was seen as suffused with all that was not human.

In contradistinction to the objectivity of the world of nature, there arose amongst the romantics the view that the world of the really human, the historically human, was not subject to scientific analysis. More, since scientific analysis was delimited to objectified nature, which in its predictability was inhuman, so the truly human became the agent of pure subjectivity, of freedom from all limitations except 'natural' ones. Humans as biological entities may be comprehended by natural science, but they also are seen to possess a spiritual quality wherein resides their freedom. The familiar duality between body and mind is built into this conception, with the mind representing that quality differentiating humans from beasts lower on the evolutionary scale. Human behavior is here not the more or less predictable, probabalistic phenomenon that is amenable to social science. Instead it is more whimsical, indeterminate, and willful. And human history can never be analyzed as predictable tendencies, but can only be grasped by the intuitive understanding of free creatures.

Bakunin's anarchism is clearly situated in this romantic conception of human behavior and human history. Consequently, he not only rejects the substantive elements of Marx's materialistic analysis of history; he considers the very attempt to comprehend humans in this way as wrongheaded. It is not, then, only a case of Bakunin finding Marx's theory objectionable. He objects to the project itself disclaiming the very possibility of a rational understanding of history. The first human reality for Bakunin is the free individual whose desires and passions will lead to a free society after individuals decide to do away with the social powers that delimit their inherent freedom. This idea of the human being who is free in the natural state only to be corrupted by the powers of society again harkens more to Rousseau than to Marx.

It is, then, this romantic individualism that suffuses Bakunin's attitude toward social science. He not only did not believe it possible to develop a science of society; he thought that any attempt to do so was tyrannical since it undercut the natural human instinct to revolt against any system of rules. So, says Bakunin, social science can do little but articulate abstract laws, which cannot grasp living, concrete individuals. When Bakunin proclaims the need for science to become everyone's property, he means natural science, for this will mean the freeing of humans from pretensions to social science. It is on this basis that Marxism was always seen as not only false, but part of the intellectual apparatus of oppression Bakunin found in the whole ideological climate around him. Thus, to him, rebellion against not only the state, but against all conformity to rules, even the intellectual ones that construct knowledge, is of the essence of that freedom to which all should aspire. If he hates anything more than the state, he hates the idea of a rational theory of society and any attempt to organize around such a social science. Bakunin's long involvement with the First International initiated by Marx could rightly be seen as a conscious attempt at undermining the whole organizational thrust of the project. As justification for this position, Bakunin condemned Marxism as intrinsically tyrannical as well as Marx himself who, said Bakunin, "lacks the instinct of liberty – he remains from head to foot an authoritarian" (quoted in Sam Dolgoff, ed., *Bakunin on Anarchy*).

In the most direct way, Bakunin elaborates upon the liberal credo that power corrupts and absolute power corrupts absolutely: "Nothing is as dangerous for man's personal morality as the habit of commanding." Bakunin is distrustful not only of state power, but of any permanent groupings consciously utilizing and seeking power. He saves his most striking barbs for those revolutionary groups that are conscientiously political. If, says, Bakunin, a revolutionary group such as a Marxist one, means to organize for the control of state power, that political group and the regime it assumes, if successful, will be no different from all other states. In fact, he asserts that Marx's state "will be the reign of *scientific intelligence*, the most aristocratic, despotic, arrogant, and elitist of all regimes." Here Bakunin shows not only an antipathy for conscious political organization in either pre-state or state forms, but his profound suspicion of a scientifically-informed approach to the problem.

Underlying this rejection of political leadership, especially for those oppressed classes in need of revolution, is Bakunin's faith in the spontaneous revolutionary possibilities of those classes: "The great mass of workers ... because of its social position, is more truly socialist than all the scientific and bourgeois socialists combined." Not only does ultimate wisdom reside in the people, a view held in general by all progressive views, but immediate wisdom as well. Yet Bakunin is neither romantic nor foolish enough to believe that the people are one homogeneous and unified mass of spontaneous goodness. Oppressed classes are themselves variegated and uneven in outlook and attitude with elite members holding more advanced ideas than others. Moreover, the more backward members of these classes are in need of assistance, education, and example to facilitate their movement forward. In short there is always leadership in all social groupings and Bakunin clearly recognized that oppressed classes can only overcome their oppression with good rather than bad leadership. This leads Bakunin and all of anarchism into its most profound conundrum.

If, says Bakunin, all conscious political leadership is inherently undemocratic at the same time at which leadership is a necessary element in revolutionary transformation, then how is it possible to square this circle? Bakunin's solution, the one which has been common to anarchism throughout contemporary history, appears in a way to compound the dilemma. The revolution to succeed needs a directorate, one that is secretive, and in its secretiveness influences rather than commands the already revolutionary ideas of the populace. It is necessary, says Bakunin,

> for the triumph of the Revolution over reaction that the unity of ideas and of revolutionary action find an *organ* in the midst of the popular anarchy, which will be the life and the energy of the Revolution. This organ should be the secret and universal association of the International brothers. There need not be a great number of these men. One hundred revolutionaries, strongly and earnestly allied, would suffice for the international organization of all of Europe. (Quoted in Sam Dolgoff, ed., *Bakunin on Anarchy*, italics in original unless noted)

The people in revolt are the ultimate arbiters of their own fate, but they need a catalyst. This secret band of revolutionary brotherhood is supposed to act everywhere to maintain the revolutionary direction of the people's raw energy. Upon revolutionary victory, the band will simply disappear as the federation of autonomous localities and regions will usher in the future in need of no leadership and no state. Bakunin thus solves the problem of political corruptibility by postulating a temporary body of leaders; leaders, he asserts, without *leadership*, which he abjures. In his own life time he remained true to his creed as he was perpetually recruiting (often after one night of heated discussion) people into secret revolutionary brotherhoods and perpetually expelling them in moments of disagreement and conflict. His hatred of leadership (while spending his life trying to lead) is so great that he was forever critical of all public and open manifestations of political action while he hatched secret societies whose existence is often lodged only in his imagination.

This mixture of rejection of intelligible understanding and adherence to secret organization to lead without leading makes the anarchist project of this arch anarchist a strange one. How is it decided, it may be asked, who deserves to belong to the brotherhood (sic) of revolutionaries? Since anarchist thought denies the possibility of a body of principles by which revolutionaries may band together, in fact it considers the very idea of such principles a symptom of dreaded political authority, and since anarchist thought only accepts leadership that is in continual opposition to its right to lead, the basis of recruitment to the brotherhood is extremely tenuous and hazy. I am sure that more stable anarchist character types would consider that Bakunin's creation and re-creation of real and imaginary anarchist organization is simply a product of his peculiar personality. Other personalities, it would be assumed, would be more careful and more sensible in their choice of political comrades. It seems, however, that this kind of political fickleness is not a product of personality, but is endemic to this kind of political outlook. It is manifested not only by Bakunin but by much of anarchism since his time, most extraordinarily by a recent manifestation of this process – new leftism in the 1960s and early '70s. Without any principles for membership, with only begrudging acceptance of the need for criteria of recruitment, anarchist organization is usually based on the vagaries of style or presumed high moral sentiments.

Bakunin's antipathy to Marxist theory, indeed to all attempts at theory, is connected to his commitment to the spontaneous rebellion of sections of the population whenever and wherever it may occur. The major reason for which one section appears to be given attention seems to be the *degree* of rebellion it demonstrates. The more intense the upsurge against the established order by any group, the greater the probability that Bakunin will define this group as the revolutionary hope of the moment. Moreover, Bakunin and much of later anarchism as well is always preparing for the great Revolution, which will destroy the past and usher in the future at one stroke. Those strata or classes, which appear to be demanding change in a piecemeal fashion through relatively stable organizations, are condemned for their dull, plodding reformism, for their absence of true revolutionary militancy; for example, Marx's engagement with the construction of working-class trade unions involved with bettering immediate economic conditions is seen by Bakunin as a dampening of real revolutionary militancy. Conflict that is in any way institutionalized is, to Bakunin, no conflict at all. Rather than analyzing the contradictions of reformist practices or understanding them tactically, Bakunin rejects any measure short of immediate revolution.

This passion for spontaneous upsurge or nothing at all leads Bakunin to downplay the industrial working class because it appears to be integrated in the new industrial order. He expected much greater things from other classes because their marginality appeared to generate more overt and intense passion. In the latter case, the peasantry comes in for special treatment by Bakunin. In contradiction to Marx's reference to rural idiocy, which is an idea rooted in a whole theory of social development, Bakunin raises the peasantry to the heights of revolutionary grandeur. The peasants, says Bakunin, are the most significant actors in the revolutionary movement, which must be spontaneous, uncompromising, passionate, anarchic, and destructive. The reason that the peasantry is so suited for this type of action is because, being only slightly affected by the pernicious influence of bourgeois society, the peasants still retain "their native energy and simple unsophisticated folkways." Bakunin goes on to indicate the anti-working class nature of this embrace of the peasant: "The more sophisticated and by that very circumstance, slightly bourgeois-tinged-socialism of the city workers, misunderstands, scorns, and mistrusts the vigorous, primitive peasant socialism, and tries to overshadow it."

In these passages we see many of Bakunin's assumptions about the social order and his ideas about its transformation. He distrusts any theory that is based on the predictable behavior of any class, a predictability which could lead to sustained and long-range organization and activity by that class. A sustained class-consciousness is, according to Bakunin, corrupted just because it is regular and predictable. He can thus reject not only Marx's theory, which perceives one class as more revolutionary as a product of the predictable dynamics of the capitalist system, but also that very class because it demonstrates its predictability through organizational forms. It is not that Bakunin rejects, for example, working-class trade unions because they manifest bourgeois characteristics; it is rather that he sees the very existence of such organizations as retrogressive. On the other side of the coin, Bakunin glorifies the peasantry for its lack of regularized connection to capitalism and its potential for chaotic rebellion without organization. For Bakunin's anarchism, the stratum that seems most active in rebellion at any time is the most revolutionary stratum; it must be against the whole system ready to destroy it at a moment; if it cannot do this, it will be condemned as co-opted, sold out, and reformist.

In both the economic and political realm, Bakunin scorns programme in the name of total revolution: "Let us *talk less* about revolution and do a great deal more. Let others concern themselves with the theoretical development of the principles of the Social Revolution, while we content ourselves with spreading these principles everywhere, *incarnating them into facts.*" This amounts to eschewing theory in the name of revolutionary action. What defines revolutionary action is the totally pure activity devoid of the taint of compromise. Since all social theory, Marxist or otherwise, is built on the basis of some order of factual regularity, and since all action based on such theory must take into account the dealing with such regularity, then some aspect of compromise (with reality) is demanded by theoretically-based action. Bakunin will have none of this. In the realm of economic action he scorns the everyday demands of the trade unions for better working conditions. These predictable demands of a class developing its own organization are dangerous compromises to Bakunin since they undermine the instinctive desire of the class to completely overthrow the whole system. To Bakunin, then, all demands for economic reform are by definition *reformism*, and all political activists advocating such reforms are sellouts.

It is not that Bakunin is so foolish as to believe that bread and butter issues are not important to the growth of working-class consciousness, but his approach to how this awareness develops is particular to anarchism. The militant worker, says Bakunin, by slow accretion of real experience in struggle and solidarity, "ends by recognizing himself as a revolutionist, an anarchist, and an atheist, without in the least knowing how he became such." Implicit in this statement is not only a rejection of theory as concomitant of experience, but also a single-purposed attitude toward the economic demands of trade unionists. These demands, to Bakunin, are not deserving of respect in their own terms, but only as stimuli (and unconscious ones at that) to higher more noble purposes. While Marxists have often been accused of taking an instrumentalist approach to the everyday demands of the working class – an accusation stating that Marxists are only using these demands as a springboard to revolution – this argument about instrumentalism appears to apply much better to anarchism. In its dedication to the Revolution as the great conflagration that, in a moment, destroys the past and creates the future, anarchism usually defines anything less than Revolution as ignoble or, at best, useful for the higher end.

Bakunin, however, still recognizes the efficacy of economic demands in leading toward his desired revolution and, while remaining antipathetic to the idea of organization in general, accepts the necessity of trade union organization for the working class. In his commitment to localism as the ultimate source of real democracy, he also sees trade unions as the potential building blocks of the future (and here he prepares the way for later syndicalist directions). These building blocks, however, are given a curious existence since everyday demands are typically condemned as reformist by Bakunin. Some degree of social organization is acceptable, even a good thing, but the parameters of this organizational form (trade unions) are quite circumscribed.

In his attitude towards more distinctly political activity, Bakunin reveals a more fundamental intransigence. He is not so foolish as to reject politics in its broadest sense since he clearly realizes that ideological positions of all stamps have implications for change of the society. Rather, he opposes all actions that can be defined as political in the narrower sense of accepting the need for state power. Here Bakunin reveals the most basic idea of all anarchism, the idea which demarcates it from all other creeds. Ultimately to him, the state is the source and origin of all evil. Any actions that accept, either implicitly or explicitly, its presence are counterrevolutionary. "The state," say Bakunin, "is the most flagrant, the most cynical, and the most complete negation of humanity."

Bakunin and the State

THERE IS OFTEN misunderstanding of the difference between anarchism and Marxism on the question of the state since both viewpoints consider the state as a pernicious agency and both favour its dissolution. But Marxism sees the origin of a centralized organization of violence (its definition of a state) in the rise of class societies and sees its dissolution to result only from the creation of a classless society. Anarchism, as stated before, does not appear to have a theory of the state (or of classes), which leads it to postulating that a ruling class which controls property and a ruling group which controls power are often one and the same thing. In fact in much anarchist writing, the state is given primacy over all other institutions and is therefore seen as the most fundamental roadblock to social transformation. Thus, in discussing the elements of a successful revolution, Bakunin says that "it is necessary to attack conditions and material goods; to destroy property and the state." But he goes further: "The revolution as we understand it will have to destroy the state and all the institutions of the state, radically and completely, from its very first day."

On the basis of this position, Bakunin attacks Marxism for its acceptance of a state form upon the accession to revolutionary power. Revolutionary Marxism of both Marx in his discussion of the Paris Commune and Lenin in *State and Revolution* sees a socialist revolution as demanding the destruction of the old state, the bourgeois state, but not the destruction of all states all at once. Instead, they say, a new type of transitional state must be created, a working-class state, which is supposed to prepare the way for future classlessness and statelessness. Bakunin saves his most pointed barbs for this idea. Any revolution, he says, which intends to construct a "powerfully centralized revolutionary state, would inevitably result in military dictatorship and a new master." Thus, for Bakunin and for all anarchism, the Marxist idea that the working class should fight for state power is considered a fundamentally counterrevolutionary idea. Whether the state proclaims itself capitalist or socialist makes little difference since its very existence makes that state equally pernicious. Given that twentieth century revolutions that have created proletarian states have moved neither to classlessness nor statelessness has clearly strengthened the prophecies of doom on the score articulated by anarchism since Bakunin.

Bakunin's hostility to all states is broader than the simple demand for the destruction of the state on the day of The Revolution. His aversion for political action involves the rejection of all dealings with existing states. From this aversion stems the common anarchist attitude toward engagement in existing government bodies in capitalist democracies. To Bakunin, political power is so corrupting that revolutionary integrity demands having no truck with it at any time. For a revolutionary even to run for office in a bourgeois parliament is proof that such a revolutionary was one in name only. All the paraphernalia of running for office – organizing, funding, speechmaking – are so much bourgeois claptrap to Bakunin and are to be categorically avoided. The true anarchist will have nothing to do with government in the present other than to attack it and keep the spirit alive for its future destruction. And to Bakunin, "keeping the spirit alive" seems to sum up a creed which spurns any political programme other than preparing at all times for that great conflagration that will settle things once and for all. This boycotting of everyday politics, and again a condemnation of all who engage in such programmes, is one of the central sentiments in the anarchist creed. At the time of the split in the International Workingmen's Association between Bakunin and Marx near the end of Bakunin's life, Bakunin was advocating that all political questions should be banned from the International and that "we should seek to strengthen this association solely in the field of economic solidarity."

Since Bakunin demonstrates a reluctance to get involved with daily economic demands because their satisfaction can, and will, lead to cooptation, what can he mean by the "field of economic solidarity"? This phrase can be understood only by recognizing that the real emphasis by Bakunin is on the solidarity. But, again, what can one mean by a solidarity that rejects either an economic or political programme, which might build and maintain collective strength? Solidarity in Bakunin's sense can only mean the unity and collective spirit that arises and continues to percolate from the spontaneous rebellion of working people as a dominated class. And it is only one aspect of that spirit that interests Bakunin, that aspect which, with a mighty violent swoop, will destroy the old order and usher in the new. It is the revolutionary solidarity of the working class that Bakunin means to sustain, but a solidarity that appears to exist in pure form simply waiting for the day of reckoning. While it waits, anarchism has the right and the duty to disparage and destroy all organizations that work upon the idea that solidarity is a social process which, to be built, must have a developmental plan based on theory and analysis.

It is in response to this last position that Marx castigated Bakunin for being a destructive force in the First International. Since anything the International did of an economic nature was considered by Bakunin a compromise with the existing order and anything that accepted either a present or a future state was condemned as reactionary by Bakunin, then anarchism represented a major divisive force in the organization. Yet it would be unfair to claim that Bakunin and anarchism are hostile to all working-class organization since it is clear that he is sincere in his desire to strengthen this organization by his call for "economic solidarity." It is the nature and theoretical meaning of such organization, which is a distinguishing feature of anarchist thought. Since, according to Bakunin, an oppressed class is by nature revolutionary, by which he means that it is in perpetual revolt against all injustice, then the unfettered connection between members of that class will not only bring about a future of justice, but already carries the seeds of that future in themselves. The triumph of revolution is no more than the spontaneous growth of the "goddess of revolt." The organization that develops spontaneously is, to Bakunin, the actual microcosm of a revolutionary society. On these grounds he can claim that:

> The true program, I will repeat it a thousand times, is quite simple and moderate: *the organization of solidarity in the economic struggle of labour against capitalism.* On this foundation, at first exclusively natural, will rise the intellectual and moral pillars of the new society.

As the above passage indicates, Bakunin does see developmental stages in the growth of organization (the emphasis for example on material factors first) but the development does not refer to real change as much as expansion of what, to him, is already there at the beginning. The spirit of revolt, which assumes a metaphysical character in Bakunin, is the driving force of revolutions and more important than any economic programme: "We are concerned," Bakunin says, "that the masses of the people carry in themselves, in their instincts (more or less developed by history), in their daily necessities, and in their conscious and unconscious aspirations, all the elements of the future social organization." At the same time at which he extols the primitive goodness of people in revolt, Bakunin admits that the people need adherents from the bourgeois world who "can contribute expert knowledge, the capacity for abstract thought and generalization, and the ability to organize and coordinate – qualities that constitute the creative force without which any victory is impossible." Perhaps Bakunin feels this comment is necessary to justify his own right to revolutionary legitimacy since he originated in the Russian landowning class, but it is a strange admission from one who downgrades all theory and leadership in the name of popular revolutionary instinct.

In any case, two major anarchist ideas flow from the glorification of spontaneous rebellion. The first is distrust of all social groupings other than the most local ones. Rebellion occurs in its only true form at the immediate and face-to-face level. The second idea is the expectation that broader types of social organization in a future society will involve the automatic and voluntary confederation of local groups. If the state is to be rejected in all its forms, then only voluntary association can be the glue of wider social formations. By seeing rebellion in this instinctive form as not only the source of revolutionary change, but even apparently as the microcosmic blueprint for all future change, the anarchist tends to see him/herself and his/her closest political grouping as the living locus of the new society. As a consequence, this seemingly most broad spirited and often most international sounding viewpoint, by rejecting analysis and the systematic presentation of ideas about groups, processes, and future change, actually often ends up with little more than the strongly held sentiment by each anarchist that the revolution, *C'est moi*, or, if not exactly *moi*, then at best the revolution, *C'est nous*. Bakunin's thought at the beginning of modern anarchism leads in this direction, and is more forcefully articulated in later manifestations, especially among new leftists of the 1960s.

Bakunin's continual condemnation of the state in all its forms indicates, in its lack of theoretical clarity (a clarity that, as stated above, is rejected anyway), another characteristic common to anarchism. This is the confusion about the idea of the state, of government, and of leadership, terms which Bakunin throughout his written works, uses almost interchangeably. For example, James Guillaume's sympathetic biographical sketch of Bakunin quotes him as saying that "it is absolutely impossible for a man who wields power to remain a moral man." In this statement, Bakunin is rejecting the very idea of societal power, regardless of the particular manifestations it may take. But, it may be asked, is it possible to imagine any social formation without some aspects of power in it? Even a friendship between two people is not based on the absence of power but on equal acceptance of the effective energy of each partner in the friendship. When we come to more complex social groupings characterized by a complicated division of labour, then some sort of coordinating or managing role becomes necessary. The operation of a complex group demands some sort of authoritative direction (which in itself says nothing about the means of recruiting such direction or the relation between coordinators and others in the unit). Bakunin's view appears to reject this view in principle; to suggest that any and all authority is illegitimate, and that the only legitimate action is the individually directed one.

Both Bakunin's and Marx's thought, as has been suggested, is rooted in the great eighteenth century Enlightenment distrust of government. The difference between them lies in Bakunin's conflation of government into all forms of authority and his conception of freedom as a condition of voluntary rejection of all authority. Here, unlike Marx, Bakunin remains rooted in the libertarian side of Enlightenment thought, that side which sees society, or at least the good society, as a free and voluntary contract of individuals. Thus, what to Marx in his conception of the withering away of the state is the diminution of oppressive and repressive aspects of societal authority is to Bakunin the rejection of authority in *all* of its guises. Here it must be said that Bakunin, as a purposefully unsystematic thinker, often sounds as if he agrees with Marx on this point, but in much of his thought, and almost all of his action, this profound difference is most telling.

Although, at the end of Bakunin's life, the difference between his outlook and Marx's was symbolized by Bakunin and his group being expelled from the International in the early 1870s, the truly great divide between anarchism and Marxism does not assume real importance until well after the death of the originators of these two movements. The reasons for this interval are manifold. In the first place, socialist thought first arose in the nineteenth century, and all its early protagonists were busy affirming its first principles and demarcating it from non-socialist thought. Although divisions quite obviously arose in the socialist movement itself, divisions that are already mentioned in Marx and Engels' *Communist Manifesto* of 1848, these differences were often theoretical. The working class movement itself was still small and immature, and while many shades and nuances contended within it, these were all tolerated in the face of much larger and more powerful enemies. Even a concept that became so central to Marxism, "the dictatorship of the proletariat," did not take theoretical form until the working class faced its first real possibility of holding power in the Paris Commune of 1871. And this concept most clearly demarcates the Marxist from the anarchist viewpoints on the nature of the state. Thus, although there was much rancour and distrust between anarchism and Marxism in these early formative years, it can be said that both were recognized as legitimate progressive forces, fighting in sometimes different ways for common goals.

Revolution by the Deed

MUCH OF THIS CHANGES in the late nineteenth century, especially when the working class became a real force on the political scene, and what appeared earlier to be 'mere' theoretical difficulties became divisions of greater practical significance. Anarchism itself also developed certain terrorist strands, which often stamped it with images still extant in popular consciousness. It is unfair to see terrorism as the central activity of anarchism since this viewpoint is an obvious attempt by ruling ideologies to brand anarchists as no more than violent criminals. In the hands of certain rather unscrupulous types probably found in any movement, anarchist ideas are often linked with apparently self-aggrandizing violence. The notorious Russian Nihilist Sergei Nechaev comes to mind in this context. A collaborator for a time with Bakunin, he preached the right of a revolutionary to sanctify any action, no matter how dishonest, deceptive, or violent, in the name of revolution. Bakunin in the end broke with Nechaev, but there is some uncertainty as to whether the break was one of principle or because Nechaev had acted scandalously toward him. In any case, Bakunin had the honesty to admit to being a fool in his infatuation for Nechaev.

Although it is not fair to equate nihilism, the philosophy that justifies any activity on the altar of individual freedom, with anarchism, it is still true that much of the political terrorism of the late nineteenth and early twentieth centuries has a logical connection to anarchist thought. And it was so recognized by noted anarchists at the time. If anarchism mistrusts theory and glorifies action, if it mistrusts the long tedious planning that goes into conceiving of revolution as a historical process, if it defines revolution by the moral fervour and dedication of revolutionary practitioners, then it would follow that anarchism would come to extol what came to be called "revolution by the deed." What more dramatic deed could there be than the assassination of some notable figure representing reactionary power?

According to anarchism, the masses of oppressed people are naturally rebellious against authority, and the realization of their freedom from authority will come with the revolutionary destruction of all authority, which will then usher in the realm of freedom for all. This conception of the rebellious mass comes up against one all too recalcitrant set of facts. Revolutionary moments, although they may be central in their transformatory effects on human history, are still only moments. The mass of people most of the time are not in a state of revolutionary turmoil. For the anarchist who is waiting for this moment as proof of the validity of his/her whole outlook, the problem is what to do in the meantime. If the masses are by nature revolutionary, then their quiescence at normal times must be unnatural. Moreover, anarchism, in its antipathy to smaller rebellion, which it sees as cooptation, disdains long-term engagement with mass action, condemning such engagement as reformism. Thus the anarchist as a logical outgrowth of anarchist thought, again finds him/herself both isolated from and potentially disappointed in those masses who are defined as the locus of revolution. In historical situations in which this hiatus between anarchists and popular sentiment is at its greatest, then anarchism turns to individual dramatic acts as its most common manifestation. With varying emphasis in different countries, this appears to have occurred in the late nineteenth and early twentieth centuries.

It is often said that the terrorist deed is an act of despair and hopelessness done by the anarchist, but this interpretation appears to be missing the point. To the anarchist, the glorious individual act, in which all bridges to safety and security are burned, is an exalted act. If anarchism extols the moral rectitude of dramatic action, if it condemns the spinelessness of everyday conformity to dull, conventional routine, if it believes that the destruction of the powerful and decadent is also an act of revolutionary construction, then those facts that demonstrate a willingness to sacrifice oneself in the destruction of evil become the highest form of anarchist action. These assumptions are the ideological underpinning for attempts at assassination of figures of power. Moreover, to anarchists who subscribe to this aspect of anarchism – and not all do since many consider assassination as foolish, senseless, and impolitic – these acts are not acts of terror. They are not arbitrary attacks on innocent people, but planned, rational annihilation of what to anarchists are clearly parties guilty of atrocities against humankind. The anarchist act of assassination is not only conceived as a revolutionary act because of its internal virtue. To repeat, anarchism commonly sees oppressed masses of people as perhaps quiescent, but, if sleeping, it is the sleep of a giant on the verge of a thunderous awakening. All these masses need, according to anarchism, is the catalyst that will set it into revolutionary motion. The dramatic deed is seen as a potential stimulus to rouse the masses into this action. And even if a particular deed does not affect a mass response, the deed contains its own internal virtue and becomes part of a tradition of martyrs to the people's cause, a tradition that can be called on as a stimulus to future action. Thus, to anarchism, the blatant attack on symbols of the world's evil is a noble act which, in a sense, takes on a magical quality. If it is repeated often enough in the right way at the right time, it is bound to have the beneficial effect of rousing the masses to revolutionary action.

This terrorist aspect of anarchism is most clearly manifested in the period from the end of the First International in the early 1870s until the First World War. The numerous attempts to assassinate the Tsar in Russia and the assassination of President McKinley in the United States at the beginning of the twentieth century are only a small example of this phenomenon. This was also a period in which working-class movements, which in the life of Marx were still theoretical probabilities because in practice they were small and marginal, became large, permanent, and consolidated. It was anarchism that was, in the main, marginal to these growing movements. And anarchism in its marginality and by its very nature seldom finds solidified, organized movements revolutionary enough (or revolutionary at all). In Russia at the time, the opposite apparently is the case; the use of terror by populist anarchists in the late nineteenth century appears connected to the absence of a working class movement. Anarchism there defined the vast Russian peasantry as the potentially revolutionary class (showing again its penchant for using sympathy with oppression rather than analysis as a basis for action) and conceived of the terrorist deed as the catalyst for upheaval by what anarchism itself saw as an "inert mass of peasantry." In the West European and North America situation, where the working class at that time was growing as a political force, the use of terror there appears to be connected more to anarchism's failure to integrate with this movement or, at the least, to anarchism's perception of the movement as not revolutionary enough without some dramatic impetus. In either case, it seems that there is a relationship between marginality and a turn to terror.

Significantly, this fairly short period of violent anarchist attacks has been the basis for the bourgeois press and media to paint all of anarchism with the terrorist brush. More than that, in its fear and hatred of working class revolt, it has smeared much of working-class militancy by calling it anarchist and terrorist. For example, the first acquisition of working class power in the Paris Commune of 1871 was not only defeated by the superior military power of the ruling bourgeoisie, but was climaxed by a brutal massacre of ordinary men, women, and children. The forces of law and order justified such wanton cruelty on the grounds that the Paris Commune was lawless, violent, and anarchist. Ever since, it has taken very little militancy of the working-class in its desire to better its lot for the bourgeois establishment to raise the spectre of anarchism, and to use this spectre to vindicate the more systematic use of terror. In more recent times, it has been the common fate of national liberation movements to be defined by official power as lawless renegades and put down with brutal state force.

It has been already stated that anarchism, although always sympathetic with oppressed and exploited groups, denies any systematic theory to identify those groups that have greater or lesser capacity for progressive action. Its only theoretical postulate is a rejection of all political authority, but it is a rejection in the name of the people in an often abstract sense or in the name of specific groups, which to anarchism at any particular time seem more oppressed than others. During the same period in which the highly individualized "revolution of the deed" became more common among anarchists, the working-class movement in the industrialized West grew to unprecedented heights both at the trade union and political party level. In Germany, which in many ways appeared to be the wave of the working class future, large numbers of an expanding industrial workforce joined the trade union movement. And the German Social Democratic Party, which openly represented the working class and espoused revolutionary Marxist principles (formally, at least until The First World War), became a consolidated and formidable political force. In short, the industrial working class was where the action was, and where there is action there predictably will be anarchist engagement with it.

Syndicalism

THE PARTICULAR DIRECTION that anarchism gives to a working class movement is anarcho-syndicalism or syndicalism, for short. Syndicalism can take a specifically reform coloration, but a revolutionary animus is the specific guise given to it by anarchism. For syndicalism, the working-class trade union is the beginning and the end of revolutionary action, and since it involves anarchism in day-to-day demands within ongoing organization, the syndicalist is often seen as the practical rather than the wild-eyed anarchist. In line with the anarchist rejection of any organization that openly vies for political power, syndicalism involves a total dedication to the trade union not only as the locus of revolutionary action, but as an opposition force to all political parties, even those which putatively (to anarchism) represent the working class.

The theoretical initiator of anarcho-syndicalism was Georges Sorel who, as Bose says, proclaimed that: "The future of socialism is to be found in the development of self-governing Trade Unions." For Sorel, the trade union is the most immediate locus of revolutionary action, and for anarchism the most immediate locus is always the best since immediacy is always to be preferred over demands of a more distant kind. Sorel's revolution by trade unions or syndicates also accords with other already familiar tenets of anarchism. First, Sorel rejects all political parties claiming that bonds of party membership are artificial and less real than the material class bonds of trade union membership. Second, Sorel was extremely distrustful of demands by trade unions for everyday reform of working and living conditions, putting all his hope in the fateful day of insurrection. Accordingly, the final goal of the revolutionary syndicalist was the general strike, that moment when all workers down their tools, bring capital to its knees, and usher in the new world of collective control of productive force through a voluntary confederation of trade unions. In their rejection of any cumulative sense of economic and political programme, anarcho-syndicalism stimulates militancy as the preparation for the great revolution – the general strike. Again, like all anarchism, it has respect only for grand gestures and little respect for the accretion of small victories over concrete issues.

What is also significant about Sorel's syndicalism, "the orientation of anarchism to fit the industrial age," Bose says, is his emphasis on the need for what he called revolutionary myth. Since anarchism abrogates the use of reason to analyze conditions and construct programme, and since the working class (in the syndicalist version of anarchism) is the repository of the instinct to revolutionary action, then what is needed to stimulate the instinct is the "magic power of myth." This myth, said Sorel, involves an image of the future suffused with faith in the efficacy of revolt. Revolutionary myths "are not descriptions of things, but expression of a determination to act." Along with this typically anarchist dedication to militant, instinctively-based action is a rejection of "allegedly inactive theoreticians. The proletarian must learn to think for himself without the guidance of middle class intellectuals." The peculiar amalgam of idealistic inspiration without theory and action based on faith makes Sorel often attractive to fascism, such that Mussolini, who himself was considered left wing early in life, could state that Sorel was the most important inspirer of fascism.

The fascist interpretation of syndicalism notwithstanding, this variety of anarchism has had great appeal to certain parts of the working class, more so in some countries than others. And while its revolutionary aspect is most significant historically, the outlook is spongy enough to go in other directions as well. For example G. D. H. Cole has suggested that guild socialism, which emphasizes the need for reform in a gradualist way, is syndicalist in inspiration. However, the Latin countries of Italy and especially Spain, which nourished anarchism at its origins, have been particularly receptive to anarcho-syndicalism.

In the United State during the early part of the twentieth century, syndicalism saw its greatest success in the International Workers of the World (IWW). This movement espoused local militant organizing and rejected gradualist action. It also rejected dealings with or for state power. The IWW had tremendous appeal for unskilled immigrant labour at a time when the existing trade unions were friendly to neither the unskilled nor the state. When immigration to the United States was essentially stopped in the 1920s and with the IWW attacked from all sides, many of its members joined the new Communist Party initiated in the aftermath of the Russian Revolution, and others simply drifted away. Specific historic reasons aside, this tendency of anarcho-syndicalist movements to rise with great exhilaration and militant energy only to last for a relatively short time and then to wither away is characteristic of a doctrine which eschews any theoretical or organizational basis for its survival.

Perhaps the most successful example of revolutionary syndicalist activities occurred in Spain during the pre-Civil War and Civil War period of the 1920s and 1930s. Organized in the Catalan Labor Federation (CNT) and Iberian Anarchist Federation (FAI), and having their greatest strength in the province of Catalonia (with Barcelona its capital), many industrial workers and farm labourers flocked to its banner. Bose, who wrote his history of anarchism as a strong sympathizer, says that the anarchist organizations in pre-Franco Spain were a continually divisive force because of their abstention from all reform. However, the fascist threat to Spain was met by anarchists with great courage and tenacity. In the face of the armed fascist attack, the anarcho-syndicalist movement in Spain responded with armed resistance, collectivization of land (done in the main on a voluntary basis), and the take-over of factories by trade unions. They also, within their own military units, broke down the traditional hierarchical order of officers and non-officers by democratizing the army under its influence. The province of Catalonia was basically under the control of anarchism at the beginning of the Civil War in Spain in 1936 and anarchist success was so notable that this period in Spain is now seen by contemporary anarchists as the high point of its movement as well as the example of its practical possibility.

The Spanish anarchist experiment was defeated, and it is unfair to see the main reasons for the defeat as due to causes internal to anarchism itself. After all, anarchism was only one element among many other forces brutally repressed in Republican Spain, and repressed not only by Franco's fascism but also by fascist assistance from Hitler's Germany and Mussolini's Italy in a general Western climate of active neutrality (essentially meaning that Western democracies let Spain go fascist). Yet looking at this one, and perhaps only, example of partial anarchist success, its failure does appear rooted in the dilemmas of anarchism as a social and political doctrine. Since anarchism demands not only the completely free right of members of trade unions to join or leave at will, but also the voluntary right of unions to federate or not to federate with other unions, successful anarchism in Catalonia immediately faced problems which its own doctrine could not by its very nature resolve (in fact, to put the matter more precisely, it was a doctrine which often exacerbated such problems).

In the first place, the anarchist accession to power occurred in a region isolated from other regions in which anti-fascist forces were run on other bases. It had to deal with these other regions both for common military purposes and for necessary economic interchange. Since it could not accept, or at least many of its local units could not accept, any unified structure to make decisions (this would be a hated state), coordination with external regions became difficult and chaotic. Second, at the internal level, there was an immediate need for coordination of producing units under anarchist control, a need clearly apparent to many anarchists themselves. The military units of the anarchist front also faced difficulties in allowing each fighting column to have the voluntary right to combine or not to combine with other columns. Thus, in this unusual example of anarchist success in spontaneously taking over the productive apparatus of a whole region of a country, the need to deal with outside regions as well as the need to produce and defend themselves in a time of great crisis made untenable the anarchist doctrine of completely voluntary recruitment to local units and of completely voluntary confederation of these units into larger regional bodies. Since revolutionary opportunities always occur in conditions similar to this and since crises demanding strong coordination and control are also common to revolutionary situations, it seems evident that these insoluble dilemmas will always face anarchism in these unusual circumstances of strong anarchist success. This sense of anarchist failure being built into its first and only success is summed up by Bose when he says: "For nearly a hundred years revolutionary anarchism ran its course. It ran its best lap in Spain." Interestingly enough, Bose wrote this epitaph for anarchism in the late 1960s at a time that anarchism under another name appeared to be proving itself far from dead.

The preceding chronicling of anarchist history, from Bakunin's engagement with the International through terrorism, anarcho-syndicalism to the partial success of Spanish anarchism, gives the outlook a certain coherence which, at other places in this essay, it has been seen to lack. The reason for this apparent coherence is because of the fact that the growth of the working-class movement in the past century with some form of Marxism as its theoretical summation has been so singularly impressive that it is all too easy to chronicle the meaning of anarchism with regard to the working class alone. But as has been already said, the most important feature in the anarchist credo is its lack of theoretical coherence, which gives it the capacity to gather all and sundry under its banner. To give an extreme, but perhaps telling example, the ideas of the arch reactionary Ayn Rand expressed in her novels extol the virtue of absolute individual freedom against all notions of social responsibility and could, without too much difficulty, be seen as a variety of anarchism; that is, anarchist ideas can take completely right-wing directions and still, in some terms, be true to some of its basic assumptions.

Communitarianism

WHEN WE LOOK outside the working class movement during the same nineteenth and twentieth century period, we find many thinkers and movements still encompassed by anarchism. The United States in the nineteenth century saw a whole series of communitarian experiences. At the roots of these experiments in constructing communities isolated from dominant industrializing systems is a basic rejection of any possibility of effectively transforming industrial capitalism for the better. There are obviously many forms of escapism possible in liberal capitalism, many of which by no stretch of the imagination could be called anarchist. Anarchist escapism is characterized by its emphasis on the experimental quality of its community building and by its commitment to immediate equality and cooperative living. What characterizes much of anarchism of this type is also a rejection of what it considers the corroding qualities of material wealth; hence the distrust of the way the fruits of industrial civilization affect the people living in it. Thus, the utopian nineteenth-century communities of New Harmony and Oneida remained predominantly agricultural, and while stressing the need for community self-reliance, they did not go beyond craft production.

The mood of rural utopianism is one of austerity and simplicity. Although sometimes these communities had hopes of affecting the surrounding society by their moral example and thereby affecting other people to break away from what was considered a life of indulgence or boredom, the more common predisposition of these communities was toward a better life for themselves, and devil take the hindmost. That is, the emphasis, as with much anarchism, is often more with the integrity and conscience of the anarchist than it is with the effect of anarchist action on the wider society.

Perhaps no one better sums up in one life these twin themes of escape to simple life and a commitment to individual conscience against existing authority than the life of Thoreau. For Thoreau lived both in society and attempted to live outside it in his famous retreat alone to Walden Pond. Whether in or out, however, he claimed himself to be in continual disobedience to the state and its laws insofar as these laws interfered with the rules of his own individual conscience. And the demands of this conscience are those of simplicity and austerity as well as an accent on as complete self-reliance as possible. What is unique to Thoreau's thought, which puts him into one of the main streams of the broad anarchist current, is his assumptions about the origins of individual conscience. These assumptions, almost always unquestioned, placed the beginnings of conscience in the realm of original human nature. It seems, according to this view, that something like the integrity of each individual exists at birth and that life is a continual battle to maintain it against the unjust demands of an inherently unjust state. This mode of thinking may often be incisive in perceiving the social origins of those without conscience, but as for itself, it is usually blind to its own connections to society. In fact, it often finds almost all others wanting in conscience since they appear to be living in continual compromise with unjust social institutions. This perpetual individual embattlement is what gives Thoreau that quality of encrusted curmudgeonry so often sanctified by those who romanticize eccentric nonconformity. The social and ideological roots of this outlook, although not addressed by the outlook itself, appear abundantly clear.

A central quality of the Thoreau-type anarchism, then, is its extreme individualism. It tends to posit a divide between the individual and society with the former colored with positive qualities of freedom, autonomy, and the potential for self-reliance and the latter tinged with negative qualities of oppressiveness, dull conformity, and tyranny. While it is true that anarchism focuses upon the state as the major repository of evil, it commonly, and especially in its most individualistic form, makes little distinction between the state and society. In fact, insofar as this kind of anarchism considers the problem of the relationship of state and society, then the state is seen as the organized reflection of popular sentiment. And popular sentiment for the individualist is suffused with the imagery of mob rule. This ideological current, which conceives of the courageous and rational individual standing apart from or standing against the arbitrary stupidity of large collectivities, has deep roots in modern Western history. No doubt one of its earliest representatives is the Robinson Crusoe myth of the single, strong (male) individual maintaining himself alone and unafraid without need of anyone else (except, interestingly enough, a black slave who is picked up on his island retreat). The same refrain occurs again and again in, for example, Ibsen's presentation of the heroic man of principle in conflict with the bigoted sentiments and ideas of the majority in his play *Enemy of the People*. Or in much of the ideology of the mass media, the strong individual of principle confronts the prejudice of the mob (witness, for example, the hero in the movies *High Noon* and *Bridge of Spies*).

The great hiatus between individual conscience and conscienceless collectivities as an ideological standpoint is so central to Western capitalism that, as was said before, it can easily take reactionary directions, as it does, for example, in the lionization of the charismatic leader who is obliged to control and manipulate the allegedly sheep-like masses. Often the central basis on which anarchistic individualism differs from fascist individualism is the fact that anarchism always demonstrates sympathy for the plight of the People whereas fascism is contemptuous of the People. This does mean something significant in political programme since there is a clear-cut difference between Thoreau or Tolstoy or Gandhi on the one hand, all of whom represent variations on this theme of individualistic integrity, and Hitler and Mussolini on the other. And it is this contempt for the People that allows the latter to embrace state power in such a cynical way. To the anarchists of this type's credit, they remain distant from power and often lead exemplary and self-sacrificing lies.

It could also be contended that the numerous elite/mass theories that dot the social scientific landscape evidence the same ideological undercurrent and similar political distinctions. And again, although the most left wing among them indicate definite anarchist assumptions, these theories can cover the spectrum.

A thinker such as Vilfredo Pareto, who postulated a theory of continual circulation of elites dominating a relatively inert populace, has often been a stimulus for fascist political conclusions along with similar thoughts attributable to José Ortega y Gasset. Robert Michel's theory of the iron law of oligarchy that sees all social organizations, regardless of their degree of democratic pretension, as tending toward domination by the few is another example of this type of thought. On the left, a thinker as critical of the status quo as C. Wright Mills links his criticism to what he considers the massive homogenization of American culture by an irresponsible power elite. And as with much of individualistic anarchism, his critique is done from a lofty moral peak from which he and those who wish to join him can hurl down their barbs of criticism.

As said earlier, the defeat of the anarchists in the more general defeat of progressive forces in Spain in the 1930s is often thought to represent the termination of the anarchist project. This interpretation, however, is neither true historically nor does it show a clear understanding of the place of anarchism in modern society. The individualist rebellion against authority has its origins in the whole bourgeois rupture with feudalism and continues in so many forms as to suffuse the whole ideological climate of liberal capitalism. And anarchism is one of its most dramatic and excessive forms since it commonly involves grand gestures and no compromise. Anarchism is so potentially common a response in this kind of society that it can arise with little awareness of itself and can call itself by other names. This is the case with the last great anarchist revival, the new left of the 1960s and '70s. Although not calling itself anarchist and often denied the term by older anarchist sympathizers, the characteristics of this movement appear so quintessentially anarchist that it cannot go by any other name. In fact, there are features in the new left that often make it appear more anarchist than any previous movements of this kind.

The New Left

THE NEW LEFT as a mass movement was located in that part of the population most prone to theoretical expression without consistency, to individualistic rebellion tinged with arrogance, and to political activism suffused with vacillation – young people and especially young students. Historians of the period in the United States link the new left to earlier individualized rebellion against the dominant system by the beats in the 1950s, the distinguishing difference of course being the much greater politicization in the new left and its far bigger mass following. Regardless of its specific historical antecedents, the 1960s and early 1970s, with varying intensity and varying policy in different Western capitalist countries, saw the eruption of fairly large movements of youth rebellion characterizing themselves as a new left.

What is peculiar about this rebellion is that its most articulate and well-known spokespersons did not see themselves as anarchists at all, but rather as part of a revival of Marxism. This peculiarity appears due to a number of causes. By the 1960s there was so little remnant of the anarchist tradition that a new rebellion, even while inspired by an anarchist animus, had little possibility of recognizing its linkage to a long dead past. Moreover, the new left, even more perhaps than all earlier anarchism, showed almost no interest in history, its own or anyone else's. Finally, the left-wing political landscape had for so long been almost coterminous with Marxism that a new movement had little option but to take on a Marxist coloration.

Seeing itself as a *new left* meant that the major reference point in launching the movement was the conception of an *old* left. Here too, the ahistorical nature of the movement, its predominant sense that it had sprung de novo onto the stage of history, dictated that it tended to create a past *for its own purposes* rather than to clearly understand that past. For its major purposes in dealing with the old left was to prove how defunct and useless that left-wing tradition had been with the result that the new left could shine in the glory of a never-before-seen eruption of revolutionary consciousness. The old left was excoriated on two grounds, one moral and one organizational. On the moral plane, it was condemned for its compromise with the status quo, for its flabby, dull, merely reformist character. Both the social democratic and communist parties everywhere were subject to this critique. At the organizational level, the communist parties, as major symbols of the old left, were seen as overcentralized dinosaurs, which had committed and continued to commit great crimes against the people in the name of socialism.

In the American context in which the new left had tremendous success, being fueled by the twin injustices of blatant racism (with actual apartheid in the South) and an imperialist war in Vietnam, the attack on the old left there had a particular flavour. This particularity was a result of the fact that there was so little of an old left to attack there. The combination of rising living standards brought on by post-Second World War prosperity plus the McCarthyist decimation of progressive forces meant that there was little remaining of an old left. The old left was literally invented by the new left as a basis for generating its own special sense of historic mission and moral fervour. In short, in the United States at the time, the old left was a straw man of little substance created mainly as a necessary myth to bolster the new left image of itself. This analysis is, of course, less true in Europe where thriving social democratic and communist parties existed and where new left critique came closer to real contention with living social forces.

In any case, the new left is considered by almost all progressive analysts as a major progressive force in this era, one which stimulated and mobilized large numbers of people around major issues such as racial oppression and imperialist war. This analysis of the new left as progressive stems, it seems to us, from a misunderstanding, but a misunderstanding that is logical to make in a predominantly anarchist movement. As with all preceding collectivist types of anarchism, the new left as a theoretical tendency rejected the idea that mass movements need organized leadership to coordinate and direct them. Central to the new left's critique of the old left was the latter's willingness to form political parties, which attempt to sum up the theoretical direction of working classes and to take and maintain power in their name. In contrast to all existing political parties, the new left eschewed any interest in political power and rejected the need to organize parties directed toward attaining such power. Its substantive attack on social democratic parties is similar in many ways to a revolutionary Marxist attack. Social democracy, said the new left, is essentially reformist with the result that it assists in the ongoing integration of oppressed groups into capitalism.

The most pointed barbs of new leftism were directed toward Leninist Marxism renouncing what may be the two most central features of Lenin's contribution to Marxism (see Chapter Three). The first feature revolves around Lenin's contention that the working class *left to itself* will remain mired in everyday economic demands. It needs theoretical direction, which in early stages of transition must come from intellectuals outside the working class who sum up and sustain the overall revolutionary movement of the class. Lenin's position on this matter is expressed well in his statement that "without revolutionary theory, there can be no revolution." Stemming from the need for theory to be developed by intellectuals is the second major feature initiated by Lenin – the demand for a highly organized body of professional revolutionaries who form a political party for and with the working class.

The new left fundamentally rejected these twin premises of Leninism, but usually considering itself revolutionary Marxist and therefore supposedly sympathetic to Lenin, its rejection was often roundabout and indirect. Insofar as it rejected the need for any type of leadership, its attack upon the failure of older existing political parties was couched in exclusively immediate factual examples. The new left, for example, was forever denouncing the arbitrary, bureaucratic, and privileged activities of existing communist parties but almost never dealt with Lenin's arguments about the necessity for professional revolutionary parties nor did they deal with the early successes of Bolshevik-type parties. It was relatively easy for the new left to attack these later parties for their 'Stalinism' implying by this attack that all such parties are doomed to this fate from the beginning. And given the real degeneration occurring in these parties everywhere, the case was a strong one. What is being suggested here is that the new left never contended with this all important issue frontally with an examination of Lenin and the real history of Leninist parties. Instead, the later 'Stalinist' versions became easy targets for the familiar anarchist attack on *all* attempts at political leadership.

On the issue of the source of revolutionary inspiration and direction for social transformation, the new left also clearly demonstrated its anarchist spirit. In the first place, concomitant with a rejection of the need for theory came tremendous vacillation in the new left about where the source of social change was located. Sometimes stressing blacks, at other times imperialized peoples, still at other times underclasses at the margins of capitalist society, the only consistent aspect of new left analysis was its inconsistency. In the May events of 1968 in Paris where French students joined with the working class to literally bring France to a standstill, the linkage was made between the new left and the working class, but this linkage was a response to events rather than a theoretical decision about the significance of that class for social change. And that is exactly the point. New left theory, insofar as there was any theorizing, focused upon the importance of any oppressed group that seemed to be immediately in motion. As has been true for anarchism since Bakunin, the accent in new left activities is upon the glorification of mass rebellious energy, which then demands of the anarchist that s/he gives full dedication to joining whatever group of people is expressing this outburst. Then that outburst was theoretically validated as a new wave of revolutionary possibility until it petered out and another group became the heroes of the moment. Instead of theory leading practice, practice becomes its own validation. To the idea that the working classes or any group in rebellion needs direction both to consolidate and channel their energies into progressive directions and to educate them for the long historical haul, the new left counterposed the idea of the purity of spontaneous rebellion. What it considered newest about its leftism was the commitment to revolutionary change as immediate daily acts. To new leftism, revolution was the moral energy and attitude suffusing whatever it was doing at any particular time. Without long range analysis of the contours of society, without analysis of their own place in society, new leftists were committed to the view that revolution is defined by the quality and quantity of activities they performed rather than the connection of those acts to other groups and the real effects such acts were having. Moreover, the more revolutionary an act appeared, the less compromising with hated power, the more it was defined as revolutionary. Any long range tactical programme was seen as selling out, as part of the compromises of the (to them) defunct old left.

The glorification of spontaneous immediate rebellion by the new left meant that social transformation was viewed as an automatic unfolding of a pre-existing revolutionary spirit. To the new left, the people or those parts of the people who are seething with rebellion are already possessed of all virtue and need no stimulus other than the fostering of this revolutionary demiurge. This trust in spontaneous upsurge combined with an absence of coherent analysis of the society in which it lived often left this movement isolated and drove the new left continuously to its own ranks for political sustenance, its own ranks being the student youth movement out of which it originated. Thus, although the new left, in the main, was intent upon the total transformation of society and was therefore aware of the need for connection to larger sectors of oppression, its implicit assumptions led it ultimately to fall back upon its own constituents. As long as blacks were in motion for civil rights or even greater numbers from all classes against imperialist war, then new leftism could be energized and maintain its role as the most revolutionary outlook in a large heterogeneous movement. But when the single issues that motivated these movements were resolved (or usually apparently resolved enough to take the steam out of the movement), then new leftists had only themselves to confirm how revolutionary they were. Moreover, as is true of revolutionary anarchism in general, the people may be glorified for their revolutionary spontaneity, but such zeal is seldom permanent or revolutionary enough for the anarchists. In the end, new leftists like their anarchist forbears were disappointed with the people they sanctify and in the end fell back upon themselves.

Two other aspects of new left history demonstrate its clear links to anarchism. One aspect involved the generation of a new communitarian experience. The 1960s saw the rebirth of utopian communities often in rural areas, but even in cities in what were called urban communes. The urge to create the microcosm of a new world in the immediate confines of private existence was extremely strong in the new left period. The proliferation of this kind of communitarian experimentation was wondrous with many types rising and falling, people moving from one to the other, with varying emphases in domestic arrangement and moral justification. The impetus toward the privatization of revolutionary experience in the new left went deeper than its attempted fulfillment in communal experiments. Often each single act by a new left activist was defined as embodying the wave of the future. Famous epigrams such as, "When I make love, I am making the revolution," indicate the significance of this viewpoint. Moreover, there was often little difference between the communal and the individual manifestations of this outlook since the same people expressed and lived both variations of these themes. The emphasis here on private existence is mainly encompassed in a domestic or rural social situation since often the idea of structured, modern paid work was rejected by the new left. Commenting on Paris in 1968, Richard Gombin sums up this attitude as follows: "To be completely emancipated, the individual must be the creator of his (sic) own existence and he must shake off the shackles which hinder him. One of these shackles is work." Emancipation among new leftists usually implied that individuals created their own revolutionary existence, and work played a small part in this creation. The major emphasis in all of this is the idea that the revolution must begin and end within militants themselves rather than with the external effects of action.

Even the new left's activities within situations which, on the surface, involve traditional strikes or factory takeovers (as in France of 1968) took on a distinctly anarchist flavour. What is deemed important by the new left in these activities is the quality of the action, the way in which the action reflects a total revolutionary viewpoint. All preexisting structures of parties, unions, and even programmes were rejected in the name of the pure quality of the revolutionary action. This action was seen as a new 'happening' symbolic of the creation of a new world inherent in the action itself. Again, even in linkage to working class groups in revolt, the new leftist attitude was not analysis and programme, but an all or nothing expression of what they considered their own already internally created revolutionary stance toward the world.

The other aspect of new left history, which links it clearly to anarchism, occurred later during this period at a time when the mass youth movement within which it was closely integrated had clearly run out of steam. By the early 1970s, broader movements that nurtured the new left, such as the civil rights movement and the anti-war movement, had either been co-opted or had been partially successful (as with, for example, the end of the draft in the United States and the coming victory of the National Liberation Front – NLF – in the Vietnamese War). As had happened in the past when anarchism lost linkages to broader movements (or were rejected by them), the response by the new left to similar circumstance was despair and disillusionment; and as with anarchists in late nineteenth and early twentieth century Europe, the new left, or remnants of this ever diminishing movement in the early 1970s turned to individual terrorism. The group calling themselves the Weatherpersons in the United States was a clear manifestation of this tendency. It was initiated, went underground, and committed a number of dramatic acts reminiscent of earlier acts of "revolution by the deed." In their belief that such acts were proof of revolutionary purity and that this purity must be kept alive because of the conservative miasma around them, this latter-day terrorism seems to embody the same viewpoint as earlier anarchist terror (while not recognizing this or any other connection). And as with the earlier variety, police repression and the almost complete lack of popular support for these deeds led to the demise of this manifestation of anarchism. Thus, terrorism erupted and died as the last gasp of new leftism.

It seems apparent, then, that the rise of the new left, its ideological justifications, its mode of operation, and its evolution and denouement all bear the stamp of anarchism. Many of its sympathizers reject this analysis and see little that connects new leftism to anarchism. Part of the reason for this rejection is that anarchism, even on the left, already had a harmful reputation by the 1960s, or it was so little known that it bore too quaint a ring for these very 'modern' revolutionaries. As was mentioned earlier, considering itself newly Marxist was much the most appealing appellation for themselves. Another reason for the new left disdain for the anarchist label is connected to its deeper distaste for any general conception of itself. New leftism had to see itself as historically unprecedented, as something never seen before, in fact as a movement erupting out of the purely and newly discovered revolutionary spirit in themselves. If what is revolutionary is what new leftists may do at any movement, an unpredictable flowering of an inner fire, then they were not only "indifferent to labels," but downright hostile to them. In this context, the rejection of the label anarchist is not only predictable but is actually part and parcel of the anarchist outlook itself.

The end of the new left period was due not only to the diminution of wider social forces, which nurtured this political phenomenon, although this is certainly an important factor in its denouement. Given the absence of easy separation between the new left and these wider forces, in fact given the new left proclivity to reject the need for such differentiation, it would follow that the end of the Vietnamese War and the Civil Rights movement would also take the wind out of new left sails. But its death is also due to ideas inherent to new leftism itself, ideas that it shares with the broader anarchist tradition. Rejecting analysis, programme, and theory breeds the very instability which gives anarchism that sense of meteoric rise and tragic fall, and this sense is certainly a major aspect of new left history. Moreover, the new left and anarchism in general can be characterized by a type of morally purified zeal that, by its very nature, cannot last long. Burnout is not uncommon in all political movements fighting against strong tides, but the burnout of young anarchist activists in the first place is the logical outcome of the nature and intensity of the flame and, as well, the lack of connection to respectable status (especially academic where you can be paid to be steeped in many forms of idealism).

The end of new leftism appeared to be the last major occurrence in the anarchist project, an end which led even sympathizers to ask whether it might not have been the last spasm of anarchism, presumably never to be heard from again. And the end of anarchism is a theme often heard at varying times from many shades of political opinion. Lenin, for example, saw the growth and influence of anarchism as due to the immaturity of the working class movement. It was, according to him, a passing thing that would disappear with the growing strength and political maturity of the working class. In response to questions about anarchists in Germany following the Russian Revolution, Lenin wrote:

> By polemicising with them we merely give them publicity. They are too unintelligent; it is wrong to take them seriously; and it is not worth being angry with them. They have no influence among the masses, and will acquire none, unless we make mistakes. Let us leave this tiny trend to die a natural death; the workers themselves will realize that it is worthless.

Anarchism did not die the natural death predicted by Lenin since it has seen major rebirths in Spain, in the new left, and in various other upsurges to the present. Whether this is due to the continuing political immaturity of the working class as Lenin contended (an immaturity which he saw as nearly over in his own time) appears debatable. Even if this immaturity remains a factor in explaining the staying power of anarchism – and "unintelligent" seems far off the mark – it must be considered that other forces are at work here. Any lull in anarchist activity does not signify the death knell of this political outlook since extreme highs and extreme lows seem inherent to this type of political manifestation. And if it is a result of immaturity, it does not appear to be something that is normally and easily outgrown. Certainly, there was little analysis in the wake of the new left demise that would suggest a critical break with anarchism. The major responses on the left involved either despair about the loss of something or soon afterwards a spate of books full of nostalgia for those bygone wonderful days of the 1960s.

We have, contrary to Lenin, taken anarchism seriously. The staying power of the anarchist demiurge is demonstrated rather dramatically by the rise in this new century of what can only be called the *new* new left. It is premised consciously on assumptions very similar to the movements of the late nineteen sixties and early seventies – a conscientious ignorance of history, an emphasis on local communal gathering, a ring of strong moral revolutionizing, some dedication to revolutionary exhibitionism, hostility to the very idea of political power, and opposition to permanent leadership – all these are ideas that suffused the earlier new left. Yet there are significant differences in historical context and emphasis in this new eruption that make it different and more positive than the last version. The new left occurred in more prosperous times and was activated by youth who still had a more bounteous future in a still prosperous capitalism (as proven by the very standard economic success enjoyed by so many ex-new leftists). Youth at present face a more disastrous and doubtful future, a situation that gives their rebellion potentially greater staying power. Also recent militancy in its very inexperience does not show a categorical rejection of an old left, making it much more open to the possibility of acceptance of Marxist theory and practice. Finally, the initiation of the Occupy movement gave radical thought a geographic permanence that has brought militant ideas to the forefront of even conventional political debate. In spite of the all too easy destruction of Occupy sites by police power, this new movement has given credence to an open criticism of capitalism with its dramatic slogan of the 1% dominating the 99%. Given the recent bank crisis and the deepening economic instability of the capitalist system as well as the overwhelming significance of environmental disaster, it is hard to imagine that anarchistic rebellion will so easily wither away; in fact the time seems ripe that some of its militants may develop a more lasting engagement with concrete planning and organizing.

Anarchism, it has been suggested here, may erupt, dazzle, and then die, but it will not automatically go away because it is rooted in very deep-seated aspects of the modem social fabric. It is so central to that fabric that anarchist possibilities suffuse modem life even at those times when they do not congeal into the pyrotechnical manifestations, which are most characteristic of this phenomenon. Anarchism, it is being suggested here, is a central mood of the whole capitalist epoch.

That body of ideological assumptions flowing out of the Enlightenment sanctified the idea of the individual in splendid isolation from the rest of society and often in perpetual rebellion against existing authority. The rebellion that defines the bourgeois revolution was against not only the feudal monarchy, but was also suspicious of all authority, especially when it takes state form. The liberal idea that the best state is that which governs least is a clear representation of this profound suspicion of government. Connected to this suspicion is the right of individual disobedience, of individual conscience against unjust government. In certain ways, Marxism shares in this Enlightenment tradition by perceiving of the state not only as an enemy to be overthrown, but as an institution which must and will wither away. Where Marxism and anarchism part ways is on the question of transition to statelessness. Anarchism sees the need to abolish the state immediately upon the triumph of the revolution whereas Marxism advocates a change in state form as the prelude to its withering away.

Given the common roots of liberalism, Marxism, and anarchism in their rebellion against authority, especially state authority, their more fundamental differences rest upon the question of for whom or what forces, the rebellion is done. Here the more central links of liberalism and anarchism have already been indicated. Whereas Marxism is a theory which focuses on social classes in conflict and the working class in rebellion as the potential resolver of that conflict, the focus of rebellion in both liberalism and anarchism is the individual. It is the infringement on individual liberty by state power, which is the starting point of both these outlooks. The liberal rebellion against feudal authority saw individual property owning as the guarantee of liberty and ultimately accommodates to that state which defends property (even as the latter becomes de-individualized through monopoly). Anarchism carries the liberal project to its logical conclusion by rejecting authority in all its forms – government authority, business authority, religious authority, family authority.

The sovereignty of individual liberty and its right to rebel against all limitations is the bedrock of anarchism and it is also perhaps the central ideological undercurrent of Western capitalism. Given that the structural foundations of individualism, the world of small property and small government has been superseded by a world of bigness, which sets more and more limits on the potential for individual liberty, then the groundswell of individuated rebellion so common to this system is even further stimulated. Only a consolidated socialist and collective form of organization could counter this bigness in a new way, but the tradition of individualism is deep and strong. The appeal of left-wing anarchism, which promises both socialism and individual sovereignty and which appears to give an immediately new world while still fulfilling the old promises of individuated liberty, becomes, in this context, an extremely alluring appeal.

It has often been said that anarchists and Marxists are working for the same historical future – a classless society without the need for repressive state power – and that their only difference is the means to get there. And there is enough truth to this statement that they often partake of the same criticism of the status quo and are often found on the same side in concrete political activities. At a deeper level, however, it appears that the ends to which these movements strive are not basically the same; and certainly the means they employ lead to very different ends anyway.

The first and central plank of anarchist theory and practice is individual liberty and the rejection of all limitations and regulations in the name of this liberty. Even when anarchism finds itself in the socialist camp, it carefully delineates itself from other forms of socialism by declaring itself *libertarian* socialist. This liberty is not fundamentally a freedom that derives from and is fostered by social circumstances, but is a disembodied mystique of pure voluntary will. While anarchism seemingly objects only to state power over the individual, it actually rejects the limits set by any social organizational form. The anarchist is an uneasy member of any social organization always prepared to reject its dictates for the sake of individual want, need, or whim. Moreover, since s/he also rejects the need for any theory that gives justification for such membership, the anarchist is always capable of finding justification for quitting membership in any group. Single-issue politics joined at the height of militancy only to be dropped with the rise of another exciting issue is most common to anarchist activity because this mode of politics fits so well with this restless, continually rebellious spirit.

If anarchism is more of a mood than a stable theory and analysis, then the core political emphasis of this mood is perpetual impatience. For the anarchist, nothing ever seems to work; failure is the end result of whatever is being done, which if it does not lead to burnout, spurs him/her on to a new round of militant rebellion in the next issue of the movement. Since it is likely that the crisis-ridden nature of modern capitalism will undoubtedly generate issues and militant responses by certain groups around these issues, it is also likely that anarchism will continue to erupt and join these movements. Anarchism cannot be seen, then, as a congealed doctrine, which fights and either clearly wins or clearly loses, an interpretation that is implicit in the view that the new left, having been defeated, is the last gasp of anarchism. Rather, anarchism as a persistent undercurrent of liberalism is always part of a society that nurtures liberal individualism and will remain so as long as the liberal tradition holds sway in the world. The idea of consumer sovereignty, of individual destiny, of do-your-own-thingism, which are the bedrock of modern liberal ideology, are also the ideas that nurture the more extreme liberalism of the anarchist. Anarchism more blatantly shows itself in periods of popular discontent and there is every reason to believe that such discontent will not disappear from modern capitalism.

It appears wrong, then, to see anarchism and Marxism as heading toward similar ultimate ends with only different means to get there. They differ profoundly about intermediate ends on the road to the future and their differences in means result in such continual conflict that it should come as no surprise that they end up in perpetual enmity. To be uncompromising about reform (and therefore unreliable in those inevitable cases where anarchists are engaged in reform), to reject organization (even when forced to form and join organizations of their own), to abstain from leadership (even while defining themselves as the leading revolutionaries of any movement), and to rebel against all power (even though power is thrust upon them by circumstances, as in 1930s Spain), makes anarchists very uneasy allies with Marxism (or with anything else). And their extreme individualism makes anarchists uneasy allies with each other.

Although anarchism is often characterized as the most extreme rejection of modern capitalism, in a very real sense it is doubtful if it could exist to the same intensity anywhere else. The kind of individuated rebellion that defines anarchism is continually generated by liberal ideology, which most easily justifies, sanctions, and tolerates this form of rebellion. Thus, it is one of the more profound ironies of history that anarchism, which in the contemporary West conjures up images of chaos, is at the same time an outlook endemic to the liberal spirit of individualism and individualized rebellion against authority. This most uncomfortable of doctrines is comfortably ensconced in the milieu it so normally excoriates.

We are finally left with the question whether anarchism is a progressive outlook. Although anarchism, as has been suggested, can take a blatantly right-wing form and can be used to justify the need for a fascist superman, anarchism has most commonly been characterized as part of the left; that is, as a critique of capitalism from the point of view of one of its many oppressed groups. The question of anarchism's progressive credentials must then be addressed to this latter form. The standard Marxist answer to this question has been clear and unequivocal. For Marxism, anarchism is a barrage of revolutionary rhetoric whose consequences not only conserve the status quo but do real damage to progressive movements and possibilities. Engels' response to the anarchist engagement with the Paris Commune (in "On Authority") is quite representative of his and Marx's views on the subject: "either the anti-authoritarians [meaning anarchists] don't know what they are talking about, in which case they are creating nothing but confusion; or they do know, and in that case they are betraying the movement of the proletariat. In either case they serve the reaction." Lenin, writing at a time when the issue of right-wing reformism was more pointed and directly involved in the problem of revolutionary transformation, was also forceful in his condemnation of anarchism. He asserts that anarchism has "no doctrine, revolutionary teaching, or theory. – Fragmentation of the working-class movement. – Complete fiasco in the experiments of the revolutionary movement (Proudhonism, 1871; Bakuninism; 1873). – Subordination of the working class to *bourgeois* politics in the guise of the negation of politics" (from "Anarchism and Socialism"). The allusion by Lenin to bourgeois politics refers to the overall consequences of anarchist activity; that it results in the conserving of the bourgeois order of things. Marxism would consider that anarchism's emphasis on individual liberty means that its origins and manifestations are petit bourgeois; that is, rooted in small property ideology.

Conclusion

THIS SURVEY of anarchist thinkers and movements and of the undercurrents that undergird them demonstrates that this viewpoint is extremely far-flung and diffuse. It also demonstrates that the overall theoretical summation of anarchism by revolutionary Marxism appears fundamentally correct although the application of that theory to actual thinkers and activities must be done with care and discretion. By definition, anarchism, bred in individual rebellion, is not all of a piece and in certain circumstances the activities of specific anarchists do play a progressive role. Anarchism often appears, in the present, to be the only game in town. Just as many ex-new left activists found respectable careers in the 1970s, at best in professions that allowed them a continued involvement with progressive work (legal aid, environmentalism, book publishing, journalism, and especially academia), contemporary anarchist intellectuals continue in this vein. What goes under the rubric of theory is, again, rebellion against unjust authority, love for the people in revolt, and opposition, not just to tyrannical dictatorships, but to authority of all stripes. For example, in the United States today, the foremost progressive social critic known worldwide for his exhaustive and invigorating critique of American foreign policy and of the intellectual prostitution of its academic establishment is undoubtedly Noam Chomsky. And Noam Chomsky is a self-proclaimed exponent of much of the anarchist tradition. At this time, to condemn Chomsky *in toto* for his anarchism is to undermine a unique progressive voice in a mainly conservative wilderness.

In the actual concrete struggles of the present, principled differences on the left are not articulated. And we acknowledge that in non-revolutionary moments that demand progressive action, Marxists put aside these differences and engage fully. But it is our fundamental contention that, in general, differences of political principle must be understood, articulated, and used to guide tactical alliances and long-term revolutionary strategy.

Much of the purely individualistic rebellion found in the many acts of individual workers bears the stamp of anarchism, since they are done as a spontaneous outburst without possibility of success. If a worker pickets alone against injustice to him/herself or in despair climbs up on a crane to stop the operations of a whole factory (both of these events have happened in Nova Scotia in the not-too-distant past), then their acts of courage and nobility set examples for others and are undoubtedly progressive. But single acts like this often disillusion the most courageous, so that without the disciplined optimism that only organized progressive action can bring, the spontaneous anarchist act is usually turned into something else. Moreover, at times of crisis where only theoretically-based organized action can lead to real progressive movement, then individuated rebellion often becomes counterproductive. The intellectual defenders of this kind of rebellion, the true anarchists, then oppose organization, theory, and disciplined leadership in the name of liberty. The more successful the progressive movement, the more oppositional anarchism becomes. In this latter context, anarchism shows its truest colors, the colors of petit bourgeois rebellion beclouding and obstructing the potential movement forward.

CHAPTER THREE

Social Democracy and Reformism

WHEN ROSA Luxemburg declared, in the revolutionary fervour of early twentieth century Europe, that the choice for the future was between barbarism and revolution, she dismissed by omission any notion of a peaceful, evolutionary path to socialism. Although Luxemburg proved to be prescient with respect to the fate of the 1919 German insurrection, the chimera of an intermediate path to socialism has continued to confound revolutionary Marxism. Various schemes for socialist transition have persisted to the present either as putative alternatives to or distorted images of Marxism in such guises as Swedish social democracy, African socialism, or Euro-communism. Whatever limited success such endeavours have had in resource redistribution, power sharing, or economic development, they have been historically specific and regionally limited. Ultimately all these 'middle ways' have collapsed as models for the future of socialism in the face of the relentless globalization of capitalism as a world system. In fact, it is as much the failures of European social democracy in the late twentieth century as the precipitous collapse of socialism in Eastern Europe that led many Western intellectuals to embrace the theoretical nihilism of post-modernism.

Unlike the underground role that anarchism has played in the history of the left, social democracy has been front and centre. The roots of social democracy extend to the early days of pre-Marxian socialism. It has been the dominant form of 'left' theory and practice in the core capitalist countries and has had an ambiguous relationship at various times and places with revolutionary socialism. In the contemporary era of global imperialism, the question of the survival of social democracy is high on the progressive agenda. In this chapter, we intend to provide an overview of the emergence and characteristics of social democracy. While the social democratic outlook emerged prior to Marxism, in its most significant political manifestation it represented a reformist offshoot from revolutionary Marxism. We will tread some familiar territory, reviewing the reformist tendencies in Lassallean socialism and the revisionist controversy in social democracy at the turn of the twentieth century. Ultimately, the fundamental question now facing revolutionary Marxism is the need for consistent articulation of the principles of revolutionary Marxism in a situation where, in the West, there are opportunities only for reform, and while revolutionary opportunities are problematic elsewhere.

Social Democracy and Revisionism

ORIGINALLY, the term 'social democracy' meant that a political party was committed to a revolutionary Marxist programme. By the 1890s, serious divisions became apparent within the national parties that composed the social democratic movement. To simplify the ideological divisions, the movement was rent by a crucial debate about strategy. The essential disagreement was whether capitalism could be transformed into socialism peacefully, through parliamentary legislation or whether such a fundamental social change could not be accomplished without a violent revolution. The idea of peaceful, evolutionary change was promulgated most forcefully in Germany within the largest and most successful social democratic party. In contrast, those who believed that only a revolution could bring about a socialist society termed the movement for socialism by slow evolution 'revisionism' when it referred to Marxist theory and reformism when the focus was on practical activities.

The revisionists believed that revolution was no longer historically probable or necessary as a means to socialism. They claimed it was possible for a socialist transformation to occur through bourgeois parliamentarianism and a slow enactment of reforms designed to eventually transform capitalism to socialism. In the eyes of its adherents, this strategy amounted to more than the struggle to wring reforms from the capitalist state within the strictures of capitalist relations of production, a position associated with social liberalism in England. The theory of peaceful transition had some support in fragments of the later political writings of Marx and Engels; the debate, however, rested less on an appeal to 'authority' than on the interpretation of the laws of capitalist development and political economy.

In most European parties, until the First World War, both the revisionist and the revolutionary points of view coexisted within social democratic parties in Europe. After the Bolshevik Revolution and the failure of the German uprising of 1919, the practical and theoretical disagreement led to an organizational split. The revolutionaries in Europe differentiated themselves from the reformists by calling themselves communists and by organizing communist parties throughout the world.

As revolutionaries withdrew from the existing parties to form an explicitly revolutionary movement, the term 'social democracy' came to refer more explicitly to a commitment to the doctrine of peaceful transition from capitalism to socialism and adherence to the democratic procedures established in bourgeois nations, such as Britain and Weimar Germany. In their political evolution, social democratic parties became increasingly similar to other 'leftist' or workers' parties that had not been influenced by revolutionary Marxism, such as the British Labour Party. Many social democrats still embraced extra-parliamentary legal tactics as well as parliamentarianism, but overall, the contradiction between a single-minded focus on achieving a parliamentary majority and the use of extra-legal, mass tactics was resolved within social democracy in favour of the former. As the political lines were drawn in the 1920s and 1930s, numerous individuals who said they were committed to revolutionary Marxism, but not to the precepts and policies of the Russian Bolsheviks, were left in a political vacuum. Trotskyism was one such organizational outlet that is analysed below. In the following section we intend to examine the evolution of social democracy in more detail, beginning with the roots of social democracy in the pre-Marxian period.

One of the difficulties of analysing anarchism, discussed in the previous chapter, is its heterogeneity resulting from its dependence on the brilliance and energy of individual revolutionaries. The problem of analysing social democracy is its chameleon-like character, which allows it to take many different forms in different social conjunctures. While Marxism has categorically rejected anarchism, the relationship of Marxism to social democracy is much more ambiguous. This is not only because in certain of its variants, such as German Social Democracy of the Second International or Euro-Communism in the 1970s, social democratic theory and practice has emerged directly out of Marxism, but because of the complex relationship between the movement for reforms of the existing system and the movement to overthrow it. The relationship between reform and revolution, between social democracy and Marxism, is shaped by time and place, by the objective circumstances and possibilities for social change and the subjective consciousness of the working class and other social strata. The history of the left, as with all history, is the development of subjectivity, of theory and programme, in the context of changing circumstances.

The history of social democracy is clouded by its tendency to evolve towards liberalism making the classification of social democracy as a form of 'leftism' problematic. Nowhere is the relativistic nature of the term 'left' more apparent than with the variants of social democracy. Unlike anarchism, which in its purest form is atheoretical rebellion – anarchists want to remake the world in their image by the force of will – social democracy is rooted more in ad hoc justifications for existing practicalities. So, while social democracy is not without a consistent accumulation of theories and ideas, theory is subservient to immediate needs.

Like anarchism, both socialist and communist ideologies preceded Marxism. Varieties of socialist theory subsequently co-existed with Marxism; in fact, Marx developed his own theory in the context of a life-long debate with other variants of socialism. From the beginning, however, socialist ideologies sprang from the unrealised goals of the bourgeois revolution.

Conservative Anti-Capitalism and Romantic Socialism

IT IS VIRTUALLY axiomatic in Marxism that – specific to time and place – capitalism has been socially progressive. In their bare-bones *Communist Manifesto*, Marx and Engels acknowledged the revolutionary role played by the bourgeoisie in liberating the forces of production from the traditional restraints of pre-capitalist social relations.

Necessarily, Marx studied Britain most extensively. Analysing economic change in the midst of the prolonged transition from a traditional to an industrial capitalist society, Marx attempted to distil the essence of capitalist development from its historically-rooted manifestation. In this sense, Marx believed that Britain heralded the future for all nations because the principles of capitalist development were global in their implications. The "laws of capitalist development" were deemed universal, but because Britain was the first industrial capitalist economy, that country could not be the historical model for successive developments of capitalism elsewhere. The mere existence of one industrial capitalist power altered fundamentally the conditions of existence of all other economies and the subsequent international as well as local manifestations of capitalist development. England, then, was unique in a particular way. The transition to industrial capitalism had proceeded in Britain over generations in a completely uncharted way that could be understood *as a transition to capitalism* only in hindsight.

Marx abstracted from the development of capitalism in Britain specific universal features, such as the increasing commodification of values, the proletarianization of the workforce, the tendency for capital to accumulate and become centralized, and the globalization of capital. Intrinsic to British capitalism was also an ideological revolution. In a very practical way, the English bourgeoisie brought the concepts of individualism, equality (before the law), (limited) democracy, and above all, economic freedom, into the modern world. Implied in the concept of a bourgeois revolution is the potential radicalism of these ideas, expressed more fully in the ideologies of liberty and equality of the French Revolution. It is too great a stretch of the historical record to claim that the English bourgeoisie emerged as a radical under-class under the domination of a traditional, landed elite; but England was and is a society in which *social class* lines historically have been sharply drawn and have shaped the consciousness of people within them (as the Southern United States may be said to have been shaped ideologically by the colour line). The bourgeoisie evinced a new ideology that was significantly at odds with the dominant views of its time. In an era dominated by notions of hierarchy, inherited privilege, legal inequality, political and economic patronage, and the inherent superiority of the upper class, counter-hegemonic claims to legal equality, propertied democracy, religious liberty, and free commerce were radical.

Yet, were these ideologies intrinsic to industrial capitalism the way that commodification and globalization were? Following the experience of twentieth century fascism and the rise of brutal neo-liberal dictatorships in the twentieth century, the belief in the inevitability of any link between capitalism and any of these liberal ideas has been thoroughly disproven. A variety of political institutions and social systems have been shown to be compatible with capitalist relations of production. But economic individualism and laissez-faire political economy were inscribed in the ideology and legitimation of the capitalist system. By the early 1800s in England, Adam Smith's laissez-faire dogma and Thomas Malthus' flint-hard utilitarianism had carried the day. The so-called gentry and Aristocracy – where they were not capitalists themselves – may still have looked down on the purveyors of trade and commerce as their social inferiors, but they were deeply in their financial debt and busily promoting the miscegenation of the new and old upper classes.

In its early period, laissez-faire generates both economic development and the extreme polarization of wealth and poverty. In the shadows of laissez-faire, the wretched and oppressive living and working conditions of the labouring poor in Britain were being exposed by the Chartists and other movements of the artisan class and by budding socialists such as Friedrich Engels, who published his *Conditions of the Working Class in England* in 1843. They were joined by middle class reformers of several political stripes.

Eighteenth century conservatives were attached to rural and traditional ways of life. As commercial and then industrial capitalism transformed the rural landscape, as the rural population was uprooted from home and hearth and crowded into the burgeoning urban slums, staid and provincial village life had never seemed so attractive. Anti-industrial social criticism evinced an attachment to the land, to simple technology, and handcraft production. This ideology survives in contemporary capitalism in the social recesses of petty bourgeois artisanship and in a romantic anti-rationalism, which feeds into fundamentalist religious movements and a variety of romantic social theories.

If the conservatives mourned the passing of traditional society and temporarily marginalized themselves in the new world of industrial capitalism, a more radical and complex movement of middle class revolutionaries did the conservatives one better by attempting to establish new societies based on a juxtaposition of traditional economies with more advanced social relations. Romantic socialism took the uprooted away from the urban jungles and transplanted them back to the rural landscape, where a new village communalism was supposedly to become a model for the redemption of the whole society (as discussed in Chapter Two). On the foundation of agriculture and artisanship, the new society would graft radical new conceptions of egalitarianism and communal property in place of the socially divisive practices of individualism and private ownership. Marx referred to these communitarian experiments as utopian socialism. These isolated pockets of technological backwardness eventually succumbed to the world of commodification and technological complexity, but they symbolized the potential transformation of oppressive industrial capitalism and envisaged a socialist future. That there are more recent examples with similar consequences is shown in the Israeli kibbutz movement.

For Marx, the distinguishing feature of genuine socialism was the transformation of the relations of production. Socialism was not defined principally by the equitable distribution of wealth but, rather, by the transformation of production. For Marx, no amount of redistribution, such as may be achieved through progressive income taxes or other forms of appropriation from the capitalist class would amount to the fundamental transformation of the relationships of people to people and people to things that would occur in a socialist society. Socialism was incompatible in principle with the commodification of labour. Hypothetically, within the domination of capitalist relations of production, the distribution of income could be made less unfair. For Marx, however, such 'fairness' would be illusory if it occurred within capitalist relations of exploitation. More practically, there were absolute limits to the degree of redistribution possible in capitalism. Beyond this limit, which would vary in time and space, capital accumulation would be adversely affected. Revolutionary Marxism was predicated on a transformation of the relations of production that would, in turn, affect more than only distribution relations.

For the labouring poor, however, more immediate and pressing problems dominated their horizons. The proletariat was the special creation of and the necessary condition for the continuous expansion of capital. The proletariat was both an economic class – a group of people existing in a specific relationship to capital – and a self-conscious entity with a growing awareness of the common interests of its class. Where there was collective employment, there was collective resistance; within the boundaries of national labour mobility, there was a labour movement. Most workers knew there was no going back to village life, which was receding intergenerationally. Their ideologists grasped the radical ideas of the bourgeois revolution and applied them to their class – the organized working class sought such goals as equality before the law, freedom of the press, and universal suffrage.

They also revived older ideas of collective rights of association and attached to them the practicalities that are the core of trade union demands to this day. Trade unions were concerned with more than only the price of the sale of labour power. Labour power is unlike any other commodity in that the sellers of labour power are vitally interested in the conditions under which their commodity is sold; that is, the conditions of work. Hours of labour, worker safety, relations with direct supervisors, control over the work process, all are fundamental issues of negotiation with employers. A collective agreement, however, represents at best a limited compromise between the interests of labour and capital in a situation where capital is the strongest party. Within the limits of the domination of capital and the capitalists' absolute need to accumulate, there is room for reforms of working conditions; but they do not substitute for the revolutionizing of the relations of production.

Trade unions, almost by definition, are collective organizations that seek to assist workers to achieve the best possible terms for the sale of their labour power to capital. In other words, accepting the commodification of labour as a given, the role of the trade union is to affect change in the distribution of wealth in favour of labour. The ruling classes resisted unionization precisely on these grounds. As laissez faire industrial capitalism became increasingly the dominant mode of production in the nineteenth century, workers in Europe rose spontaneously in unorganized rebellions, which peaked first in the revolutionary year 1848. Marx argued that the defeats of 1848 demonstrated that the working class was not politically ready to challenge the bourgeoisie for power. The stronger the socialist movement, the more the bourgeoisie is forced to respond with reforms to ameliorate the worst abuses and placate labour.

Reformism was the third possibility Luxemburg omitted from her famous epigram about revolution or reaction. The question of reform has bedevilled Marxism from the beginning. Theoretically and practically, 'reform' is an ambiguous political process. In the face of the horrendous social costs of unrestrained, competitive capitalism, liberal theorists such as John Stuart Mill called on the ruling class to ameliorate the worst abuses of the economic system. In this sense, 'reform' is a 'social liberal' strategy for preserving the essential elements of the capitalist mode of production in the face of potentially more radical demands from the working class. The emergence of social liberalism split bourgeois ideology into two inter-related strands. Throughout the nineteenth century, laissez faire capitalism tended to predominate. Over time, however, social liberalism emerged as a counter-tendency within bourgeois ideology, achieving dominance in the West only in the post-Second World War era of Keynesianism. Keynesianism was dethroned by neo-liberalism and a return to laissez faire globalization in the 1980s. Social liberalism is clearly outside the Marxist movement. It is important to recognize this history, however, because social liberalism has merged with a right-wing, reformist movement within Marxism, which is the essential question examined in this chapter.

The social implications of bourgeois reforms were clear to the anarchists, for whom any reform was anathema, tantamount to selling out the interests of the 'People.' Bakunin, for example, rejected any measures short of system-wide revolution. For Marx, in contrast, the fight to secure reforms was an essential and progressive component of the working class movement. The question was not the reform itself, but the conditions under which it was collectively won and the class consciousness the struggle engendered. Reforms have a dual nature because reforms that are not connected to a socialist revolutionary movement feed into reformism, an illusion opposite to that of anarchism. In our terms, reforms protect workers' interests within the capitalist mode of production, and the struggle for reforms led by progressive forces can raise consciousness about the need to transform these relations of production. Reform*ism* entails the assumption that the capitalist system is susceptible only to reform, not revolutionary transformation. To anticipate the argument below, the term 'social democracy' applied originally to the Marxist movement as a whole. After 1914 – and especially after 1917 – social democracy became the ideology of reformism within the Marxist movement. When reformism becomes entrenched theoretically within the movement that was originally revolutionary Marxism, the term 'revisionism' applies.

Social Democracy and the Capitalist State

REVISIONISM ENTAILED, at the level of theory, the transformation of the necessarily short-term, tactical struggle for reforms into an ideology that replaced the necessity for revolution with the expectation that capitalism can be transformed peacefully and will evolve into socialism by the piece-meal accumulation of ameliorative changes. Reformism tends to merge in practice with bourgeois social liberalism, as described above. Insofar as social democracy proclaims the ultimate goal of replacing capitalism with socialism through evolutionary means, it is 'reformist'; when it becomes a movement for social fairness within the terms of the capitalist system, it becomes indistinguishable from social liberalism.

In this sense, the ideology of reformism is represented by evolutionary variants of socialism such as Fabianism in the 1890s and African Socialism in the 1970s, which followed a path essentially independent of Marxism, and by similar ideological developments in Marxist theory itself after Marx. All these movements have in common a condemnation of capitalism and a programme to replace capitalism with a variant of 'socialism' that does not threaten bourgeois property rights.

Within Marxism, as noted above, reformism is usually linked to a theoretical trend termed 'revisionism,' a pejorative epithet signalling the abandonment of what is essential to the Marxist revolutionary outlook. Revisionism is a term that embraces many theoretical tendencies that contradict revolutionary Marxism. In practice, revisionism reflects and feeds many forms of political opportunism, from the embarrassing denouement of the Second International in 1914 and the Menshevik support for the Provisional Government in 1917 Russia, to the electoral illusions of Euro-Communism in the 1970s. More controversially, Stalin's claim that the USSR had become a classless society, that class struggle had disappeared and the Soviet state represented the whole people, makes that theory – or at least key elements of it – a variant of revisionism. The term, 'revisionism' is reserved for movements that are within the main currents of Marxism. Ultimately, revisionism evolves into capitalism.

One of the cornerstones of the dispute among anarchists, social democrats, and Marxists concerns the nature and role of the state. Anarchists regard the state as, by definition, coercive of individual freedoms and want to replace any institution of authority with voluntary cooperativeness. Marxist social democrats (as reformists) seek to gain legal control over the institutions of government and use them to reform the existing economic system, theoretically until it is transformed into socialism. Revolutionary Marxists work towards the overthrow of the bourgeois state and its replacement by a revolutionary state, defined as an apparatus that is at once repressive (limiting the freedom of anti-socialist classes) and constructive, in the sense that it is the instrument for the conscious construction of socialist society.

Theoretically, the issue of the state revolves around the question of the degree of independence between economics and politics. The theory of the state has been subject to enormous debate among Marxists. Bourgeois economics has its origins in the movement to free economic enterprise from the domination of the mercantilist state. Under the conditions of competitive capitalism, the state satisfied the common requirements of the bourgeoisie while leaving capital as independent as possible. Throughout the era of imperialism, from the late nineteenth century, however, the capitalist state assumed increasing economic importance, regulating markets, repressing labour movements, promoting national economic growth through tariffs and protectionist measures and, at least in core capitalist countries, pursuing an aggressive colonial policy. Increasingly, the business of governments in core capitalist states became economic management within the boundaries of existing capitalist class relationships.

What, precisely, these boundaries were, however, was a crucial question. Could the autonomous state in capitalist society become the instrument for the gradual elimination of capitalism? Social democrats believed it could. There were clearly different conceptions of the 'end' of the proposed reforms, although these were not necessarily key determinants of the day-to-day tactics of social democratic parties. There were also differences over shorter-term tactics, over the speed of social transformation and the timing of specific measures, such as nationalization of industries. This reformist and ultimately social-liberal tendency has existed within the socialist movement since its inception. The fundamental questions concern the strength of various tendencies in time and space, and the state of class struggle in the given conjuncture – what Lenin called the concrete analysis of concrete conditions. In analysing this question, both the overall tendency of reformism to compromise with capitalist interests must be balanced with an understanding of objective and subjective conditions in the worker's movement.

Perhaps the earliest form of 'social democracy' in its more modern sense was derived from a titled aristocrat known as Saint-Simon. Like Marx, Saint-Simon rejected the return to petty handicraft, rural production characteristic of the Romantic socialists and, instead, believed that the future society was to be built on the foundation of modern industry. For Saint-Simon, however, the transformation to the positive society of the future was to be the work of a coalition of intellectuals and business interests, such as engineers and industrial capitalists. His ideal was a planned economy and an organized society, based on the enlightened application of reason and science to the construction of human social organization. The supposedly altruistic intellectual and business elite was expected to guide the working class in the acceptance of this new industrial order and in its construction through mass education and a new state-sponsored religion.

Saint-Simon's idea of progressive, state-sponsored reforms was inherited by a variety of reform-minded liberals and socialists, including the Fabian Society in England. Saint-Simon represented a form of 'socialism-from-above' in which an elite organized in a centralize state, guided by moral principles of fairness as well as objective models of efficiency, would engineer a more just and equitable society. The working masses would play their part as cogs in the wheel of progress and as cheerleaders for the social elite, but they would not be emancipated to control production directly or exercise any real political power. In Germany, however, a more grass-roots socialist movement emerged, which was inspired by the leadership of Ferdinand Lassalle. As in the case of Saint Simon, Lassalle focused on what he hoped would be the progressive intervention of an 'enlightened' state although, in his case, the German state was still in the hands of the traditional elite.

Lassalle, Nationalism, and Social Democracy

IN GERMANY, undergoing the tribulations of unification under the iron heel of Prussia, Ferdinand Lassalle (1825-1864) emerged for a time as the dominant revolutionary figure. In *The Main Currents of Marxism*, Leszek Kolakowski describes Lassalle as a powerful and influential orator who was instrumental in creating the first German working class association in 1862, as a voice for German workers independent of the liberal bourgeoisie. A charismatic and popular leader, Lassalle carried his convictions to the courtroom and rode them on more than one occasion to jail. More an activist than a theorist, Lassalle's theory of socialism differed from Marx's most profoundly in his conceptions of the nation and of the state. Lassalle was, above all, a nationalist who believed the German nation was destined by Providence to lead humanity. The intensity of this nationalist strain, with its roots in the conservative side of Hegelianism and its future in German National Socialism, was particularly strong, though not uniquely so, in German social democracy.

The German nation in Lassalle's day existed more as a concept than a reality. In the context of German disunity, both Marx and Lassalle regarded national independence as progressive. They differed, however, on Prussian (military and aristocratic) domination of the new Germany. For Lassalle, the state was not fundamentally an organ of class rule but a universally necessary institution that united the individuals of a nation into a moral whole. Since, for Lassalle, the nation overrides class interests, the state could become the instrument for the reconciliation of class differences in the interests of the nation. In fact, Lassalle believed that German workers should form an alliance with conservative landowners and state bureaucrats in an anti-bourgeois coalition. Not only would such an alliance fulfil the German mission to lead humanity to civilization and progress, the German state would become the instrument for the liberation of the proletariat through the formation of state-sponsored workers' co-operatives. The co-ops would replace competitive, private businesses, which were obviously inimical to the interests of workers and, more importantly for Lassalle, to the interest of the German nation as a whole.

Lassalle's worker's party remained aloof from the First International when this first attempt at institutional internationalism was founded in September, 1864, the month following Lassalle's death by misadventure. Lassalle had a very brief period of 'ministry,' but his influence in the German workers' movement extended well beyond his death.

By 1872, when the First International was effectively being dissolved (by being moved to New York), numerous other socialist parties had come into existence, including a German Social Democratic Workers Party (known as the Eisenach party) with close links to the trade unions. The Eisenach Party was founded by Wilhelm Liebknecht (1826-1900) and August Bebel (1840-1913). The differences between the Eisenach and the Lassallean wings of the German movement sharpened during the Franco-Prussian war. Consistent with their German nationalism, the Lassalleans initially supported the war. Bebel and Liebknecht refused to support war loans, demanded that Prussia extract no territorial concessions, urged a speedy peace, and were jailed for treason.

In 1875, the Lassallean and the Eisenach wings of the workers' movement held a joint conference in Gotha that united the two groups in the German Social Democratic Party (SPD) and promulgated a common platform known as the Gotha Program. Marx criticized the draft programme virtually line by line in what Engels and Kautsky published in 1891 as the *Critique of the Gotha Program*. In his critique, Marx argued that the document was inconsistent with key principles of socialism and was largely Lassallean. Until 1891, however, Marx's objections were not widely known.

The Gotha Program, claimed Marx in his *Critique*, focused attention on the fair distribution of the product rather than directly on production. What Marx called "vulgar socialism" treated the distribution of the product "as independent of the mode of production and hence [presented] socialism as turning principally on distribution" – a view he labelled "retrogressive." He located its source as an idea "taken over from the bourgeois economists." The Lassallean emphasis on distribution irrespective of the mode of production would lead to the view that the 'reform' of the distribution could be achieved within the capitalist mode of production by, for example, progressive taxation. Without the theoretical foundation that grossly unequal distribution is inherent to capitalism, Marx argued, this view feeds reformist illusions.

Second, the Gotha Program demonstrated Lassalle's 'worship' of the state. For Marx, existing capitalist society is the basis of the state; the Gotha Program "treats the state rather as an independent entity that possesses its own *intellectual, ethical, and libertarian bases*." The fundamental point, for Marx, was that the state was essentially a capitalist state; it had to be overthrown and a worker's state established in its place. While Marx was never very specific about the form that a future socialist state and society would take, in the *Critique of the Gotha Program* he speculated about the period of "socialism" that would commence following the proletarian revolution, when society was still burdened with the structures and ideologies of the past. Between bourgeois society and the future communism, Marx said, is a "political transition period in which the state can be nothing but *the revolutionary dictatorship of the proletariat.*" Marx's discussion of the period of transition was to be central to Lenin's conception and practice of socialist construction, and to the later Chinese revolution.

Lassalle's flirtation with Bismarck, Marx said, was echoed in the Gotha Program's call for "'the establishment of producers' co-operative societies *with state aid.*'" These co-operatives were not to be established by the workers in "the revolutionary process of transformation of society" but, rather, were to be called into being by the German state. For Lassalle and his followers, it wasn't even necessary to have a working class majority in the Reichstag (German parliament); the existing German state (an alliance of conservatives and militarists) could be convinced to implement, by themselves, progressive goals; working class institutions could be built through state aid, Lassalle said, "on such a scale that the socialist organization of the total labor will arise from them." Bismarck did pass some social legislation, such as workers' pensions but only following a period when, under the anti-socialist laws, social democratic and trade union agitation had been banned. Bismarck maintained control over the labour movement through both repression and piecemeal reform, depending on the circumstances. Repression was periodically an essential state tool, but it was a less successful long-term programme of domination than reform.

When Marx's *Critique* was finally published in 1891, it was intended as an intervention in the midst of another debate about the theoretical and practical orientation of the German Social Democratic Party. According to David MacLellan (*The Thought of Karl Marx*), while Lassalle's legacy predominated in the German SPD, his influence was gradually eroded by the anti-socialist legislation promulgated by Bismarck (1879-1890). Rather than becoming a partner in the building of democratic reforms and co-operative socialism, the German state appeared ever more clearly to be the tool of an alliance between the landowners and the industrial bourgeoisie, not Lassalle's chimera of an alliance between anti-capitalist conservatives and workers. The Gotha Program, which had imagined a policy of seeking peaceful reforms through the Bismarck-dominated state, revealed the German state, Marx said, to be a "police-guarded military despotism." Even the bourgeois democrats, Marx replied, did not commit themselves to keeping "within the limits of what is permitted by the police."

After Bismarck repealed the anti-socialist laws, however, and trade unions became reactivated, the German SPD used its mass base to insert itself increasingly and successfully into the parliamentary forum. Lassalle might have been wrong about the progressive nature of the Junker state, but the electoral successes of the German Social Democratic Party in the 1890s fostered a vision of 'capturing' parliament peacefully. In fact, the popular electoral swing towards the SPD was linked to a series of reforms implemented by the German state, particularly in the period of German prosperity and expansionism in the 1890s. As the century neared an end and capitalism entered a distinctly new phase, the question arose whether Marx's economic theories were still applicable in the context of the rise of monopoly capitalism and modern imperialism, a period dominated by the ideology of what Samir Amin calls "monopolistic nationalist liberalism." Did the era of monopoly capitalism necessitate a changed Marxist practice and theory? If so, what should be changed and what aspects were still fundamental? Within the German Social Democratic Party, the model Marxist party of its time, a revisionist point of view emerged in opposition to Marx's revolutionism.

The split personality evinced by the German SPD in its early period continued in a new form in the period of legality. During the 1890s, a left-wing intelligentsia led by Karl Kautsky dominated theoretical debates and advocated revolutionary Marxism. At the same time, the practice of the Party was confined to demands for trade union rights and for the liberties of bourgeois democracy. These two tendencies, MacLellan points out, were reflected in the new party programme drafted in Erfurt in 1891. Engels, who lived until 1895 and was the remaining organic link between the German SPD and Marx, approved the draft. Although Paul Sweezy and Harry Magdoff conclude that Marx's critique of Lassalle had won out, the Erfurt draft was a compromise between the two main tendencies within the Party. The theoretical part, drafted by Kautsky, reflected the Marxism of the *Communist Manifesto*. Eduard Bernstein drafted the more immediate and practical section. Bernstein would subsequently become the dominant figure in the controversy over the need to 'revise' Marxist political economy.

Reformism and Revisionism

BERNSTEIN HAD EMERGED as key figure in the German SPD during the period of illegality. He was initially a close collaborator of Karl Kautsky and an opponent of the wing within the German SPD, which advocated close ties with German liberals. After the death of Engels, however, Bernstein initiated a debate over revising Marxist political and economic theories in the light of the changed circumstances of late-nineteenth century capitalism. Bernstein did not create his views out of whole cloth. During the anti-socialist period in Germany he had lived in exile in England where he became a collaborator of Engels. While he was in Britain, Bernstein also became intimate with the ideas of a clearly reformist socialist group known as the Fabians. When Bernstein returned to Germany in time for the Erfurt Conference in 1891, he began to infuse Fabian ideas into the German SPD.

The Fabian Society in Britain, founded in 1883, assumed that capitalism had changed fundamentally since 1848 and that a revolution was not necessary to achieve the goals of the socialist movement. The transition from capitalism to socialism was to be a gradual process. Industry was to be socialized through the peaceful use of the existing economic and political agencies. The extension of the franchise to the working class, the Fabians said, had made Britain 'genuinely' democratic and created, in Parliament, the instrument that could slowly reform capitalism out of existence. The agent for this change was, above all, the emerging 'middle class' which, Harry Laidler said (*A History of Socialist Thought*), could be won by "arousing ... the social conscience of the community in favor of the socialist ideal." The middle class would develop the techniques of administration with which they would administer the new social order. Socialism – like temperance – was, essentially, a moral movement that could win over the educated middle class and the literate workers.

Fabian socialism was evolutionary and positivist. The socialist future would evolve out of the principles of equality and freedom enunciated by the bourgeois revolution, bringing these ideals to actualization. Liberalism had created the political institution appropriate for slowly modifying society by enacting progressive legislation; the task of the state was to create *economic* democracy through state ownership and planning. Fabianism was an intellectual movement that condemned capitalism on moral grounds. Lenin was thoroughly dismissive of this version of English socialism, regarding the Fabians as liberals in socialist clothing and approving Engels' summation that they were "a band of careerists." For Lenin,

> Fear of the revolution is their fundamental principle. They are the 'educated' *par excellence*. This socialism of theirs is ... presented as an extreme but inevitable consequence of bourgeois liberalism; hence their tactics, not of decisively opposing the liberals as adversaries but of ... intriguing with them, or permeating liberalism with socialism.... With great industry they have published ... some good propagandist writings.... But as soon as they get on to their specific tactics of hushing up the class struggle, it all turns putrid.... These people have of course many bourgeois followers and therefore money.

Where the socialist party was not sufficiently strong to gain a parliamentary majority, reformists such as the Fabians advocated an alliance with the Liberals to influence the direction of legislation. The Fabian perspective was advocated by the Independent Labour Party (ILP) in Britain. For the ILP, in Lenin's words, "the great function of the House of Commons ... is to translate into legislation the socialism that is preached in the country." To achieve this result, the ILP sought to co-operate with the liberals, leading Lenin to conclude that the ILP was "independent of socialism but dependent on the liberals." Lenin attributed this reformism to "the specific historical conditions of the latter half of the nineteenth century in Britain, when the 'aristocracy of labour' shared to some extent in the particularly high profits of British capital."

Generally for social democracy, participation in a bourgeois government was not supposed to be an end in itself, but to be a springboard for subsequently achieving a majority and easing the nation into socialism. In France in 1899, Alexandre Millerand became the first socialist to be enlisted by a liberal government and given a position in the Cabinet. The tactic was supposed to reveal what one socialist could accomplish with a modicum of political power, throwing into relief the possibility of what an elected socialist government could do, and throwing into the dustbin the call for revolution. Millerand later abandoned socialism altogether, a denouement that strengthens the argument that such tactics, if they do not inevitably lead to cooptation, at least generally risk sacrificing the long term interests of socialism for immediate, and often personal, advantage.

Reformism was not confined to France and Britain. The Fabians provided the model for a reformist trend within the German SPD. It is ironic, Sweezy and Magdoff point out, that at the time the German SPD adopted the Marxian Erfurt Program and was "becoming something of a model for the whole international socialist movement, in practice it was becoming more and more reformist," the contradiction between theory and practice being reconciled in favour of the latter.

For Lenin, once Marxism achieved some theoretical dominance, the struggle over ideology and practice became internal to the Marxist parties rather than external to them. In practice, the issue facing revolutionary Marxism outside Russia was how to respond to demands for immediate reforms in a way that helped realize them and also fulfilled the ultimate aim of revolution, thereby avoiding 'reformism.' While many anarchists dismissed social 'reforms' as illusory and counter-productive, reforms are a necessary component of class struggle. Lenin argued that he was not opposing reforms, only *reformists*: those "who, directly or indirectly, restrict the aims and activities of the working class to the winning of reforms. Reformism is bourgeois deception of the workers who, despite individual improvements, will always remain wage-slaves as long as there is the domination of capital."

Just as reforms of existing circumstances cannot be rejected out of hand, despite their inherently dual nature, so, too, must theory be modified as a result of changed circumstances. Concerning the question of theory, to fail to 'revise' Marxism consistent with new contingencies makes it an article of faith, a theology. Arguably, no Marxist revised Marxism more significantly than Lenin. The debate over revisionism, then, is a debate about the ways that concrete economic and social conditions had changed since the principles of Marxism were enunciated, and to what extent, if at all, Marxist theory ought to change to better guide practice. For revisionists, such as Bernstein, circumstances had changed so fundamentally in the core capitalist countries that many key elements of Marxism, including the necessity for a revolutionary break with bourgeois society, far from being inevitable, were no longer necessary or possible.

Bernstein and Revisionism

IN MANY WAYS, the 1890s in Western Europe were decades where reform appeared to be possible and revolution impossible. The massacre of the French Communards was still recent memory. Autocratic governments predominated on continental Europe. Socialist parties were involved in the day-to-day practicalities of the class struggle, none more than the largest and most influential party, the German SPD. Even the revolutionary wing of the German party was concerned to prevent 'adventurism' in a political context where class consciousness among the working class seldom extended beyond trade union demands, a situation they blamed on the working class and not the failure of revolutionary leadership. When the Second International was established in Paris in 1889, on the anniversary of the French Revolution, Warren Lerner notes (*A History of Socialism and Communism in Modern Times*), its criteria for membership embraced political parties that held socialism to be their aim, and also agreed that "legislative and parliamentary action [w]as one of the necessary means of attaining that end." The qualification meant that parties that adopted revolutionary means were not excluded provided they also accepted – as the anarchists did not – the need to engage, in the short run at least, in legal parliamentary tactics. But no reformist party that eschewed revolution could be similarly excluded. As in the German SPD, the official ideology of the Second International was revolutionary Marxism, while the dominant practical orientation of the organizations that comprised the Second International was reformist. And the practice reflected the class consciousness of most trade unionists and parliamentary deputies in the party.

Among the first prominent members of the German SPD to take an openly reformist position was Georg von Vollmar, a Munich deputy in the Reichstag who, Laidler says, preached "slow organic evolution" to socialism. Gradually, Bernstein was converted to this view. In 1895, the year of Engels' death, Bernstein began to print criticisms of Marx's revolutionary theory in the SPD journal, arguing that Marx's theories had to be substantially revised to meet contemporary social and economic conditions. The title of Bernstein's influential pamphlet *Evolutionary Socialism* expressed the essence of his gradualist view. The SPD's Hanover Congress in 1899 spent three days debating Bernstein's views and passed a resolution dissenting from them. This vote revealed the considerable gap between the official Marxist ideology of the SPD and the increasingly reformist practice of the party.

Bernstein based his arguments on what he saw as a series of economic changes sweeping Germany in the 1890s. The working class was not growing absolutely poorer; the peasantry and middle class generally was not disappearing; class polarization was not taking place; a "new middle class" had emerged as a product of the new economy; property ownership was becoming more widespread as a result of the creation of joint stock companies; capitalist crises appeared to be becoming less severe and were better managed by the capitalist state; and capitalism was becoming more pacific. Capitalism and imperialism rested on a foundation of extensive trade that required a degree of national state regulation and international military domination. In these circumstances, the objective conditions necessary for revolution in Europe were becoming more remote.

After the SPD and the trade unions were legalized in late nineteenth century Germany, Sweezy and Magdoff say, they "set about winning for their workers a share in the prosperity of the burgeoning German economy." Thanks to their own strong organizations and a paternalistic state with access to expanding resources of surplus value, the German workers fared well by capitalist standards in the decades before the First World War, as Bernstein realized. An important part of the process, as both cause and effect, was the proliferation of large political (party) and economic (trade union) bureaucracies firmly rooted in the existing socio-economic order. Lenin had argued that the highly productive economy of monopoly capitalism permitted the progressive bourgeoisie to implement a conscious strategy of reform in opposition to revolution. In short, objective conditions in Germany (and monopoly capitalism generally) engendered both a decline in class consciousness among the masses and careerism among the leadership.

In addition, Bernstein said, capitalism was organically linked to the expansion of liberal democracy. The bourgeois state may be under the predominant influence of the bourgeoisie, but given universal suffrage, an educated workforce, and the moral superiority of such socialist policies as equal distribution and industrial democracy, a parliament with a majority of socialists could quicken the pace of social reform and pave the way for socialism. In *Evolutionary Socialism*, Bernstein postulated a steady advance towards socialism, which relied on the methods of bourgeois democracy:

> The right to vote in a democracy makes its members virtually partners in the community, and their virtual partnership must in the end lead to real partnership. With a working class undeveloped in numbers and culture, the general right to vote may long appear as the right to choose the 'butcher.' With the growing number and knowledge of the workers, it is changed, however, to the implement by which to transform the representatives of the people from masters into real servants of the people....
>
> Universal franchise is the alternative to a violent revolution.

Above all else it was the successful growth of capitalism and its political ideology, liberalism, which made a peaceful transition possible. Socialism was the legitimate heir of liberalism. According to Bernstein, "Feudalism ... had to be destroyed nearly everywhere by violence. The liberal organizations of modern society are distinguished from those exactly because they are flexible and capable of change and development. They do not need to be destroyed but only further developed." Bernstein concludes that the German SPD must "emancipate itself from a [revolutionary] phraseology which is actually outworn." The phrase about dictatorship of the proletariat was antiquated and no longer fit the new political reality of liberal 'democracy.' The SPD should openly proclaim itself what Bernstein believed it actually was: "a democratic socialist party of reform.... [A] party that strives after the socialist transformation of society by the means of democratic and economic reform."

For Bernstein, in one of his most memorable phrases, the movement is everything, the end nothing, by which he makes a principle of pragmatic reforms. This slogan connects Bernstein with mechanical, evolutionary Marxism by assuming that the goal (socialism) was implicit in piecemeal reform. It also reflects the liberal argument that you cannot achieve a just and democratic outcome if you do not use just and democratic means to bring about social change. Social democratic governments accept, in principle, the rules of this game according to which the loss of a socialist parliamentary majority in a subsequent 'free' election, resulting in the reversal of the socialist-tending reforms, must be accepted as the will of the majority. In the long run, reformists maintain, the socialist mission will proceed. It is the only course of history that is consistent with the highest moral precepts; it is the only system that represents the real interests of the majority of the population; ultimately it is the end to which the capitalist system is (unconsciously) tending. The eventual victory of socialism is inevitable.

As revolutionary potential shifted in the new era of imperialism to the periphery, and as core capitalist countries became, in the normal run of affairs, non-revolutionary, the question arose: what is the role of a revolutionary party? Bernstein's answer was that you don't need a revolutionary party in a situation where revolution is impossible. Bernstein, and Kautsky later, claimed that all that is necessary is to win the battle of democracy. The same economic conditions that make revolution increasingly unlikely are creating the conditions for a peaceful transition. Once again, as in the origins of the socialist movement (and as in Fabianism), socialism is essentially a moral idea. The existing distribution of the product is unjust, and properly-educated people can come to perceive it as wrong. Since only the SPD stands for economic and social justice for the majority, under conditions of bourgeois freedoms, the SPD can win the battle for democracy.

Certain aspects of Marxist orthodoxy supported Bernstein's revision of Marx. Against the orthodox position of the early Kautsky and of Luxemburg, who held that capitalism was heading, by inexorable law, to a final breakdown, Bernstein adopted a position that was similar in its ultimate determinism but different in its conclusion. Engels had argued that the replacement of competitive capitalism by monopoly capitalism and the accompanying expanded role of the state as economic manager were evolutionary steps in the direction of socialism. This positivist argument was consistent with Bernstein's theory, although his argument rested more on the moral claim that socialism was just and would therefore be seen to be superior. Ultimately, however, socialism was the end to which capitalism was slowly evolving, politically, morally, and economically. Consequently, it was counter-productive to attempt to hasten this evolution. Hence, the movement was everything for Bernstein; the end was inevitable.

Within the German SPD in the 1890s, the revolutionary wing, led by Bebel, Liebknecht, Luxemburg, and Kautsky, opposed Bernstein. Bebel introduced resolutions at both the Hansa (1899) and the Lubeck (1901) conferences against the revisionists, the latter directly specifying Bernstein. As Laidler points out, however, at neither conference was Bernstein expelled, nor were any of his followers. The Party ideology continued to reflect the long-standing principles of revolutionary Marxism. Even the revolutionary wing, however, was concerned to avoid 'adventurism.' After the 1905 revolution in Russia, the revolutionary perspective appeared to be vindicated. The SPD adopted the tactic of the mass strike. However, over time, so many conditions were imposed on actually calling such an action that it became nothing but a dead letter. Above all, most of the revolutionaries (Rosa Luxemburg was the most prominent exception) feared arousing repression from the state. It was a sharply ironic position. On the one hand, state repression would slow down the inevitable progress of the SPD in bourgeois elections. On the other hand, however, the fundamental question was just how far the bourgeois state would go in allowing the SPD to gain formal power and, more fundamentally, actually implement changes that would undermine capitalism. Social democracy makes a fetish of the rule of law in a situation where the dominant class is wedding only to power, not to the formal mechanisms of exercising it. For Lenin, the nature of revisionism is best summed up by:

> ... its attitude to the ultimate aim of the socialist movement. 'The movement is everything, the ultimate aim is nothing' – this catch phrase of Bernstein's expresses the essence of revisionism.... To determine its

conduct from case to case, to adapt itself to the events of the day and to the chopping and changing of petty policies, to forget the primary interests of the proletariat and the basic features of the whole capitalist system, of all capitalist evolution, to sacrifice these primary interests for the real or assumed advantages of the moment – such is the policy of revisionism. And it patently follows from the very nature of this policy that it may assume an infinite variety of forms and that ... every more or less unexpected and unforeseen turn of events ... will always inevitably give rise to one variety of revisionism or another.

In Lenin's view, the reformists and revisionists in the German SPD were "thoroughly imbued with faith in bourgeois legality" and "steeped in constitutional illusions." They did not understand "the historical limits of this legality" nor the "historical *conditionality* of constitutional institutions." Bourgeois legality was assumed to be permanent. It was necessary, Lenin countered, to see historical circumstances as specific. In his view, "real ... history includes ... both slow evolution and rapid leaps, breaks in continuity." Despite the legalities of parliamentarianism, should a social democratic party achieve control of the legislative arm of the state, Lenin argued, it could maintain its toehold in the state only as long as it took no bold, socialist steps. Any movement in the direction of actual socialism would be met by force. Violence would come anyway; the only way to avoid it would be to renounce making any real changes to capitalist relations of production.

Within the German SPD, the most implacable opponent of revisionism was Rosa Luxemburg, whose *Reform or Revolution?* is a refutation of Bernstein. In her view, Bernstein had effectively renounced the goal of all genuine socialists, thereby placing "him squarely among the bourgeois democrats." As with Lenin, Luxemburg argued that Bernstein's "clear distinction between reform and revolution was basically the presentation of the petty-bourgeois trend in the labour movement." Revisionism amounted to passing off the views of vulgar bourgeois economics as socialism and was theoretically grounded on a theory of capitalist standstill rather than breakdown. Bernstein concluded that, with the exception of certain imbalances, the capitalist system (through credit, cartels, government regulation) had solved its major contradictions and that, consequently, it was unrealistic to hope for a final collapse. Luxemburg demonstrated, however, that the contradictions of capitalism had not ceased to operate and that the mechanisms of stability outlined by Bernstein contained, themselves, the germs of future crises.

For the revolutionaries, reforms merely prepared the subjective conditions for revolution while, "for Bernstein and Co., they objectively realized socialism!" Luxemburg agreed that the development of the productive forces leads necessarily towards greater socialization, but argued that the political and juridical relations had developed in an increasingly capitalist direction.

Reformism and revisionism were, therefore, reactionary rather than progressive, Luxemburg concluded. They do not "lead to the final goal of socialism but move in a precisely opposite direction." Reformism, whether in the hands of self-proclaimed bourgeois democrats or revisionists, becomes a means for shoring up capitalism rather than a means for its destruction. It attempts to smooth over contradictions and reconcile class antagonisms and is, therefore, class-collaborationist. Revisionism, Luxemburg argues, might be the best means to control the class struggle and preserve capitalism, making it effectively a counter-revolutionary movement.

The Denouement: 1914-1919

BERNSTEIN DID NOT succeed, before 1914, in having party theory revised to be consistent with the reformist practice. In the end, however, it did not matter. When, at the outbreak of the European War of 1914, the SPD voted in its normal bloc-vote pattern to authorize war credits, the party effectively abandoned revolutionary Marxism in favour of German nationalism. Germany was not alone. European Marxist parties everywhere followed suit in supporting their national (bourgeois or authoritarian) governments and renouncing the principle of internationalism.

In the political theory of social democracy, revolutionaries are as much a problem as the capitalist class, and potentially more of a problem. The German SPD was already conscious of the problem of 'adventurism' – taking precipitous revolutionary actions in situations in which such actions are doomed to failure. They are dangerous because precipitous actions can cause the state, still in the hands of the ruling class, to react with repression, and to undermine any bourgeois freedoms that are assumed to be the necessary conditions for the peaceful, electoral victory of socialism. As Luxemburg had said, in such a situation social democracy becomes counter-revolutionary. Her words were prophetic. In the confusion following the First World War, Friedrich Ebert, a right-wing member of the SPD, established a provisional government. In 1919, believing Germany to be in a crisis parallel to that facing Lenin in 1917, German revolutionaries launched an insurrection. With the support of the 'socialist' government, however, the police and the army, the military arm of the state, smashed the rebellion, massacred revolutionaries and activists, and murdered Luxemburg and Liebknecht. By its pivotal role in the defeat of the 1919 revolution in Germany, the right-wing of the SPD revealed the counter-revolutionary nature of social democracy in that type of conjuncture. The weakness of the SPD was revealed, above all, not in its failure to secure legislative office, but by its actions once it had achieved a modicum of power within the state.

In 1933, social democracy in Germany stood in the Reichstag and voted against Hitler's vain attempt to cover his putsch with a thin tissue of legitimacy. They could believe they had preserved their individual morality, but without even the attempt to organize against fascist violence, they effectively rolled over in the face of Nazism. Fascism triumphed in Germany on the basis of extra-parliamentary violence and terror – what Jack London had called the "iron heel." Big business had funded the Nazi Party in the interests of counter-revolution. Fascism was, essentially, monopoly capitalism exercising power through anti-liberal political means.

The German SPD subsequently became in theory what it had been in practice: openly reformist. In fact, as this term is defined above, the SPD ceased even being 'reformist' in favour of advocating some state oversight of the manner in which the capitalist class conducted business as usual. The victory of Marxism over Lassalleanism in the 1891 Erfurt Program had been entirely hollow. Eventually the SPD eschewed any connection with Marxism altogether, becoming a social liberal party associated with Keynesian reforms, which through the welfare state during its heyday in the 1960s and 1970s, modified somewhat the distribution of wealth in Germany.

Post-1945 Social Democracy

THE HISTORY of the enmity between social democracy and communism before the Second World War is understandable in light of the history of counter-revolution. During the Great Depression, in liberal Western countries that did not succumb to variants of fascism, Communist parties organized by the Third International had assumed that the collapse of capitalism was immanent and that revolutionary tactics were appropriate. Social democrats, in this context, were defined as counter-revolutionaries in the workers' movement. The rise of fascism in Germany and elsewhere changed the conjuncture of forces. As fascism became the principal enemy, communists moved to join a united front of liberals, social democrats, and other anti-fascist forces in a tactical alliance.

The 1914-18 conflict had precipitated revolution in Russia and near-revolution in Italy and Germany. The defeat of fascism in 1945 did not bring about revolutionary situations in the defeated countries of Europe. Rather, as Lenin had argued, the revolutionary potential had shifted to the colonized world. China's revolution, for example, grew out of the anti-colonial struggle against Japan. Elsewhere, resistance against Japan and various European imperial powers frequently took socialist directions. The countries of Eastern Europe that were liberated by the Red Army or by their indigenous socialist resistance (Yugoslavia) emerged from the war into governments dominated by Communist parties, most of which formed a bloc with the USSR.

In liberal democratic countries, the political system could be leveraged by working-class parties in alliance with progressive forces, including enlightened capitalists, to bring reforms to the economic system. Social democratic parties based to a degree on the interests of the working class within the existing relations of production, were elected into legislative power in many European nations in the post-1945 world, most notably in the Scandinavian countries. Sweden became synonymous with social democracy in the postwar world. Sweden had remained officially neutral during the anti-fascist war and emerged from the conflict in a strong economic position. With a corporatist history that sometimes leaned towards fascism, Sweden's national economy was characterized by government regulation, tri-partite associations, and wage controls, as Sweden developed a model welfare-capitalist state.

Perhaps more radical was the British Labour government (1945-1951), which embarked on an unprecedented wave of nationalization, including transportation, utilities, the iron and steel industries, and the coal mines. Even the Bank of England was nationalized. The Labour government established a welfare state, the heart of which was nationalized medicine. It appeared to be a promising beginning to the gradual socialization of the means of production. In fact, there was no armed revolt of capital in Britain to protect its interests. Perhaps the rhetoric of having fought a war for democracy against fascism weighed against a military putsch.

However, in many respects, the times were not propitious for civil unrest, and capital had other weapons in its arsenal short of a putsch. The Marshall Plan re-built the economy of Germany to become a bulwark against presumed Russian expansion, but it ignored Britain. The British appeared to the Americans to be engaged in a socialist experiment of their own. They faced rationing years after 1945 and many Britons complained bitterly that Germany, in effect, had won the war. Perhaps the greatest irony in the Labour Party's move towards socialism with a British face was that, when Labour acquiesced in the loss of its parliamentary majority in favour of a Conservative government, the Conservative Party did not dismantle the system wholesale. For decades the Conservatives preserved much of the edifice of the welfare state as well as many of the nationalized industries. The political spectrum had taken a left-wing lurch that was not reversed until 1979 with the election of Margaret Thatcher. Only then would the British experiment in a 'mixed-economy' be reversed.

Social democratic parties might have been the most consistently Keynesian, but they were not exclusively so. The British experiment in state capitalism demonstrated, above all, the limits that reform could achieve in practice in the most propitious period. In the post-WW II world, social democracy has undergone a transmogrification, repudiating its Marxist heritage in favour of explicit acceptance of the parliamentary rules of the political game and the permanent domination of private capital.

Nationalization on the scale of the British Labour Party of 1945-51 was never attempted again by a social democratic party. When the Social Democratic Party came to power in Germany, it did so following an explicit disavowal of Marxian socialism and an acceptance of the pre-eminence of the capitalist market. Nationalization might be advocated in specific dying and unprofitable industries, in order to sustain regional economies or national interests, as well as political pluralities, but it did not have any of the ideological meaning suggestive of a step towards socialism (except in the rhetorical posturing of the extreme Right). Rather, a notion of the 'mixed economy' prevailed; some state ownership of isolated islands in the sea of private enterprise, connected to a pastiche social security net. The welfare state was the fruit of social liberalism in its social democratic guise. In the sense it is being used here, it was not even the fruit of reformism, which implies a political programme putatively committed to the goal of socialism.

Over the course of the twentieth century in advanced capitalism, the actual evolutionary path has not been from capitalism to socialism, conceived as alternative relations of production; rather, it has occurred within the social democratic parties themselves as they have evolved away from socialism. In countries where they have won electoral majorities, social democratic parties, both practically and theoretically, became managers of corporate capitalism and the welfare state. In the process, they explicitly abandoned any vestiges of Marxist theory and rhetoric in the interests of developing a broader class alliance for fighting electoral contests. 'Socialism' was explicitly abandoned as a goal of social democracy, which limited itself to a semi-regulated economy (including public ownership in cases of necessary but unprofitable enterprises), perhaps industrial democracy in its tri-partite disguise, and the welfare state – measures that themselves become defined as 'socialist' by the Right. Social Democracy, at best, became embedded in monopoly capitalism as the conscience of the system, emerging first as the most Keynesian, and then evolving in the contemporary era of neo-liberalism and global imperialism as the party that dismantles the welfare state in the most apologetic manner.

It is certainly an historical irony that, after the social rebellions of the 1960s collapsed, many Communist Parties in Western Europe followed the same track that had been laid down by the social democrats after the First World War. As social democracy became explicitly committed to the economic as well as the political status quo and eschewed its socialist past, the remnants of the Third International were shunted onto the vacated platform, becoming new reformists and revisionists. As the social democrats became born-again social liberals, the communist parties of Western Europe identified a vacuum on the reformist left. Following a path already blazed by the parties of the Second International, European communist parties disavowed Marxist-Leninist politics, discarded the rhetoric about the need for a "dictatorship of the proletariat," and distanced themselves from the policies of the Soviet Union (discredited by its repressive policy in Eastern Europe, principally in Poland in 1956 and Czechoslovakia in 1968). The

Euro-Communists, as they were known, cut adrift what they regarded as their revolutionary Marxist baggage in favour of explicit reformism and parliamentary democracy. In 1975, the Italian and French Communist Parties explicitly defined their policy as following the democratic road to socialism. They participated as one among a plurality of parties competing in the electoral process. Despite their renunciation, however, parliamentary successes of any significant kind did not follow. Just as history repeats itself a second time as farce, the Euro-Communists did not follow the social democrats into political power, despite some temporary vote-shifting. By the 1990s, as neo-conservatism triumphed and the erstwhile social democrats moved even more explicitly to the right (as in Britain's 'New' Labour), reformist-communists became an absurdity in more than merely name. Without question, however, they precipitated a crisis of terminology similar to the decision to differentiate 'communists' from 'social democrats' in the early part of the last century.

What of the new left, then? We have already discussed the individualistic and anarchistic tendencies that were apparent among the new left. To call the new left a failure is to imply that there was anything in it that had a chance of genuine social transformation. The new left fed into a number of political options, including urban terrorism, ultra-leftist glorification of Mao, and Trotskyism (which is never short of new, youthful, idealistic recruits), as well as into 'new social movements' such as feminism and environmentalism. One of the typical outcomes of this radicalism was a rediscovery of Marxist theory and the multiplication of numerous neo-Marxist theoreticians securely rooted in the universities. We don't intend to differentiate among the various contending schools of neo-Marxism. In general, they confined their increasingly esoteric attention to political economy rather than political theory.

Among many of them, however, including some who passed through the New-Communist movement of the 1970s, the question of political involvement was still salient. Aside from active involvement in the myriad of social movements that have accompanied globalization, perhaps the most typical path of political engagement for neo-Marxist academics was into the existing social democratic parties. Inevitably, this meant an internal 'left' presence and implied a notion of boring-from-within, of pushing the party – or 'waffling' to use a Canadian phrase – leftwards. While the results of this strategy were minimal, the counter-tendency has been overwhelming. Social democratic parties have stampeded to the right. In the process, they have created a serious dilemma for those social democrats still committed in their ideology to socialism of a more profound sort than welfare capitalism, but who are still opposed to the Leninist model of organization. More broadly, as formal social democratic parties abandon everything except the contest for electoral victory, most contemporary leftists embrace any form of extra-parliamentary activism, seeking to find the elusive Holy Grail: a successful, non-Leninist, mass strategy.

But if only reforms are on the agenda in the core countries, a second question naturally arises: Does social democracy have a future in the West? Social democratic parties are constrained by national boundaries. Insofar as social democracy reflects some liberal and national sentiments, it is a less bad alternative than the Right. At best, it may minimize the effects of globalization in the interests of preserving the remnants of the welfare state and a national policy. And what of organized labour? Historically, social democracy has been inextricably tied to national labour movements. While capital has been globalized, no equivalent 'liberalization' has occurred for labour. In this sense, labour is increasingly unfree relative to capital.

But national Keynesianism has had its day. What, then, of global Keynesianism? As the contradictions of *laissez-faire* globalization exacerbate social inequalities and foment local rebellions that have the potential for wider linkages, does capitalism still have up its sleeve a global social liberalism and welfare super-state? Social liberalism and social democracy achieved some very modest redistribution of income in the core and semi-core capitalist nations. Is a similar small-scale redistribution of income possible on a world scale? Arguably, of course, a redistribution has already occurred as a result of neo-liberalism – from the poor to the rich everywhere, and from the poor countries to significantly large strata among the rich countries. Ironically, however, where people do turn to supposedly social democratic parties (as in Britain or France), or to presumably more social liberal ones (as in Canada and the US Democratic Party), the entire political spectrum has rotated on a right-wing axis. The imperatives of neo-liberal globalization are the accepted parameters within which the interests of capital must be considered. Fundamentally, however, despite these obvious global contradictions, no political structure of an equivalent global magnitude is on the historical horizon. It is the state within the nation that negotiates trade concessions and accepts the dismantling of the welfare reforms of Keynesianism. Formal social democracy is forced, more and more, to abandon its roots in the capitalist nation state and succumb (or champion, as in the case of New Labour), globalization and modern imperialism.

Conclusion

THE CRUCIAL THEORETICAL question concerns the relationship of the state to civil society. For Bernstein, bourgeois liberalism was an inevitable stage in the evolutionary development of society, and there was a necessary causal link between the development of capitalism and the evolution of bourgeois democracy. But, as Luxemburg demonstrated, there was no necessary connection; bourgeois democracy is a rarity rather than a norm. Furthermore, she argued that the trend towards militarism (and imperialism) would force bourgeois democracy into the arms of reaction.

As Luxemburg pointed out, Bernstein held a metaphysical view of the state as representing the whole of society rather than being a class state. Hence, she argued for the crucial importance of distinguishing between 'parliament' and the 'state.' The state is fundamentally a repressive institution, which controls overt instruments of power (police, prisons, standing army). The state may, as well, include some forms of bourgeois democracy, but the attachment of any ruling class to one method or another of political rule depends on expediency and class interest.

It is generally recognized that Marx did not explore political theory thoroughly in his writings. Marxism was conceived in an era of revolution – the 1840s – when the issue of revolutionary consciousness at first seemed unproblematic. When the revolutions of 1848 were defeated, Marx sought an explanation for the failure and found the answer, not in political theory, but in political economy. The proletariat was not sufficiently developed as a class to lead a revolution in its own interests; at best, in central and Eastern Europe, bourgeois revolutions were imminent. Marx focused his analysis on the objective conditions of revolution, on the dynamics of the capitalist mode of production that were creating the proletariat, and the crisis tendencies that would ultimately push it to revolution.

Marx developed his political economy after 1848 at a time when revolution was not practically imminent. Marx often spoke as though he expected a revolution in his lifetime, but this wasn't because he sensed the emergence of mass revolutionary consciousness; rather, he believed that the laws of capitalism were creating the conditions that would lead to the development of such consciousness. A theory of political revolution in embryo does emerge from Marx's analysis of the Paris Commune, but it remained fragmentary.

The experience of the Commune was very important because it revealed that a revolutionary situation emerges out of crises that do not necessarily originate directly from the contradictions of capitalism. It confirmed Marx's belief that the proletariat was a revolutionary class, that it had the potential to rise in open rebellion and, once again as in 1848, that the bourgeois state would be vicious in its repression. Yet, even in his critique of the Gotha Program, Marx does not develop a theory of revolutionary leadership. There is a sense of inevitability in Marx's political economy that allows one to assume that, given the appropriate economic conditions, capitalism will be unable to resolve its internal contradictions and, in such a circumstance, the development of revolutionary consciousness is unproblematic.

Bernstein, for his part, did not develop his reformist theory in a period of mass revolutionary action but in the era of imperialism and monopoly capitalism. It cannot be said absolutely that, at that time, revolutionary potential had shifted away from the core capitalist countries into the periphery (or the semi-periphery, Lenin having demonstrated that Russia had a small, but significant and class conscious industrial proletariat). The point of Lenin's *Imperialism* was to identify Russia as the weak link and to anticipate revolution in the East. Even then, there were still questions about the type of revolution it would be, the role Russian socialists should play in it, and whether revolution in the East would be the spark to ignite a revolution in the West.

For reformists, the 1880-1914 era in western and central Europe was essentially non-revolutionary. Arguably, imperialism was a short-term solution to the problems inherent in the capital accumulation process. But turn-of-the-century imperialism brought in its wake a political crisis because imperialism implied international rivalry and war. Again, just as in Paris in 1871, a revolutionary situation developed in Russia and then, subsequently, in Germany, that had less to do with the "laws of motion" of competitive capitalism and more to do with the consequences of capitalism in its phase of imperialist rivalry and, particularly, out of the concrete conditions that arose from military defeat and the breakdown – not of capitalism – but of the state. In Russia, the state of the Tsar could no longer rule, and the subsequent rule of the bourgeoisie and its supporters deepened the crisis in the whole social formation seriously undermining, most crucially, the repressive agencies of state power. In Germany, however, the wider state apparatuses, the police and the army, were still intact – the Kaiser was gone but the generals were still in power – and the revolution was snuffed.

The era of imperialism shifted the more severe contradictions of the capitalist system to the periphery where, in the context of political and economic imperialism, nationalist and potentially socialist revolutions were both possible and achievable. What of the otherwise essentially non-revolutionary situation in the West, however? It is important not least because the same situation faced the West throughout the twentieth century, with a few exceptions that arose in the more semi-peripheral nations (Spain, Greece) and in central Europe as a result of the aftermath of the Second World War. The point, however, is that non-revolutionary times predominated. What is the role of a revolutionary party in non-revolutionary circumstances?

One answer was to fight for reforms that are achievable within the bourgeois state. Where the old aristocracy and not the bourgeoisie was a dominant force, and therefore, where a bourgeois revolution was the most likely political consequence (except in peripheral capitalist countries where they were too weak to rule), the revolutionary party would support reforms that were achievable within bourgeois democracy, and that would allow the working classes to organize separately and carry out its own agenda. The organization of the working classes, the dissemination of propaganda, the development of class consciousness, were all less problematic under the conditions of bourgeois freedoms, such as a free press, freedom of assembly, legal trade unions, and so on. It has commonly been remarked that the programme of the First International, the demands set out in the *Communist Manifesto*, and the practical elements of the Erfurt Program endorsed by Engels, did not go much beyond bourgeois reforms.

But in the absence of a political theory, the implication is that revolutionary consciousness arises spontaneously from the effects of a crisis in which political agitation conducted by revolutionaries has a ready-made subject. If Marx saw revolution as essentially unproblematic, and as a consequence of the right objective conditions; if, as Luxemburg claimed, revolution would arise spontaneously from a class conscious proletariat, then political theory need not be developed in any systematic way. The proletariat would take power. The experience of 1871 indicated that there would probably be a short period of dictatorship given the difficult situation at the moment of revolution and the need to overcome the resistance of the expropriated classes. Otherwise, the political dimension of the newly created socialist society would have to be developed through praxis, reflective of the concrete conditions of the nation within which the revolution occurred.

The relationship between political leadership and the working class is a crucial matter of political theory and practice. As Mao summed up the situation, political problems derive from too great a separation between class leadership and the masses. Party leaders may err by being either too far in front of the masses (adventurism) or too far behind them (tailism). Anarchists anticipate that their sacrifice and rebellion can inspire the masses to imitate them; hence they are often isolated and successes are short-lived. While social democrats may be more rooted among the masses (although this is not true in its more Right-wing, bureaucratic form), they have a tendency to assume that ordinary people, through their genuine humanity and decency, already possess the qualities necessary for social progress.

The revolutionaries' relationship to the 'masses' is somewhat more problematic. In times of revolutionary war, the guerrilla is likely to be the "fish in the sea" of the aroused and conscious people. Theoretically, however, the Marxist revolutionary in non-revolutionary times is expected to be rooted in a fraction of the class-conscious working class dubbed the "vanguard." In the 1930s and '40s, communists in the West were active in labour unions and peoples' struggles. Even a superficial overview of this period in communist history indicates a number of disastrous policies. With the Great Depression, the Comintern concluded that the objective conditions for revolution had finally materialized in the West. Given the standard positivist assumptions, class consciousness could not be far behind. The memory of the German "white terror" and the role of the SPD in counter-revolution was barely a decade old. Accordingly, the Third International defined as "social fascist" any left organization that, while calling itself socialist, actively worked against revolution and limited its goals to reforms within the capitalist system. This harmful and divisive definition derived from both an overestimation of the objective factors – the assumed final breakdown of capitalism – and an overestimation of subjective factors – given the circumstances, workers' experiences would ordinarily lead them to recognize the leadership role of the CP except that social democratic misleadership prevented the workers from developing revolutionary consciousness. Hence, the argument went, social democrats were the capitalists' best friends. Ironically, at the time, the Communists may have been the fascists' best friends.

In *What is to be Done?* and in his later writings, including on the "renegade" Kautsky, Lenin had drawn the sharpest demarcation between revolutionaries and reformists. Political theory, however, is not just a matter of making clear demarcations. That is not to say that there aren't times and circumstances where "which side are you on" has a very polarized meaning; but not in the 1930s in the face of the rise of fascism. The Comintern abandoned the ultra-left, social fascist tactic, replacing it with a united front against fascism, but not without serious political consequences. Not to be outdone, in 1939 with the opportunistic Stalin-Hitler pact, the united front was abandoned, and wasn't revived until Germany invaded the USSR. If revisionism is replacing principle with expediency, then the USSR had succumbed to revisionism.

Marx accepted the struggle for bourgeois reforms not as ends in themselves but as means to further develop the class struggle, keeping the proletariat interest separate and understanding that, at some point, the interests of the proletariat and the bourgeoisie would completely diverge. But with reform, the issue of power is central because, by definition in a situation where any party – even a revolutionary one – is struggling to achieve reforms, the capitalist state is still dominated by the bourgeoisie. Legal tactics means playing their game, even if such tactics may achieve some small successes, if nothing else, deflecting the worst neo-liberal policies. Ultimately, though, power talks. So the correct tactic must be to involve the widest body of people as possible, to propel them into the most action possible under the circumstances – illegal action if they are properly prepared – to both learn and lead simultaneously, and to connect the present struggle with larger issues.

Organized, collective action can sometimes force power's hand much more readily than supplication.

In this context, the neo-liberal globalization of the turn-of-the-century may be a dominant feature of political economy, but it is not an entirely new stage for which the revolutionary dramas of the past are obsolete. Oppression is never unopposed. Conglomerate *laissez faire*, represented by the global institutions such as the World Trade Organization (WTO) and the International Monetary Fund (IMF), along with the emergence of large, regional trading blocs, are already generating their own opposition. Just as capital has burst through national boundaries, to some extent so too have the movements of opposition, although such movements take on a myriad of forms, both progressive, such as peasant rebellion in Mexico, anti-free trade activism in the core capitalist countries, or variants of socialist reforms in Venezuela and Ecuador. They also take reactionary forms, such as religious fundamentalism in the Near East and the revival of neo-Nazism in the West.

Lenin's absolute demarcation between revolutionaries and reformists was not just a reflection of an era of high revolutionary potential; it reflected a theoretical summation of the tendency towards reformism and revisionism in the Marxist movement. Present-day social democratic parties in the West have devolved into social liberalism at best and apologists for neo-liberalism at worst. It is an illusion to think they can be transformed from within. At best, extra-parliamentary activism can force some liberal concessions in the struggle to retain some of the gains of social democracy from the past. Lenin argued at the beginning of the twentieth-century that revolutionary potential had shifted away from Europe to the colonized world. In the opening decades of the twenty-first century, perhaps social democracy has not exhausted its potential for social reform in the peripheral counties of contemporary capitalism or in what might be termed post-socialist, revisionist capitalism. In this century, as evidenced in much of Latin America, we find supposedly new social democratic paths to socialism. Their opposition to or perhaps ignorance of the need for Leninist party organization, we are afraid, will lead to a repeat of errors of the past.

It is our main contention that it is essential to reiterate the fundamentals of revolutionary Marxist political theory even – perhaps especially – in the contemporary context when revolution is unlikely in the West or, indeed, globally. The crucial point is that, while practical activities are constrained within the limitations of reform, it is essential to retain a focus on the socialist 'end' to avoid the errors of the past. Now, as always, developing theory and organization are crucial tasks for social activists committed to the long-term goals of social revolution.

CHAPTER FOUR

Lenin and Leninism

THE FUNDAMENTALS of Marxism both as a theory of capitalism and its development, and as a political theory outlining the principles and practices necessary to transform and transcend capitalism, were articulated by Marx and Engels in the nineteenth century. To summarize our argument above, when compared with other social theories, the validity of the political economy side of Marxism has retained quite extraordinary staying power. Unlike the myriad theories that see capitalism as a prosperous and felicitous system, the best of all possible worlds and the end of history, Marxism perceives the historical nature of capitalism, pinpointing how it operates and its essentially crisis-ridden characteristics. From its beginnings, Marxism successfully projected the tremendous productivity of the system and its tendency to encapsulate the whole world into one common system of wealth accumulation occurring under the domination of increasing concentration and centralization of wealth. Even the changes wrought by imperialist expansion are well incorporated into predictions about the operation of modern monopoly capitalism.

There has been a growth in respectability of a certain kind of Marxism in Western academic and intellectual life. This has been true in Europe at least since the end of the Second World War; but in North America until the 1970s, Marxism in academic and intellectual life had either no official existence of was given merely token, and often quite distorted recognition. The infusion of Marxist ideas into scholarship was a healthy corrective to the cold war iceberg that so paralyzed social thought up through the 1960s.

Yet even with a thaw in academic thought, certain deep and entrenched assumptions still delimit what is considered appropriate to respectable analysis, and such assumptions continue to avoid or misunderstand distinguishing features of the Marxist mode. Perhaps the most recalcitrant reluctance to fully engage contemporary Marxism is reflected in attitudes toward V. I. Lenin and his contribution to the development of modern Marxism. If Marx's ideas were either distorted or almost completely neglected in social and political thought, it is nothing compared to the veritable wall of silence surrounding the work of Lenin.

Marx once proclaimed that the traditions of the past lay "like an Alp" upon the minds of the living. It is never easy for a contemporary of any intellectual system to perceive the fundamental assumptions of one's own times, and this is true of Marx and Engels as it would be true of anyone else. The almost completely dominant world view of science in the nineteenth century, one that still holds strong sway in present popular thought, was positivism. This view postulates a deterministic and progressive direction both to scientific knowledge and to history. Its negative effects seem less significant in the natural sciences where relativity, change, and probability have weakened the idea of pre-determined absolute truth, but in the human historical sciences the deleterious effects of determined scientific truth are still palpable. Bourgeois social science with its usual fixed engagement with the present as history and its almost complete contempt for history per se remains rooted in positivism, whereas one would not expect positivism to remain part of Marxism that embraced a Hegelian sense of change and sees itself fundamentally as a rational understanding of history. In subtle and significant political ways, however, Marxism had positivist aspects at its inception, aspects which, in the political realm, continue into the present. As mentioned in earlier chapters, this positivism is shown most clearly in Marx's belief that he was articulating the "laws of motion" of capitalist society. While the idea of motion accepts change as central to capitalism, the use of the idea of laws includes an ambiguity since laws suggest the discovery of some final truth. The great methodological truth embodied in modern science that scientific knowledge is a matter of probability rather than law explodes any positivist pretentions in Marxism or any other theory. In the face of his more positivist side rising to dominance in the Marxist community, Marx later in life, in a fit of irony, proclaimed that he was not a Marxist. In hindsight, it can be seen that he was too late since by the late nineteenth century, positivist-style Marxism already held sway in burgeoning European social democracy. In this positivist style, in which the materialist core determined the social superstructure, lay the seeds of later revisionism, as demonstrated in Chapter Three.

Implicit in this latter discussion involves an answer to fundamental questions about post-Marx Marxism. These questions ask: why does revolutionary Marxism add the name of Lenin to its fundamental lexicon and make his name synonymous with revolutionary Marxism? We believe that this new appellation is well warranted, for the following reasons.

What is unique to Lenin and the times in which he lived is that he was himself surrounded by a European Marxist movement suffused with positivism and revisionism, a movement that was of greater strength than anything in the nineteenth century. This was so much the case that we are not sure that Lenin recognized the full extent of his break with that tradition. In fact, Lenin still carried aspects of that outlook until the end of his days, but more on that later. Living in a context in which socialist revolution had become a living possibility, Lenin was a more quintessentially political actor than Marx. Marx's main battles were with those ideas that he considered essential to the understanding of capitalist dynamics while Lenin dealt with the political application of these ideas to Russia and the world. That is, he recognized that Marxist political economy had so clearly won the day that the major intellectual battles would be fought within Marxism itself. It is significant that the question of opportunism was not at all raised during Marx and Engel's time since, for them, differences of opinion appeared to be a matter of education, of convincing opposition through argument and evidence.

Background to the Russian Revolution

THE RUSSIAN SITUATION at the turn of the last century presented a particular dilemma for Marxist theory and practice. On the eve of the Soviet Revolution, Russia was a predominantly semi-feudal country ruled by an absolute monarchy. The class control of Russia included a long-term established monarchy and landed aristocracy supported by primitive levels of technology and low productivity. The majority of the population lived in rural areas working either in serf-like bondage (official serfdom had been repealed in 1860) to the landed aristocracy or farming small parcels of land with relatively primitive tools. This was not a situation conducive, according to nineteenth century Marxist theory, to a socialist transformation (and this view has shown a good deal of staying power). According to that theory, only the full development of society's productive forces generated by centralized and coordinated mechanized factories could prepare the way for socialism. Historically it had been capitalism through its ceaseless drive to accumulate wealth that had generated these productive forces, conditions which inexorably replaced primitive with mechanized agricultural production while forcing much of the farming population into modern factory labour. It is this modern factory run by capitalists that becomes the locus for the development of the new industrial proletarian class, which in its perpetual conflict with its capitalist masters, is the harbinger of the future classless society. Without this level of development, a society remains mired in scarcity, and scarcity engenders a low standard of living as well as inequality for the population.

No one in the socialist tradition has imagined that a classless society would involve little more than the equal sharing of poverty. Moreover, many Marxists went further than requiring a full development of economic conditions as a prerequisite to socialism. Social democrats saw certain political features of mature capitalism as not only necessary for socialism, but they elevated to the status of strategic principle such institutions as parliamentary democracy, a free press, and a multi-party electoral system. In short, socialism was unthinkable without the total ripening of what are considered the most progressive features of advanced capitalism. In this scenario, only the mere existence of the capitalist class becomes an obstacle to the realization of socialism while the totality of bourgeois institutions supporting that class takes on a progressive nature.

The expectation and the great hope for socialism in the Marxist theory, which Lenin had inherited, resided in the advanced capitalist world. Marxism paradoxically not only represents the most fundamental opposition to the bourgeois class, which introduced the central features of modern society; it is at the same time one of the strongest supporters of many of these central features. In contrast to all former ruling classes, the modern bourgeoisie generates a world that, along with fostering hitherto unprecedented material wealth, breaks down centuries of traditional cultural backwardness, superstition, and obscurantism. The ideas supporting democracy, science, and rational inquiry are all unthinkable without their introduction by the modern bourgeoisie.

If Russia was to have a revolution, it would have to be along the lines of the earlier French Revolutions where conditions were similar to those facing Russia. The ball and chain of landed property, aristocracy, and Tsardom must be replaced by an industrializing capitalist class and a modern democracy, a parliament, and all the other forms of freedom associated with these political institutions. In a country with only a small industrial working class and an underdeveloped bourgeoisie, it was considered, by most of Marxism at the time, unrealistic and foolhardy to expect or work for anything else.

Political Development of Marxism

IN TRANSCENDING the positivist side of Marxist politics, Lenin did not critically refer to it by this name since he appeared implicitly to understand the taken for granted nature of that aspect. Furthermore, its command over the Marxist political economy landscape was so overwhelming that little would be gained by a fundamental break with it (although it is possible that the absence of critique indicates Lenin's own connection to it). In openly accepting the genius of Marxist political economy and the revolutionary spirit that motivated Marx and Engel's work, in his political writings, Lenin referred mainly to the later revolutionary ideas found in the later Marx and built upon them. Nothing could be gained by apparently exposing the founders' weaknesses in their early work, even though it is just those weaknesses that had been built into more systematic organizational form in the revisionism of Lenin's time. More to the point, the most clear-cut revolutionary summation of Marx's ideas are found only in his very late analysis of the Paris Commune such that Lenin had much less in the whole corpus of Marx and Engels' work to refer to when attempting to update Marxist political theory.

Let us be more specific about these limitations often implicit in this earlier work to demonstrate how Lenin could transcend them, still recognizing the foundational value of all that had gone before. For Marx and Engels, two major events punctuated the nineteenth century. The first was the widespread revolutionary outbreaks in many European countries in 1848 and the second was the Paris Commune of 1871. Britain and France in those times were still struggling in the midst of consolidating bourgeois rule over the remnants of a feudal past, a struggle which was weak and ambiguous since bourgeois economic dominance was so well entrenched that it could afford to act kindly in the political realm to feudal and aristocratic remnants. In central and southern Europe, particularly in Germany, industrial capitalism emerged as the fruit of an unholy alliance between the traditional landed aristocracy and the urban bourgeoisie. In either case, what was coming to be recognized by the new ruling class was the growing danger of a rising industrial working class and attendant socialism. Marx and Engels were fully cognizant of this situation and were active participants in the ensuing struggles. However, their political activism had built into it ideas, which only in hindsight can be seen as taken-for-granted positivism. These ideas regard the nature of the working class and the kind of leadership necessary to lead it.

The failure of the 1848 revolution in Marxist terms was a great shock and disappointment to the founders of Marxism. They were not surprised at the solidification of bourgeois rule since their very prescient understanding of capitalist dynamics clearly predicted it and, where bourgeois rule had not yet been consolidated, their political involvement actively supported this outcome. Their disappointment stemmed from the utter defeat, in fact dissolution, of this first rising of the modern working class as a political force. Their explanation of that defeat, however, symbolizes the existence of a positivist impetus. It is summed up in a phrase that now has a continuing history in Marxist politics: "the working class was not yet ripe for political power." Central to nineteenth century Marxism was the idea that the introduction of socialism demanded the full development of the capitalist system. This meant that its productive forces must be fully developed by a growing industrial working class, which in the context of collective experience in the modern factory would become conscious of its exploitation and of its potential power. At this juncture, it was expected that the working class in fully-industrialized nations would overthrow the capitalist class and initiate a new socialist future. In short, it was assumed that the private ownership that was controlling already socialized production would be seen as superfluous and unnecessary to continue. From this outlook, however, came the view that the working class could not and should not press for full political power until this full development of productive forces had occurred. Accordingly, for those societies in which full development had not been reached, it was the duty of revolutionary politics to support a bourgeois democratic revolution as a necessary stage in the movement toward socialist revolution.

What followed for Marx's understanding of the defeat of any socialist possibilities in the 1848 revolutions was a turn to the objective limitations of the situation. We would suggest that this viewpoint, quite understandable in the nineteenth century context, becomes much more than that with later developments, developments that, in the main, are a result of totally new initiatives introduced by Lenin. Implicit in this initiative is a different conception of objective and subjective factors in the process of socialist revolutionary change. Anarchism assumes that the exploited classes are always potentially revolutionary and need only an activist, subjective spark to set them in revolutionary motion. For positivist Marxism, the subjective condition of the working class is fully dependent upon the objective conditions in which the class is situated. For this Marxist outlook, the working class can come into revolutionary consciousness only when the objective conditions generate that consciousness. Marxist politics may nudge it along and do some educating along the way, but it cannot push the working class beyond the consciousness imposed by the objective conditions in which it lives. This assumption is strongly implied as well in the famous Marxist methodological dictum that being determines consciousness, the dictum by which Marxism and, in fact, the whole bourgeois revolutionary tradition broke with traditional philosophic idealism. By the 1870s in industrialized capitalist nations, however, a disjunction had appeared between the advanced productive forces and the consciousness of the majority of the proletariat. Apparently propitious objective conditions were not automatically reflective of revolutionary consciousness, prompting Marx and Engels to speculate about false consciousness and the labour aristocracy.

The divide between reformism and revolutionary Marxism is already foreshadowed in Marx's time, as we said before, with his incisive critique of the German Social Democratic programme in the late nineteenth century in the *Critique of the Gotha Program*. Marx appears there, however, to be treating reformism as a remediable and somewhat transient problem to be dealt with by more education. By the first decade of the twentieth century, the division within social democracy between reform and revolutionary Marxism had become far from transient. It had become solidified although it did not assume a clear organizational schism until the beginning of the First World War. There had been basic agreement in all parties until then that the working class of all nations must be international in its outlook, that it should never fight a war and die for its own national capitalists, that war should be seen as only benefitting capital and can be superseded only by the overthrow of the capitalist class in each nation. Reformist Marxism in practice put this overthrow into a distant future, and accordingly, these parties voted to support the wars initiated by their national bourgeoisies. This adherence to war accorded well for parties that had proclaimed the small gains made by trade union bargaining and worker-friendly parliamentary legislation to be the be-all and end-all of Marxist politics.

It is clear and definitive in Marx and Engels' writings that history is made not primarily by the actions of kings, generals, and the like, but by ordinary people. This is potentially even more so in the case of industrial capitalism, which for the first time creates a class that can be fully conscious of its place in society and of its capacity to govern a new society for the benefit of all. The future, said Marx and Engels, depends upon the actions of these new "free" propertyless proletarians. As early as the *Communist Manifesto*, they reinforced the view already formulated in the great cauldron of the French Revolution that the people are the major agents of history. But they saw "the people" not in the sense of everybody, but in the specifically class terms generated by the growth of capitalism. It is the new industrial working class created within the specific conditions of capital accumulation, which will be the creators of modern history. And being a class without property and without any hope of ever owning productive property, it will be a class that will create, for the first time, a society transcending the very need for private property.

The question left somewhat ambiguous by the founders of Marxism was the nature of leadership of the working class. That leadership was necessary was unequivocal as the active political life of Marx and Engels showed them quite ready to take on such responsibilities. Moreover, their lifelong opposition to anarchism on the question of leadership is sharp evidence of their theoretical recognition of such a need. The fundamental problem with their commitment to the leading role of the working class revolves around the question of how this class *leads*. Does its position in history mean that the class *as a whole* possesses or is in the process of possessing those qualities that assure it of leading a revolutionary transformation? Is to be born working class an assurance that revolutionary leadership will be developed in sufficient numbers by the almost automatic maturational process of working-class life? To pose the questions in this way leads in the direction of their answers, but strangely enough, Lenin was the first Marxist who dared to raise them.

Lenin's Revolutionary Break

AT A STROKE, Lenin broke with the positivist approach to revolutionary politics. In the early written *What Is to Be Done* Lenin declared that the working class "left to itself" will never make a socialist revolution. There must be another subjectivity brought into the revolutionary equation since the most potentially revolutionary class in human history is limited by its everyday working and living conditions from developing the theoretical tools for transforming the capitalist system. What the working class needed, continued Lenin, was a new kind of leadership, one that was derived from the intellectual stratum that had renounced its bourgeois origins and ideas, and chose the outlook and attitudes consistent with the potential of the working class.

Marxism had always recognized the need for leadership of that class, especially in its long struggle with anarchism, which rejected the need for anything but temporary leadership. It had also strongly criticized the idea of revolutionary change initiated by a secret conspiracy, an idea associated with the work of Louis Blanqui. But the work of Marx and Engels had never clarified the exact nature of working-class leadership, leaving the door open to the idea that leadership should simply follow the initiatives of the spontaneous strivings of a class that seemed historically destined to develop the programmes and leadership that will transform capitalism into socialism. What was unprecedented in Lenin's conception was not only that leadership must arise outside the class, but that it must be a different kind of leadership. It must be fully dedicated to the working class and its best aspirations; it must be professionally organized; and it must integrate itself into that class to prove itself worthy of the right to lead and to better assess objective and subjective conditions. By implication, integration with the working class is also necessary for the party to be accountable to the class in whose name it seeks power. Since it is implicit in Lenin's bold statement about the limitations of the working class that it lacks theoretical education about itself, so perhaps the major ideological mission of this new leadership is to bring revolutionary theory to a class in need of such theory.

Lenin in declaring a need for new leadership was rejecting all that passed for revolutionary leadership at that time. And that leadership was extremely formidable, in command of the largest working class movements ever seen. In line with essentially positivist assumptions, the leadership saw itself as guiding a class, which by the objective nature of advanced capitalist life, was discovering itself and automatically forwarding its own leadership, one which best represented this discovery. In short, Lenin faced the solidification of varieties of reformist Marxist ideas in existent and concrete political movements, including the social democrats who claimed to simply follow historical laws (the positivist side of original Marxism discussed in Chapter Three). As early as 1902, in the context of an impending social revolution in Russia, Lenin argued that these opportunist Marxist ideas had to be confronted, ultimately, as forms of collaboration with the bourgeoisie. Lenin argued that opportunism was a political force to be strongly exposed and, if possible, defeated. Even though he anticipated a bourgeois-type revolution in Russia, in *What Is to Be Done?* Lenin directly challenged the strategy of relying on economic struggle alone in what was essentially a political conflict. The recognition that the fight against capitalism must include a fight against opportunism defines the overriding impetus in Lenin's political development of Marxism. As always with Lenin, historical circumstances condition the timing and the tactics with which opportunism within Marxism is confronted.

Outside of Russia, with its apparently warring factions of small political groups, existed large, well-organized and unified Marxist parties, especially in Germany, which were well integrated into massive and growing industrial working classes in the advanced capitalist countries. And these parties were, at least rhetorically, revolutionary parties articulating a programme expressing permanent conflict between capital and labour, only resolvable by the forceful overthrow of capital. It was then not surprising that even the most revolutionary pens of the working class movement swung into action to condemn Lenin's declaration. Rosa Luxembourg and Leon Trotsky wrote pamphlets pillorying Lenin for elitism, for attempting to foist outside leadership upon a class that could depend only on its own members to lead.

The most significant opposition to Lenin's thesis on party formation in the advanced countries came from the pen of Rosa Luxembourg, a Marxist of impeccable revolutionary credentials in the German Party and in the Marxist world at large (credentials that retain much of their viability up to the present day). At an international socialist conference in Stuttgart, Germany in 1907, Luxemburg drafted a resolution demanding that the workers' movement use the opportunity of a future war to turn the tables and destroy the capitalist state. In 1914, she did not change this revolutionary position. This strategy was also precisely Lenin's. But there was little compromising on her part with Lenin's highly controversial position on party formation. For a revolutionary movement feeling its oats in advanced capitalist societies, already successful with what were considered tried and true principles, such ideas from a Russian revolutionary could be given short shrift, and they were. At best the idea of the need for a select, professional party might be acceptable for the special conditions of Tsarist Russia, but could have no general applicability (a position still expressed in socialist circles today).

In her "Leninism or Marxism?" pamphlet published in 1904, Luxembourg sets forth what she considers the fundamental relationship between the revolutionary party and the working class. In Luxembourg's view, and she would proclaim Marx's as well, it is not only that the working makes the revolution (as would be agreed by all Marxists including Lenin), but that its ideas and actions are the *leading* force in that revolution. A party to be successful can be no more than a general staff for a class in revolutionary motion, a staff composed of perhaps some intellectuals from other backgrounds, but mainly working class in origin; and this staff takes its cues and guides to action from the vitality and advanced political ideas of the working class itself.

The original title of Luxembourg's critique of Lenin's conception of the Marxist party was "Organizational Questions of the Russian Social Democracy," a much less polemical title than "Leninism or Marxism?" Significantly, the latter title was not Luxembourg's at all, but was added as late as 1935. In line with the present argument, there would be no sense to talk of "Leninism" in the first decade of the twentieth century when Lenin and Luxembourg initially wrote about this question. As a member of the powerful German Marxist party, her article takes on the colouring of a much wiser, older sister instructing a somewhat rebellious younger brother about the ways of the world. As a writer sympathetic to Lenin's aims, she does not condemn Lenin's conception outright, but attempts to see its potential justification in the unique features of backward Russia. Lenin's task, she says in "Leninism or Marxism?" is "deciding on what is the best socialist tactical policy in a country where absolute monarchy is still dominant.... The problem is how to create a Social Democratic movement at a time when the state is not yet in the hands of the bourgeoisie."

Although Luxembourg realizes that conditions specific to Russia demand a unique response and that therefore Russia need not simply repeat the experience of the advanced capitalist nations, she still asserts that absolutist, feudal Russia cannot move towards socialism without a lengthy bourgeois transition. At the same time that she was accepting bourgeois rule as the next step for Russian social democracy, both Lenin and Trotsky were formulating a policy of a working-class/peasant alliance as a means of immediately transcending bourgeois rule.

Luxembourg does not only assume a replication of general European experience for Russia; she explicitly sees the European social democratic experience as the model for Russia (and therefore for all other Marxist projects). The essay opposing Lenin's conception of the party rests on a rejection of the central axiom of his argument, the axiom that the working class *left to itself* will not come to revolutionary consciousness. Lenin continues to see the modern working class as the seedbed and the force of revolutionary transformation at the same time it is also a class of diverse ideological tendencies generated by the powerful agencies of bourgeois rule. Without dealing frontally with this idea, Luxembourg presents what must be considered (at least in hindsight) a highly romanticized version of the working class and its spontaneous revolutionary development. "The Social Democratic movement," she writes, "is the first in the history of class societies which reckons, *in all its phases and through its entire course*, on the organization and the direct, *independent action of the masses*" (italics are ours). Moreover, she accuses Lenin of rejection of this fundamental position by "slighting this fact." Instead, continues Luxembourg, Lenin is substituting a band of elite conspirators where the "preparation for the revolution concerned only the little group of revolutionists armed for the coup." Here, Luxembourg accuses Lenin using one of the strongest epithets in the early Marxist lexicon, claiming that he is a Blanquist conspirator, not a Marxist revolutionary. She finishes her critique with the much quoted statement that "Historically, the errors committed by a truly revolutionary movement are infinitely more fruitful than the infallibility of the cleverest Central Committee."

We have quoted at length from Luxembourg not because we agree with her critique (in fact in later recognizing the significance of the Bolshevik victory in 1917, she herself tempered her views), but because these are the views of a bona fide Marxist revolutionary at the time, and they represent the standard Marxist air breathed by virtually everyone in what was a burgeoning, confident working-class movement in much of Europe.

On the question of overcentralization, Lenin did not adequately address the relationship between party and class, particularly after the taking of power. The practice of democratic centralism is meant to establish the terms within which party members analyze theory and policy in changing circumstances, guide their practice, and reassess the consequences, both practically and theoretically. Despite Lenin's prestige and ability, internal disagreements in the Bolshevik party were fractious, including the decision to launch the October insurrection. Maintaining both a revolutionary practice and innerparty democracy is a thorny issue in the history of Leninist parties, and the question of how to hold party members accountable to the class they represent is even more problematic and remains so.

At its inception, Lenin's ideas did not lead to his outright rejection by the European socialist movements. After all, he was only a Russian living in the economic backwaters of Europe and perhaps he could be forgiven for such conceptions if they could be seen as necessary in still feudal conditions. This is especially true about the need for a secret leadership acting in this way since the reactionary and oppressive monarchy in Russia, and the more primitive industrial working class, could not develop or permit the apparently vibrant leadership already existent in advanced European countries. It was for this reason that Lenin was not fully condemned and that he was still accepted as a poor benighted cousin. And it was for this reason that he himself at first articulated and defended his ideas about leadership mainly in the context of Russian conditions.

What is striking about Luxembourg's thought in this regard is that she was one among a minority of social democrats to perceive the depth and breadth of opportunism in her own German social democratic movement. In fact, her confrontation with the problem in her famous *Junius* pamphlet has become one of the classic landmarks in articulating the danger of this right-wing tendency in Marxism. Writing in 1904, she was not yet aware of its real depth and danger since she believed that working class responses would always overcome what she considered temporary problems. In her *Junius* pamphlet Luxemburg strongly criticized the conservative trend in social democracy, as discussed in the previous chapter. So strong was this criticism that it can now be seen that she and Lenin were two of the first of contemporary Marxists to perceive and condemn this trend as opportunist. Unlike Lenin, however, Luxemburg maintained her connection to the positivist underpinnings of traditional Marxism by explaining the existence of opportunism as resulting from the temporary backwardness of the working class, one that would be overcome with the almost automatic development of working-class consciousness. Her pamphlet, while obviously criticizing parts of the leadership, was a helpful appeal to workers to speed up their revolutionary zeal and educate and/or reject the conservative proclivities of what was considered a minority of the leadership. Until her untimely death supported by her own social democratic party in power in 1919, Luxemburg did not relinquish this interpretation, a fact which demonstrates the great hold of positivist assumptions on social democracy from very early on.

As opposed to Luxemburg, Lenin's conception of a revolutionary party creates a new political subjectivity where the issue of opportunism takes on a striking importance. This importance is twofold. In the first instance it recognizes that opportunism is no more something that will be overcome by the laws of history, and in the second instance it sees the rejection of or denial of the need for such a party as itself a significant aspect of opportunism in the Marxist movement. More bluntly, the fight for a revolutionary party and the fight against opportunism become twin aspects of what we now mean by Leninism. Objective possibilities as well as limitations to change also take on a different meaning with Lenin since the new subjectivity, the party, must often bare primary responsibility for the way that it understands and responds to possibilities and limitations. Standard Marxism after Marx often attacks Lenin for being too critical of others, of creating disunity rather than unity when what he is criticizing is the easy unity that is common to right opportunism and reformism. Lenin and Leninist criticism, recognizing the damage done by easy acquiescence to revisionist theory and practice, is obliged to attack what it considers false theory and practice *inside* the Marxist movement, and in its own ranks as well. In saying this, we are not claiming that Leninist polemics within the 'left' are always correct or appropriate tactically or that groups and parties claiming to represent Lenin are always good representatives of revolutionary Marxism. As we state elsewhere in our critique of ultra-leftism, much of what goes under the name of Leninism is often completely sectarian and detrimental to progress, a problem often opposed by Lenin and later by Mao, but we believe, not strongly enough. We would claim more fundamentally that a rejection of the need for a revolutionary party and of the need to recognize and oppose opportunism is almost universal to reformist Marxism in the whole contemporary epoch. But, to reiterate an earlier point, the fight against opportunism is powerfully shaped by contingent circumstances. The uncontextualized rejection of anything short of pure revolutionary zeal is a hallmark of ultra-leftism.

Lenin and Positivism

THROUGHOUT THE First World War and right up to his death in 1924, Lenin's more polemical tracts treated the debacle of the Second International as temporary (as indeed with a longer view revolutionary Marxism would continue to take this position). However his more sober analysis quite clearly recognized the shift of revolutionary energy in the new imperialist era. Here his theory of uneven development explained the occurrence of successful revolutionary insurrection in Russia and pointed the way toward a more general theory of revolutionary change in the twentieth century. According to Marx, capitalist development is never homogeneous either in time or place. In chronological sequence, it always has its periods of expansion and of contraction. Within societies and between societies, it creates poles of privilege and poles of misery with varying gradations in between. In the imperialist era, according to Lenin, the exploitative character of monopoly capitalism is particularly destructive of the social systems of formerly 'traditional' societies. They are incorporated into the capitalist orbit with overt brutality and with an expansion of misery and impoverishment. Thus, these backward societies become the location of revolutionary ferment, what Lenin called the weakest link in the chain of uneven development. It was on the basis of this theory that he perceived the revolution in Tsarist Russia to be no mere historical accident, but an occurrence intrinsic to the dynamics of twentieth century development. It is often considered a blindness of Lenin's that he waited in vain for the Russian Revolution to ignite the fuse of revolutionary change in the advanced countries of Europe; yet his own theories were and continue to be the underpinning for all those later revolutions in societies that shared important characteristics with Tsarist Russia. Although an early industrializing nation, pre-socialist Russia was a predominantly peasant, backward, and imperialized society. Its revolution involved an attack on feudal vestiges and even maintained a definite capitalist economic structure in the need to mobilize all productive energies for an industrial takeoff – the New Economic Policy (NEP) of the Soviet Union in the 1920s represented a temporary commitment to capitalist economic forces. While the Russian Revolution lacked the impetus to national liberation since Russia already possessed a long tradition of political autonomy, there are still so many similarities between the Russian and subsequent cases to reject any theory of Russian exceptionalism.

Looking more concretely at Lenin's experience, however, demonstrates how deep the positivist problem has been in Marxism, how his fight against it still showed elements of the problem in Lenin himself, and how innovative and incisive has been the break he made with it. Preceding the Russian Revolution, Lenin held to the view that a socialist revolution was not on the agenda for backward, feudal Russia; that is, he was still committed to what was a relatively fixed-stage history in which humankind proceeds from slavery to peasantry to wage labour in advancing capitalism and then to socialism when the industrial proletariat was ripe for the transformation. The Russian situation at the turn of the last century, as noted above, presented a particular dilemma for Marxist theory and practice. The class control of Russia included a long-term established monarchy and landed aristocracy supported by primitive levels of technology and low productivity. It would seem that the goal of reaching socialism in these conditions would be, at best, a protracted affair and that political strategy could only prepare the way with policies that would create capitalist development. If Russia was to have a revolution, it would have to be along the lines of the earlier French Revolution where conditions were similar to those facing Russia. Huge landed property and its aristocratic owners must be overthrown and replaced by a more productive class of capitalist farmers and budding industrialists. Moreover, the ball and chain of landed property, aristocracy, and Tsardom must be replaced by an industrializing capitalist class and a modern democracy, a parliament, and all the other relative freedoms associated with these political institutions. In a country with only a small industrial working class and an underdeveloped bourgeoisie, it was considered by most of Marxism at the time unrealistic and foolhardy to expect or work for anything else.

The expectation and the great hope for socialism in Marxist theory, then, resided in the advanced capitalist world. And Russia being in the feudal stage demanded an overthrow of the monarchy (a Tsar in the Russian case) and the landed aristocracy. In the political realm, it would be a bourgeois democratic state that would be the necessary political form to facilitate the process. So strong was this outlook that Lenin's wing (the Bolshevik wing) of Russian social democracy, after the initial February, 1917 Revolution, still saw itself as a progressive force for the initiation of capitalism in Russia. Therefore, when Lenin returned to Russia after a long exile in Western Europe in April 1917 and announced to the Bolshevik Party that it should prepare to overthrow the fledgling bourgeois democracy and introduce socialism immediately in Russia, many in his own Party considered that he had gone haywire. It was only his prestige as well as the forcefulness of his ideas that won the day and put the Party on the revolutionary path. Interestingly enough, his theoretical defense of the move to socialism did not break with pre-existing ideas. He saw Russia as a "weak link" in the imperialist chain possessing a small but militant industrial working class that could introduce socialism but a socialism that would need the help of revolution in more advanced countries. If this assistance did not occur, Lenin considered that socialism in a backward country could not succeed. It was too early for him to recognize that imperialism was creating a world in which socialist revolution in underdevelopment countries was becoming the order of the future and that this new revolutionary form would face seemingly intractable problems of socialist industrialization in the midst of backwardness. To his dying day, Lenin put great hope in the impending socialist revolution in advanced Europe, especially Germany. It is only with later revolutionary development in China, Cuba, Vietnam, and elsewhere that the time-honored hope of revolution in the West was lost (for the time being) and had to be given up. And it is to the work of Mao, Castro, and Ho Chi Minh that we must look for later developments and to new problems in the revolutionary project.

Another strong remnant of positivist impetus in Lenin, it seems to us, was his treatment of ultra-leftism in his pamphlet on "left-wing infantilism" written shortly after the Bolshevik access to power. He considered this political phenomenon to be a result of youthful zealousness to be cured by working-class development. However, this type of political behavior arises so often in revolutionary history, including as we will indicate later in Mao's experience, that we think that it must be considered a much more recalcitrant and difficult problem.

Lenin's treatment of the longevity of advanced capitalism and the attendant lack of revolutionary zeal among its working class also indicates positivist inclinations. Engels had already mentioned the presence of bourgeois attitudes in the working class in late nineteenth century England, and Lenin advances the same opinion for his own time. In line, however, with older positivist wisdom, he considers attitudes as very temporary and only present in a small minority of the class, a minority that he calls a "labour aristocracy." It is assumed, therefore, that continued development of the system will expose this small aristocracy, that it will be rejected, and that the class will become progressively more revolutionary. He could not imagine that even with the continued crises engendered by capitalism, the working class could in the main either support the system or more or less silently acquiesce to its depredations. Of course, Lenin's own analysis of modern imperialism partially explains this tragic denouement within the working classes of monopoly capitalist nations.

Other elements of Lenin's work are often given credit for giving him a special place in the revolutionary pantheon, for he did unusually excellent work on a number of fronts. For example, his analysis of capitalist development in Russia in his critique of the belief that Russian cooperatives in the countryside could lead to socialism without industrialization set the stage for the acceptance of a distinctly working-class revolution there. This analysis, however brilliant it was, cannot be considered a fundamental addition to Marxism since it only had particular relevance for Russian conditions. As for his well-known book on imperialism, in this case it mainly served the purpose of attacking the Marxist position by Kautsky who was claiming that imperialism was a new progressive development of capitalism.

The book by Lenin that is often seen as the true mark of his place in Marxist theory is his last great work *State and Revolution*. According to Nadya Krupskaya, Lenin's spouse, he was strongly positive about a Russian revolution leading up to and during the War. When he returned to Russia after the February Revolution, which overthrew the Tsar, he was even positive about a socialist insurrection. He began *State and Revolution* during the July days while he was in hiding from the Provisional Government. This polemic is a set of guidelines for a socialist insurrection and transition afterwards, written as a result of percolating optimism. He thought that it was incumbent upon him to set down the basic principles of revolutionary transition in the face of then triumphant revisionism. Moreover, while he could not glean these principles from the major corpus of nineteenth century Marxism, he had to turn to Marx and Engels' later work, mainly *The Civil War in France*. There, Marx's celebration and critique of the first attempt at socialist revolution is clearly articulated. With regard to our major thesis about the positivist assumptions of traditional Marxism, Marx's discoveries of basic principles in this first attempt at revolutionary transformation (it only lasted three months) indicates certain unique features. In the first instance, the Paris Commune was recognized by Marx as a socialist revolution, yet there were no Marxists involved. All of the leading elements were followers of the outlooks of Proudhon or Blanqui or Bakunin, outlooks which Marx had solidly and critically opposed in the past. Yet his book, while strongly supporting those policies that solidify and enhance revolutionary change did not, in mentioning what was wrongly done or what should have been done, refer to the misleadership forwarding these wrongheaded viewpoints.

What do we make of this silence since, knowing Lenin, his response would have had a more distinctly polemical tone? The difference, it seems to us, lies in the complete change in context from Marx to Lenin. Marx, in essence, is criticizing the Commune for not having the proper leadership (his own) at a time when he could not get beyond the limits of his own century. He believes in his book that he is talking to the working class alone as the leader of change and giving it lessons about what it should do in the future. Lenin's advance over Marx is the recognition that in speaking for the class, you must also speak for its unique leadership and critically oppose any and all varieties of misleadership. This idea reflects the major difference and major development of Lenin's thought and actions over earlier Marxist experience.

Furthermore, Lenin demonstrated the importance of developing policy through an analysis of concrete conditions while not abandoning revolutionary theory. With the New Economic Policy (NEP) instituted after the Civil War, the Bolshevik Party reverted to capitalist relations of production in the countryside, in petty production, and even with regard to strategic foreign capital. What is crucial to note is not the temporary turn to capitalism in significant economic areas, but the clear understanding that it was a return to capitalism and that petty production engenders a new petty bourgeoisie with capitalist aspirations, which poses a distinct threat to the consolidation of socialism. By implication, class struggle necessarily continues through the stages of the revolution although, at this point, classes were still defined only in relation to the de jure ownership of the means of production. The Party made no concession in theory about the need to maintain socialist production in major sectors and build the conditions for a later, more direct transition to socialism.

Writing in the early twenty-first century, at a time when revolutionary socialism is in retreat, it is well to reiterate the historic significance of the Russian Revolution. E. H. Carr, perhaps the most illustrious historian of that Revolution, wrote in 1967 that "The October Revolution may reasonably be celebrated on its fiftieth anniversary as the greatest event of the twentieth century." Except for the brief three months of the Paris Commune of 1871, there was no example of a successful anti-capitalist revolution led by a party representing the new class created in the capitalist epoch. The Russian Revolution was the first great modern revolution ushering in a long period of hope for the introduction of a classless society based not on the scarcity of earlier tribal societies, but on the abundance borne of scientific advancement and industrial technology. For Marxism it confirmed Lenin's reiteration of a controversial idea found in Marx's later works and denied or rejected by reform Marxism – the idea of the need, in a socialist revolution, for a period of 'dictatorship' rooted in the working classes.

Luxembourg, who as we have said, strongly opposed Lenin's ideas about a revolutionary party, wrote at the inception of the Russian Revolution (and again at the end of her life) that the proof of a truly revolutionary programme in Russia was demonstrated not by "the safeguarding of bourgeois democracy, but [by] a dictatorship of the proletariat." That is, the realization of socialism cannot come about through the ritual adherence to the political rules of conventional democracy, what she and Lenin called "parliamentary cretinism." Also, the experience of the Bolshevik

Revolution indicates that the breakthrough to socialism will not come through the slow process of winning a majority to vote for apparently socialist candidates, since in that game, the capitalist class possesses the major tools to retain power. Not, continues Luxembourg, "through a majority to revolutionary tactics, but through revolutionary tactics to a majority – that is the way the road runs." Moreover, the power of the bourgeoisie is such that, after taking power, the proletariat cannot afford to return to earlier democratic forms without losing power and, with that loss, to squander revolutionary momentum as well. All successful initiations of relatively permanent revolutionary change after October learned these lessons (and other attempts to consolidate revolutionary power through liberal "democratic" means all too tragically have fallen by the wayside).

But, and this is a big 'but,' the first great socialist revolution did not occur where it was supposed to occur according to original Marxist theory. That theory proclaimed that socialist revolution would be a product of advanced capitalism, of a capitalism that had reached the end of its development. It was almost unthinkable that the classlessness promised by socialism could be created in the conditions of scarcity faced by technically undeveloped societies. But Russia was a society mired in such scarcity, a scarcity rooted in the backwardness in productive capacity. Russia in the early twentieth century was a land with a core of advanced industry (mostly foreign owned) in its two major cities and a mass of agricultural production worked either by manual labour alone or at best, the animal-driven plow. The Western leap into industrialization was based on the transformation of both the city and countryside, and it involved the twin processes of the mechanization of agriculture and the accompanying exodus of surplus labour to the cities, which were the driving forces behind industrial development. This situation was certainly not the same as the condition faced by the unexpected Russian Revolution. Along with traditional backwardness, the new Soviet Union faced the devastation of the First World War and a subsequent civil war, events which almost completely destroyed whatever industrial base had been built before. In the civil war, the very idea of socialism promised by the Revolution so frightened the ruling classes of the advanced capitalist nations that they, with their advanced military and other resources, attempted to strangle socialism at its birth. In short, as a precondition for the realization of its ideals, the Russian Revolution faced the need to industrialize under the most inauspicious conditions. These conditions along with a later brutal Nazi invasion were overwhelming obstacles for maintaining the advance of revolutionary transformation. Beyond these objective conditions, however, it is important to consider political changes within the USSR that in our opinion, as discussed in the following chapter, derailed the Russian Revolution.

To repeat part of our earlier argument, there has been a silence surrounding Lenin. We think that is a result of the continuation of the same positivism that was there at the beginning, still found even in Lenin's thought, and still too easily embraced by much of contemporary Marxism. The positivism of Marx and Engels cannot be seen as a mistake since there was little possibility of transcending positivism at that time. In fact, what makes Lenin's break so extraordinary was that positivism was more completely accepted in his time by seemingly successful Marxist parties. In his pamphlet against revisionism, Lenin points to the difference in context by alluding to the misleadership in the Marxist movement and to the opportunism and reformism upon which it was based. Moreover, he proclaims, it is the very success of Marxism as opposed to all other social outlooks that generates false leadership. Finally, Lenin could only rely on the political advances made by Marx in his later years to buttress his arguments against the burgeoning opportunism of his own time.

The bedrock of positivism lies in its assumptions about the objective and subjective factors in the process of revolutionary transformation. If, as positivism assumes, the discovery of scientific knowledge sets down the objective conditions within which the working class will come to revolutionary consciousness, then all that is necessary for revolutionary transformation to occur is the development of correct objective conditions. The development of the class and the consciousness that such development brings about are the conditions for transformation. This assumption is implied by the well-worn statement by Marx that the full development of capitalism is the pre-condition for full proletarianization both objectively and subjectively. Much of Marx and Engels' political activities belied this assumption since they spent a good deal of their lives in the education of small working classes with the hope that this would prepare them for revolution even at that early stage of development. Moreover, as mentioned before, Marx's treatment of the first experiment of socialism in the Paris Commune demonstrates that he thought it could have been victorious with different policies. Ultimately, however, rather than critically evaluating the leadership that did not forward such policies, he was left again only with the immaturity of the working class.

Only Lenin makes that leap with the recognition of the necessity of a particular kind of leadership in the revolutionary process. With this leap, he introduces a separate and unique subjectivity into Marxist politics. This is the need for a permanent, professional revolutionary party recruited at its beginning from the population of intellectuals primarily of non-proletarian origins. We are asserting strongly that this position is the essence of Leninism and that one of the first planks of ordinary opportunism within progressive platforms is the rejection or intentional silencing of any discussion of this type of party. In asserting this, we must, however, add the following reservations. The acceptance of the need to build such a party does not assure that it is an easy task. Since Leninism has commonly been added to distinguish revolutionary from reformist Marxism, groups with little else but superficial sloganeering have sprung up in many places and call themselves Leninist parties. This tendency is an example of the continuing problem of ultra-leftism, and its presence is often an index of the weakness or absence of revolutionary Marxism.

In certain circumstances, moreover, such as in Latin America in the later twentieth century, socialist programmes have been initiated and taken state power without the existence of a revolutionary party. We see no reason to denigrate such attempts, but we do think that these regimes are extremely vulnerable to attacks from without and within because of the lack of such a party. The tragic destruction of the Allende regime in Chile in 1973 and the resulting horrors thrust upon the Chilean people by the fascist government there stands as a sharp reminder of such an outcome. Of course, the lack of other guidelines originally stressed by Marx and reiterated by Lenin is also very important in giving dire warning to these still noble attempts to break the back of capitalist power. Finally, in raising the need for a revolutionary party, we must also face the fact that it has been easier for these parties in power to initiate socialism than to sustain it. We only have to look at what occurred in the two great revolutionary events in the twentieth century to make us realize what has been perhaps the major tragedies of our time. Both the Soviet Revolution of 1917 and the Chinese Revolution of 1949 have been aborted, leading to regimes where full-fledged revisionism took over power, a revisionism initiated and forwarded by Leninist-type parties. If there is a central crisis in revolutionary Marxism, then this counter-revolutionary event must fit the bill.

Still this new type of party adds a very different dimension to Marxism. The analysis and self-analysis of leadership becomes equally important to the analysis of the concrete conditions within any society. In certain circumstances it becomes all important since bad leadership can so suffuse the atmosphere that dealing with that problem can be the primary obstacle in building the necessary revolutionary cadre to get progressive work done. In addition, the question of the relationship between the party and the proletariat as well as other social classes is crucial to an understanding of the dynamics of political leadership. In adding this dimension to Marxism, Lenin at the same time re-emphasized certain features that the growing opportunism of his time was conveniently wishing to forget. The fact that Marx and Engels lived in a less revolutionary time than Lenin partially explains the difference in emphasis. In hindsight, it can now be seen that Marx and Engels established the foundations of Marxism, the outlining of the essential features of the new capitalist system and presciently predicting much of its future. Lenin, on the other hand, articulated some solutions to the problems faced in the political transformation of capitalism, solutions that the political economy side could not perceive. In this sense, Lenin represents the more political side of Marxism at a time when revolution became a real part of the historical agenda.

To stretch an analogy, original Marxism is similar in the world of human health to the basic sciences like biology or anatomy, and Leninism is similar to the health practitioner in the face of concrete cases of illness and malfunction. We are obviously speaking here in terms of emphasis because successful Marxism depends upon the integration of these two strains. Since concrete cases, however, are suffused with contingent and individual factors, more political Marxism cannot depend upon the easy application of general scientific knowledge but can only set down guidelines demanding great flexibility and sensitivity to concrete conditions. It is in this latter realm where Lenin's contribution excels and becomes part of the corpus of revolutionary Marxism. More significantly, in an era of real revolution and counter-revolution, it is sensitive to problems of bad leadership and the opportunism behind it, although not sensitive enough.

As to the problems facing Leninism, they are often the same that face Marxism in general. There has never been a successful revolution in advanced capitalist countries and there is little in the way of guidelines pointing in the right direction. The industrial working class in these countries has in significant ways shared in the bounty from the super-exploitation of the imperialized world while its very composition has changed from its blue-collar past. Trade unions have been denuded in numbers, in militancy, and in militant leadership. At the present time, the capitalist establishment has fairly successfully stripped the working classes of the gains made during more prosperous, Keynesian conditions. Moreover, attempts to create new Leninist parties have been so out of touch with the prevailing conditions that they suffered from the isolation generated by ultra-leftism.

Problems particular to Leninism have occurred in those successful revolutions in underdeveloped societies. Lenin was wrong to consider the Soviet case as unique and to wait for assistance from the West. Instead, the Soviet experience became, for a time, the wave of the future. All successful revolutionary insurrections occurred in just those societies that had neither bourgeois revolutions nor the technical advances generated by capitalism. These also differed from the Soviet case in that the class leading the revolution was not an industrial proletariat (since these societies did not have such a class in significant numbers). In fact, the attempt in China in the 1920s to copy the Soviet experience was such a failure that it led Mao to institute the successful programme of countryside liberation led by the rural working class. Significantly, however, almost all successful socialist transformations were led by Leninist parties. The only exception was the Cuban case, which it seems to us, came to power in the completely accidental condition that American imperialism was confident at the time that any Latin American insurrection would be easily controlled (as they had been in the past). Even in the Cuban case, a Leninist party was instituted almost immediately after the revolutionary movement achieved state power. The Nicaraguan revolution had a much shorter period of success before its leadership capitulated to bourgeois democracy rather than following the Cuban example. And twenty-first century socialism in Venezuela, however much it deserves critical support, has not succeed beyond the cocoon of third-path social democracy.

The crisis particular to Leninism occurred after the revolutionary access to power. Again, except for the Cuban case where socialism maintained a real but tentative and vulnerable existence for more than fifty years, all successful twentieth century socialist revolutions have been aborted and have taken the capitalist path. And Cuba is in a precarious position as we write these words. There is no easy answers as to why this has happened, but it can be said that the early fears of Trotsky and Luxemburg about the *necessarily* authoritarian direction of such a party, while wrong-headed in principal at their time, have come to roost as a realized potential in the period of socialist transition. And beyond the question of authoritarianism is the regression from socialism to capitalism. We will have more to say, at least speculatively, about these all-important problems when we discuss the Chinese experience and the role of Mao Zedong in that experience.

Conclusion

WE ARE LEFT with a summing up of the contribution of Lenin to revolutionary Marxism. Since Marx and Engels did not set down specific political guidelines for successful revolutionary transformation until late in their lives and since those guidelines were, by Lenin's time either ignored or forgotten by powerful European Marxist movements and parties, we owe to Lenin the re-discovery, systematic articulation (especially in *State and Revolution*) and successful application of these guidelines. Here we are referring to things such as the need to totally overthrow the bourgeois state and to institute a new-type ruling state. Finally, and what we consider the most unique of Lenin's contributions, he recognized and outlined the need, leading up to insurrection and into the period of socialist transformation, for a professional and disciplined revolutionary party recruited at first from the intellectual stratum of privileged classes.

It is part of the tradition of recognizing human advances in personal terms that the names of particular people are given to great historical contributions. We have been obeisant to this tradition by giving Marx (and secondarily Engels) credit for the articulation of those central ideas we associate with the initiation and generation of socialism. This is a strange tradition given that we know that such ideas were common to nineteenth century thought and that many others added elements to these ideas. And it is clearly recognized by the famous discussion about whether Darwin should be given credit for the adumbration of Darwinism since another person had already written about evolution in the same vein and earlier than Darwin. The same may be said about Marx such that his more precise contribution might lie in his greater and more elaborate articulation of already existent ideas. In short, it might be said that his ideas or some variant of them would probably have been written even if Marx had never existed. The same cannot be said about Leninism. While it must be realized that Lenin is totally dependent upon the existence of earlier Marxism in order to further develop it, it might also be said that what we have defined as the central advance of Leninism appears to be an almost unique historical phenomenon. This is why Lenin's idea of the need for a professional revolutionary party recruited from a population of privileged intellectuals fell like a thunderclap upon the Marxist world at the time. It is partly for this reason that the idea even now sits so uneasily upon the heads of left-wing intellectuals. At the level of direct political action, Lenin was not alone in suggesting that a socialist revolution could be initiated in a backward country by an alliance of a smaller working class with a much larger peasant mass. Yet, as we said earlier, when upon his return to Russia in 1917, he asserted that a socialist insurrection should immediately be planned, his own party members considered that perhaps he had gone crazy. It might be surmised that the Bolshevik Revolution might never have occurred without Lenin. Nevertheless, effective leadership has to operate within existing historical conditions and possibilities. The Bolsheviks seized the opportunity to take political power in October 1917 and consolidated the revolution in the civil war. Only afterwards did Lenin face the necessity of using state power to build a socialist society on the basis of an alliance with the peasantry in semi-feudal conditions. His immediate answer was a temporary turn to capitalism with the NEP. With his untimely death, the resolution of the contradictions established by the turn to capitalism lay in the hands of his successors.

CHAPTER FIVE

Trotsky, Trotskyism, and Stalin

THE END OF THE great experiments in "actually existing socialism" has delighted those who think that capitalism is the best of all possible social systems and nothing better can come after it. But it has also had a profound effect on the world of socialist sympathizers as well. In the latter case, it is often believed that almost all that occurred in these experiments is negative and that the only lesson to be learned from them is not to repeat anything that they have done.

We believe that this latter point of view is wrongheaded for a perspective that considers itself essentially historical. Blanket condemnation without analysis of historical phenomena is a sign of either sloppy analysis or worse, the unquestioned acceptance of easy fashionable outlooks. We gain very little, for example, by calling these experiences "communist tyrannies," for this is no more than a repeat of what passes for conventional wisdom, yet this is what has occurred for a long time even in much of what passes for left-wing literature. It is for this reason that we think we have much to learn by revisiting a controversy about which many contemporary socialists are either uninformed, or if not, consider merely historical. We allude here to the great conflict between the ideas and practice of Joseph Stalin and those of Leon Trotsky.

The struggle for power and the maintenance of that power in the Soviet Union following Lenin's death in 1924 most centrally involved the conflict between these two historic personalities – so much so that the conflict itself is often seen as little more than a question of the machinations of different personalities. We do not reject the significance of personality in this issue, and in fact the question of personality is comprehensively covered in E. H. Carr's classic *History of the Bolshevik Revolution*. Lenin's well-known "last testament" is largely an assessment of leaders' characters. But as usual in such profound historical events, there must be more than personality involved since great social forces form the background for the actions and ideas of these protagonists. More important than personality is the question of concrete conditions and policies; that is, the socialist direction of the revolution.

In Stalin's case, after intense internal struggle over the political and economic direction of the Soviet Union, he became the de facto successor to Lenin in the Soviet Union until his death in 1953. He presented himself as the sustainer of Lenin's legacy, clearly indicated by the publication of a book he called *The Foundations of Leninism*. In our view, Stalin undermined these foundations and, in the unprecedented circumstance of socialist construction, he initiated a new form of revisionism. Trotsky's connection to Lenin is equally complex, but he was easily as conscious as was Stalin in his defense of that tradition throughout his exile from the Soviet Union. However, the complexity of his connection is evidenced by the fact that he was opposed to Lenin in the original split between the Bolsheviks and the Mensheviks in 1903, a split which in his case lasted until the beginnings of revolutionary activity in 1917. Trotsky considered during this period that it was still possible to unite the left and right wings of the Russian social democratic party. As an activist committed to the revolutionary overthrow of capitalism, he was clearly restive about the reformist tendencies of Menshevism and much of European social democracy. But on the question of revolutionary leadership, he (along with such staunch revolutionaries as Rosa

Luxembourg) found Lenin's conception of the party too exclusive, elitist, and autocratic. As we have argued above, there is a contradiction in any Marxist party between leadership and class. Handling this contradiction is a question of inner-party struggle as well as in the establishment of concrete practices shaping the relationship between the two. We elaborate on this fundamental contradiction below.

After Stalin's succession to power in the mid-1920s, Trotsky was officially exiled and his early opposition to Lenin on the party question was used opportunistically as one argument to justify his exile. Furthermore, unlike Stalin, Trotsky disagreed with Lenin on specific issues during Lenin's years of leadership in the Soviet Union, at the time, disagreements that were well within the scope of democratic centralism. Trotsky in exile became perhaps the central opposition to Stalin's regime, leading to that regime condemning him as an enemy of both the Soviet Union and of socialism. For at least two decades, the ideological conflict between Stalin's and Trotsky's views dominated the Marxist left.

It is important to distinguish between Trotsky's political theory and the movement he created, although there are significant connections between them. Trotskyism is a difficult and controversial doctrine in the corpus of Marxist political theory and practice. Spawned by Trotsky after his forced exile from the Soviet Union in 1929, the doctrine carrying his name has seen a life beyond the death of its progenitor in 1940. Although never taking power in any society, Trotskyism, like anarchism, has sustained a relatively permanent, if often meager, existence almost everywhere, right up to the present day. Now with the end of the Soviet Union and the rejection by the left and the right of all that occurred under Stalin's regime, it is one of the supreme ironies of history that Trotskyism, existing in small groups in many countries of the world, remains almost alone as the manifest standard bearer of revolutionary Marxism. Trotsky himself was a Trotskyist only later in his life (indeed he never called himself such, rather considering himself merely a guardian, in the face of Stalin's betrayal, of revolutionary Marxism). Because Trotskyism has developed in often divergent forms well beyond Trotsky's life, we think it appropriate to begin our discussion of the subject by trying to separate the life and political activities of Leon Trotsky from the later doctrine in his name. After all, it is quite possible to imagine that if Trotsky could see the evolution of his thought in later concrete form, he might have, like Marx, disavowed this later development and proclaimed that he was not a Trotskyist.

During the Bolshevik accession to power in 1917, Trotsky disavowed his earlier opposition to Lenin's ideas, and he became a leading member of the Bolshevik Party and a staunch defender of Lenin for the rest of his life. He had a brilliant mind, wide learning from an early age, was a stirring orator and a dramatic writer with a striking capacity for innovative articulation. These qualities, along with a large and imperious ego, often made him speak and write with verve, but sometimes with little forethought for longer-range political consequences. His early vitriolic attack on Lenin and his ideas were so provocative and memorable that some of his words have become the stock-in-trade of anti-Leninism to this day. For it was Trotsky who said that "Lenin's methods lead to this: the party organization substitutes itself for the party, the central committee substitutes itself for the organization, and, finally, a 'dictator' substitutes himself for the central committee," words seen now as profoundly prophetic.

What must be recalled about the pre-First World War period of Marxist politics is that, in direction and even concrete programme, *revolutionary* Marxism dominated the left-wing political agenda. In Europe where capitalism was supreme both nationally and internationally, there had arisen a growing and militant working-class movement just as Marx had predicted. And, also as he had predicted, this militant movement welcomed the ideas and hopes of Marxism as a revolutionary and transformative force. Working-class political parties arose in the major European nations and, with some variations, all forwarded, at least theoretically, a revolutionary programme. This programme involved permanent working-class opposition to its capitalist masters, preparation for inevitable economic crises insoluble by capitalism, and readiness for the final crisis that would lead to the revolutionary overthrow of capitalist rule and the ushering in of the socialist future. All these parties were called social democratic, and revolutionary Marxism then was the clarion call of social democracy. It is probable, as we said in Chapter Three, that broad sections of the working-class movements of Germany and Great Britain were not prepared for the idea of revolutionary change.

While agreeing in broad outline and long-range programme, there was also often fairly clear division in Marxist ranks in everyday practice. And, as is common in such cases, schisms in practice will be reflected at first in shades of theoretical difference and, if unchecked, lead to more fundamental theoretical divides. We elaborated more fully on this issue in our discussion of social democracy, but for our purpose here, the major division involved the manner by which reform was treated in class conflict. Marx and Engels were strong supporters of the reform process in advancing capitalism as a necessary measure to both better the quality of working-class life and to act as an educational experience in deepening consciousness about the permanent rift between the classes. They never saw reform, however, as any real solution to the depredations of the capitalist system. Reform is a necessary but never sufficient policy in the struggle with capital, and this point is reiterated often, especially in their battle with Bakunin and the anarchists who argued that all reform is a fundamental compromise with the system and that immediate overthrow of capital can be the only programme for real revolutionaries.

In the pre-First World War period, Trotsky was an ardent revolutionary opponent of the reformist tendencies in social democracy. Along with activists such as Rosa Luxembourg, he waged constant battle against the integration of working-class parties and trade unions into mild and acquiescent reformism, and always upheld the need for permanent class conflict and clearly independent action by working-class organizations. As mentioned before, he and Luxembourg parted ways with Lenin at the time in their differing views about party formation and about the relationship between the proletarian party and the working class in general.

As we indicate in our chapter on Lenin, he boldly asserted that the working class without conscious and professional leadership cannot make a revolution. When this basic premise was accepted as the bedrock of contemporary revolutionary Marxism, then opposition to this premise and to the kind of party demanded by this position has become the stock-in-trade of anti-revolutionary thought and action, whether from the left or from the right. As remarked before, no one has been as vitriolic or as articulate in the attack on this position as the young Trotsky, and the attack came back to haunt him.

We think that the condemnation of Trotsky for these early ideas is unfair because they were rejected by him in his adult years. Moreover, it must be remembered that Lenin's conception of revolutionary leadership was so bold and innovative that Trotsky's rejection of it was in line with shockwaves sent throughout the broad-based Marxist movement at the time. Trotsky's turnabout and acceptance of Lenin's conception on the eve of the Bolshevik Revolution was never questioned by Lenin, and it is a conception that Trotsky held for the rest of his life. To condemn Trotsky for his early position on leadership would lead to a rejection of all socialists who were guilty of early folly. How many worthies would remain after such a purging?

It is important in dealing with the Trotsky question to recall the sketch of the historical background in Russia, which was elaborated in Chapter Four. For those of us who live not only in the aftermath of the demise and disintegration of the Soviet Union, and almost a century from the earlier years of the Soviet triumph of 1917, it is very difficult to comprehend the great, in fact the unique, drama presented by this event. More to the point, the Bolshevik Revolution was not supposed to happen, even according to the fondest hopes of most Marxist leaders who had devoted their lives to making revolution.

Revolutionary Theory

IT SHOULD COME as no surprise that Marxists embraced both the material and many of the ideational features of industrial capitalism. Many Marxists took a position that was a variation of the earlier rather roseate optimism, not by allying with the capitalist class (this would be manifestly anti-Marxist), but by attempting to separate a progressive from a conservative bourgeoisie and supporting the former. Within the large social democratic (that is, Marxist) movements in Europe at the time, this position was at the center of what has become reformist Marxism. What is less surprising still is the fact that in backward predominantly feudal countries like Russia, which had yet to have its bourgeois revolution, Marxism there would see a totally bourgeois transformation as a next historical necessity.

Trotsky at the beginning of the twentieth century, when he was very young (he was born in 1880), was one of the first thinkers to contradict this traditional Marxist thesis. In summing up the position he had always taken during a lifetime of political activity, he asserts ("Three Concepts") that "historical backwardness does not mean a mere retracing of the course of the advanced countries a hundred or two hundred years later." This thought, while dramatically relevant when applied to Russian circumstances in 1917, was not completely new to Marxism since Marx had raised it at the end of his life when proclaiming that his theory cannot be turned into a straightjacket. History is not a predetermined process moving automatically from primitive communism through ancient slavery to feudalism, capitalism, and then classless socialism. Marx also asserted that his theory cannot be a philosophy of history, but is a science of history, which must speak of trends and possibilities and not of events already predicted by philosophy. For Marx and Marxism, what has been called dialectical materialism is not philosophy in the old-fashioned sense of establishing final truth, but is a summation and social application of the principles underlying modern science. In line with this view, human history must always be studied afresh in all of its concreteness, always using theory as a guide, which was exactly what Trotsky was doing.

From his recognition that underdeveloped Russia could initiate a socialist revolution, Trotsky (along with Lenin) came to some then novel conclusions about the bourgeoisie not only in the modern era, but historically as well. At the time of the first Russian Revolution in 1905, Trotsky, a leading light in that event, proclaimed that under the domination of advanced foreign capitalism, the indigenous bourgeoisie in predominantly feudal Russia is no longer a leading progressive force. What Marx had suggested about earlier bourgeois revolutions in Europe in 1848 – that the rise of an independent working-class political voice had frightened the bourgeoisie into alliances with any retrograde forces, even the most reactionary ones like the aristocracy – Trotsky perceived in more general historical terms. He was one of the first Marxist thinkers to realize that the era of the classical bourgeois revolution like the French one in 1789 was already over in 1848, and certainly was not a realistic alternative in twentieth century conditions.

This innovative idea did not lead Trotsky to make the mistake of earlier Russian populism. If, said the populists, Russia already possesses rural cooperatives (which it did possess), then it can skip a bourgeois revolution entirely and jump directly from feudalism into socialism. This unique situation led the Narodnik populists to assert that capitalism was unnecessary for Russia. However, Lenin's first book on the Russian economy in the 1890s had demonstrated that through the intervention of modern imperialism, Russia had already become capitalist in its major cities, moreover with an unusually advanced proletariat. And Trotsky agreed with Lenin on the fundamental Marxist thesis that a predominantly feudal peasantry could not be a socialist force since its major demand would be for individual landed property. However, this demand as a rebellion against a landed aristocracy would still be progressive, especially with the leadership and assistance of a more revolutionary industrial working class. This argument was the basis for a new revolutionary strategy for underdeveloped societies in a worldwide capitalist era. A modern working class, although small, can ally itself with a more massive peasantry leading to what are essentially bourgeois revolutionary policies as a first step in a transition not to full-fledged capitalism, but ultimately to socialism.

And where does the bourgeoisie fit in this new proletarian/peasant alliance? Is it an ally, albeit a reluctant one, or an enemy during the early transition to socialism? Trotsky is unequivocal in his answer to this question in "The Motive Forces." The bourgeoisie in underdeveloped economic conditions, he proclaimed, is in the main an obstacle to progress. There are two major reasons for this. Under monopoly capitalism and imperialism, the national bourgeoisie in Russia (and in similar underdeveloped nations) is in myriad ways linked to the more powerful capitalist class in the dominant nations; it has become a predominantly comprador class. Secondly, the new threat of socialism has made this class so frightened of socialism that it is unlikely to forward independent nationalist policies. Although Russia is in need of a bourgeois economic transformation, especially in the countryside where a peasantry is dominated by feudal landowners and is thirsting for land of its own, this revolution will not be led by a now reactionary bourgeoisie. Thus, concluded Trotsky, the Russian revolution would be "bourgeois" in overcoming feudal property relations but "proletarian" in political leadership.

Capitalism had developed rapidly in Russia in the late nineteenth century, often under imperialist auspices. And with it had come a new, if relatively small, industrial working class. This class resided mainly but not exclusively in the largest cities of St. Petersburg and Moscow. The Russian working class, said Trotsky, occupies a unique historical position. The concentration of this new proletariat in the especially brutal conditions of an imperialized country made this class more predisposed to revolutionary consciousness (the more universal application of this idea awaited the later Marxism of the Chinese Revolution). Moreover, the tendency of reform Marxism to more ostensible alliance with the bourgeoisie in also more manifest there. Since Menshevism, or reformist Marxism, demanded a longer-term collaboration with capitalism, so said Trotsky in *My Life*, a clearer demarcation by the proletariat between reform and revolutionary Marxism is a more manifest political demand. In Marxism, he proclaimed, "the struggle against the Revisionists toughened us politically, as well as in the field of theory."

Thus, as alluded to above, from his earliest acceptance and commitment to Marxism, Trotsky solidly embraced its more revolutionary principles in opposition to the growth and solidification of that Marxism which was jettisoning those principles. This divide, which became the major battleground in early twentieth century Marxism, saw the revolutionary side in a clear minority. We cannot reiterate too strongly that Marxism before the First World War was the vital force in the advanced European labour movements. To be a social democrat was to be a Marxist social democrat, openly committed to a working class in perpetual conflict with capital, a conflict to be resolved only by the forceful overthrow of the ruling class. It was to the credit of Trotsky along with Lenin and Rosa Luxembourg to see the beginning of the decay of this revolutionary position, its erosion in small points of theory and in everyday acts of practice. The prescience of this early opposition to what Lenin called revisionism is clearly borne out in the devolution of these Marxist parties into the openly anti-socialist, social democratic and labour parties today. In a long lifetime of political activity, Trotsky never wavered in his fundamental opposition to a Marxism which meant to do no more than reform existing capitalism.

Trotsky's strong opposition to Lenin's dramatic thesis on the party question was in accord with literally every major revolutionary Marxist thinker at the time. When Lenin in 1903 asserted that the working class left to itself cannot make a revolution and that the class needed a professional, organizationally distinct party to lead it, this assertion was more than bold; it was almost heretical. Trotsky, it seems, not only rejected Lenin's conception of a party, but also in his commitment to a potential alliance between Mensheviks and Bolsheviks, did not understand the depth of the break that existed between these two factions until long after Lenin concluded the break was irreconcilable. In Trotsky's defense, Lenin did not clearly articulate the demand for a socialist revolution in Russia until his April Theses in 1917 and even many Bolsheviks at the time were shocked at Lenin's position. This must mean that Lenin himself may have still accepted until a late date the possibility of an alliance of the two factions in a bourgeois revolution in backward Russia. If this is so, even with the outpouring of Lenin's polemics against Trotsky at the time, Trotsky's position as a centrist does appear as little more than a mistaken judgement, which he later corrected.

Moreover, like Luxembourg, Trotsky validated his revolutionary credentials by boldly and courageously attacking the rightward drift in established Marxism, and again like Luxembourg he never varied from a keen recognition of reformism in all of its guises. However, when Lenin forwarded what must be considered the unique and highly innovative theses on party formation, Trotsky frontally attacked them for sectarianism and elitism. It was in this context that he uttered what is now considered by many, both within and without Marxism, the much quoted, often considered prophetic statement quoted above about the future 'substitutionism' of the Leninist party.

In line with his mistrust of the reformist tendencies among the Mensheviks, the young Trotsky did not, while opposing Lenin on the nature of the party, become a full-fledged Menshevik. One other factor needs mentioning with regard to the present argument about the early Trotsky. The Mensheviks and the Bolsheviks throughout the pre-First World War period were not always clear and distinct political parties; they were different groupings within what was considered a common social democratic (or Marxist) movement. Therefore, Trotsky's opposition to Lenin was simply one of the major positions among a host of critical outlooks in the movement. The rather unfortunate tendency of later Marxism in the Soviet Union to brand Trotsky as a traitor from the very beginning is, it seems to us, wrong-headed in a double sense. It is wrong because it seems clear to us from what we have presented above that Trotsky's early political activity cannot be branded as opportunist or traitorous or any of the other epithets hurled at him in the Soviet Union and in all the communist parties associated with the Soviet Union. If the young Trotsky made mistakes of the type discussed, they were nothing more than mistakes understandably made by a vast number of honest Marxist revolutionaries at the time.

This kind of judgment is also wrong-headed because the later political activities, even deleterious ones, of any person cannot automatically be transposed backward onto a whole career. One is not red or blue or anything else from the very beginning, then living out what is a predestined destiny. This kind of thinking is unworthy of any form of progressive thought. Significantly, Lenin, whose polemics against the young Trotsky were harsh and strong (as was his custom in polemics against what he considered very harmful views), never, to our knowledge, articulated a negative word about these early errors after Trotsky joined the Bolsheviks in 1917. And Lenin and Trotsky had quite heated disagreement about significant policy issues after the takeover of power. Finally, to prove the point, Lenin wrote a whole book excoriating the "renegade Kautsky" without failing to mention that the early Kautsky had been a true revolutionary.

During the whole period between Lenin's presentation of new principles of party formation in 1903 until the revolutionary upsurge in February 1917, which led to the overthrow of the Tsarist monarchy and the introduction of a provisional constitutional government, Trotsky stayed mainly on the fence in the ongoing dispute between the Mensheviks and the Bolsheviks, attempting to unify the opposing factions. He assumed, we may speculate, that their opposition was temporary and the inevitable revolutionary crises would bring them together. Moreover, while Trotsky's blanket opposition to Lenin's conception of a party has become a part of almost all anti-Marxist propaganda in our own time, some of his and Luxembourg's critique assume special relevance with the actual overcentralization and misleadership of later Leninist parties.

In reading the polemics between the Russian factions during this period, it would be easy to infer that these opponents were the harshest of enemies. Lenin especially was a master of the most irascible of polemics. As the most articulate and most formidable spokesperson for anti-party Menshevism, Trotsky was the object of Lenin's most pointed barbs throughout this period. For example, at a time when Mensheviks were attempting to downplay differences between themselves and other Marxists in order to eliminate the Bolsheviks as a separate organizational form (what Lenin called liquidationism), Trotsky was the strongest proponent claiming little difference between them. Lenin responded to Trotsky's views in this way: "That is an example of how fine words are torn into shreds by phrase-mongering intended to disguise a monstrous untruth, a monstrous deception [by] those who revel in phrase-mongering."

Trotsky is accused here as a base deceiver. And yet there is something significant that might be missed in the quote if taken out of context. Lenin is still speaking, this in 1910 or 1911, to the whole movement with Trotsky considered still a member of a common Marxist movement. In spite of the harsh polemics between the factions, Trotsky was *not* seen by Lenin as a fundamental traitor to Marxism. Trotsky was simply a wrong-headed part of a dangerous trend – wrong, opposed, but educable.

Trotsky's abnegation of his anti-party Menshevism upon Lenin's return to Russia in 1917 led to his full welcome into the Bolshevik ranks, and as far as we know, his mistaken past is never mentioned until after Lenin's death. When the Bolsheviks were consolidated into a clear-cut Party calling itself for the first time a communist party in 1919, Trotsky became a full-fledged member of the party and to the end of his life in 1940 he never wavered in his staunch defense of Bolshevik party formation and its principles of organization.

To sum up our thinking on Trotsky's early political career, we would suggest that he was a young, highly exuberant, and literate Marxist thinker and activist. At the age of twenty-five, he had already demonstrated unusual leadership abilities when he became the clear leader of the Petrograd Soviet in the revolutionary uprising of 1905. As a revolutionary orator, Trotsky was unsurpassed, demonstrating a capacity forcefully to articulate central ideas and stir revolutionary passions. At the level of theory, he was, with Lenin, one of the first thinkers to realize the socialist revolutionary potential of industrially backward Russia and that revolution can occur as an alliance of a small militant proletariat leading a much larger rural peasant mass. Trotsky also made mistakes, as who doesn't especially when they are young. But his initial opposition to Bolshevik party organization must, in historical context, be seen as extenuating. Bolshevism represented a very new approach to revolutionary activity, one which was opposed by many honest revolutionaries in a broader Marxist movement. It is no surprise and it is no egregious failing that Trotsky opposed it, and opposed it in ways which have certain prophetic relevance even today. Moreover, the unity of the social democratic (Marxist) movement was seen as both necessary and almost inevitable during this period. Bolshevism and Menshevism were considered by everyone at the time, including Lenin, as trends and not distinct antagonistic parties. The attempt by the young Trotsky was not the act of a congenitally entrenched scoundrel as he was characterized later by the Soviet-inspired communist movement.

In *Two Tactics of Social Democracy in the Democratic Revolution*, Lenin proposed a clearly demarcated two-stage process, the first of which was a bourgeois-democratic revolution based on an alliance between the peasantry and the proletariat that would culminate in a revolutionary democratic dictatorship. The first stage would strengthen bourgeois rule, but once this bourgeois revolution was underway, the proletariat would unite with the semi-proletarian peasantry in opposition to the rich peasants in developing a socialist revolution. Lenin envisaged a continuous, 'uninterrupted' revolutionary process in Russia that, nevertheless, required a European revolution to succeed. Trotsky differed from Lenin primarily in asserting that the urban proletariat was the only genuinely revolutionary force and was capable of seizing political power on its own. His experience with the Soviet in Petersburg convinced him that a workers' rebellion would win political power for the proletariat. Sustaining their position of power would necessarily lead to further socialist demands as the revolution would become continuous or 'permanent.' As noted above, Trotsky did foresee the potential for an alliance between urban workers and peasants as a first step, but it would not be possible to maintain this alliance with the peasantry, Carr says, because a fundamental conflict of interest existed between the proletariat and the peasantry. A proletarian agricultural policy would necessarily entail cooperatives or state control, and such socialist measures could only be imposed on the peasantry.

While still not a Bolshevik, Trotsky remained part of that minority of Marxists who, by opposing proletarian involvement in the First World War, kept a very fragile Marxism alive. He also supported the main policies of the Bolsheviks so that soon after the February revolution broke out in 1917, he wished to join them. Accordingly, although with some reservations from old Bolsheviks who could not forgive his past, Trotsky was welcomed into the Bolshevik ranks. From this period until he was exiled in the late 1920s, he became a major revolutionary leader, second only to Lenin in the Bolshevik accession to power and in the transformation of Russian society. Trotsky became what Isaac Deutscher in his three-volume biography called "The Prophet Armed."

Every revolutionary Marxist at the inception of the Russian triumph accepted the idea that the Revolution, standing alone, was doomed to failure. Its significance, said Lenin, Trotsky, Stalin, and all Bolshevik-minded people was as a stimulus and as an example for revolution in the advanced industrial capitalist countries. Concomitantly, it was believed, these revolutions in these advanced countries would help pull revolutionary Russia out of its technical backwardness. When Lenin died in 1924, he was still of the opinion that the Russian Revolution would be the harbinger of world-wide revolution, and would fail without it. With Luxembourg, he would have agreed that "it is only internationally that the socialist order of society can be realized." Trotsky, who lived almost twenty years longer and faced the dilemma of a Russian Revolution standing alone, maintained this position to the end.

The Bolshevik Revolution, then, was initiated in a society in which the leading force was a small industrial proletariat surrounded by a massive peasant sea. This peasantry, although no longer a class of traditional feudal serfs, still lived in conditions of semi-serfdom working for landlords on large, landed estates. While some of these estates were managed with advanced technical methods, the bulk of the Russian landed nobility still resembled the incompetent, head-in-the-clouds landlordism so well presented in Ivan Goncharov's novel *Oblomov*. The dream of the peasant in these conditions was to get rid of the landlord and have a piece of land of his own (the female peasant was the servant of the servant). To realize this dream had to be the crux of Bolshevik land policy since it was the only policy that would win the support of this vast class. To give each peasant a small piece of land to be worked with primitive technology was hardly a socialist programme, however. Breaking up the few advanced farms was often even a step backward in agricultural productivity. For industrialization to occur, a leap in agricultural production had to occur as had been the pattern in all preceding examples; the industrialization of the cities depended upon more food being produced in the countryside to feed the expanding urban workforce. In Soviet conditions, there was no blueprint to achieve this leap (again without assistance from more developed societies). Only with the Chinese Revolution was this problem confronted in a new way. In the Russian case, the problem of the technical and social disjunction between urban and rural areas haunted the Revolution from its beginnings and was never satisfactorily resolved. The fact, in the case of Trotsky, that his outlook partook in this failure can hardly be held against him since his twists and turns dealing with the problem paralleled at different periods those taken by the Soviet regime itself.

After joining the Bolshevik Party in mid-1917, Trotsky quickly became a major figure in the Bolshevik advance to power. His ascent was so swift and his revolutionary talents were so outstanding that, with the success of the Revolution only a few months later, Trotsky's position was second only to Lenin in the Russian and even the international pantheon of revolutionary leaders. As Lenin was forced into hiding in the summer of 1917, it was Trotsky who was at the center of insurrectionary planning, which led to proletarian power. After taking power, the fledgling socialist society faced not only the internal opposition of enemies from the old regime (and there were many), but also from the combined opposition of armies from fourteen outside countries, countries whose ruling classes were terrified about the potential success of socialism. For over three years, civil war raged over the vast territory of the new Soviet Union, and in hindsight, it appears miraculous that the regime survived. Throughout these overwhelmingly difficult years, it was Trotsky who led the Red Army to its victory against what seemed to be insurmountable odds.

Trotsky's contribution to the Russian Revolution in its early years, then, cannot be denied (a common denial by later attempts at re-writing history). Moreover, from the moment he joined the revolutionary movement in 1917 until his death in 1940, he was firmly committed to the Leninist form of party organization (although in hindsight, as would be expected, he had some reservations about certain features in the Party late in his life). While in the Party he did take opposing positions and even perhaps mistaken positions in Party debates, but dissent during that period was normal and common. In some cases, these positions were quite contrary to Lenin's, but it is possible to see this as a product of courage and independence; never did Lenin see such opposition as anything more than acceptable difference of opinion. Trotsky was also a premier revolutionary orator and writer. His writings are more comprehensive than those of almost any active revolutionaries ranging over subjects like literature and art to history and military organization and tactics. In short, during this brief period of the early heady years of the Russian Revolution, Trotsky's reputation as one of the world's greatest Marxist revolutionaries was based on solid contributions to that revolution, a reputation well deserved. We reiterate this point to counterpose to that type of thinking, which sees all later failings of a person as already in embryo from the very beginning, and in this case tries to undermine all of Trotsky's revolutionary contributions.

Left Opposition

TROTSKY WAS ONE who often took great risks in both theory and action, and often in a very public way. In his battle with Stalin over leadership in the Party, Trotsky's often standoffish style easily made enemies. It is often reported that he was arrogant about his political positions and probably did not suffer fools easily. This style might make close connection to a few loyal supporters, but it did not create the loyalty generated by plodding day-to-day contact with a multitude of diverse party members. Even greater modesty would be expected of a rather latecomer to the Party, and modesty was not Trotsky's long suit. To many, he was an all-too-bright interloper who assumed great power too quickly.

Then there were real issues of disagreement, issues which often can only be seen as portentous in hindsight. The Bolsheviks took power when the First World War was still raging, and Russia was participating in that war with a huge army in the field against Germany. Revolutionary Marxism was in principle against what it considered an inter-imperialist war, a war within which ordinary people would shed their blood, and capitalists of warring nations would profit from this bloodshed. In Russia, therefore, revolutionary propaganda opposed the war before and during the conflict. The proletariat, it proclaimed, should not fight its proletarian brothers in other nations, but should instead turn its guns upon the capitalists of its own nations. As with all revolutionary Marxism, this propaganda did not oppose war in general as does pacifism, but only this particular war, an outlook that was called revolutionary pacifism.

The revolutionary outlook on the war struck a responsive chord in the Russian army, which had gone from defeat to defeat – ill-fed, ill-clad, ill-equipped, and led by a feudal-type corrupt officer corps. This army, mainly of peasants who had fields to plow, was ready to abandon the war and go home. Only the Bolsheviks, courageously for it was considered treason, responded positively and openly to this desire. In response to the call to quit the war, the army started to abandon the front in droves. Of the three elements in Bolshevik strategy at the time – the call for peace, bread, and land for the peasantry – it was the weariness with war, which probably resonated most strongly in the Russian army and citizenry. And since all the other political parties including the Mensheviks wanted to continue the war, the growing hatred for these parties went hand in hand with the increasing popularity of the Bolsheviks. With the success of the popular insurrection in St. Petersburg leading to socialist power in October/November, 1917, the Bolshevik Government immediately began plans to withdraw from the war.

While quitting the war was a clear necessity for Bolshevik success, it presented the new revolutionary government with an apparently insoluble dilemma. The war continued for a year after Bolshevik accession. On the one hand, the Bolsheviks became the reigning government over a large territory whose security from foreign incursion was an obvious responsibility. On the other hand, the Bolshevik policy of immediate peace speeded up the disintegration of an already disintegrating army facing a still powerful German invading force. Also, the revolutionary government saw itself as more or less transitional, if not downright temporary, as a stimulus and even helpmate in the revolutionary transformation of more advanced capitalist nations, especially Germany. Under present conditions, the Bolsheviks were in no position to spread revolution by military means, which in principle they were opposed to. Their only policy was to spread revolutionary propaganda among the German troops hoping to stimulate them to their own revolution. A disintegrating, at best semi-literate peasant army was not a hopeful agent for such a task. The new Soviet regime was in the midst of dismantling its own army so it could neither protect itself nor spread revolutionary propaganda. Finally, the German army appeared to show little interest in the revolutionary overthrow of its officers even though it was losing the war and was only a year away from total surrender.

As would be expected in such circumstances, there were major divisions in the Bolshevik ranks. Lenin asserted in the name of realism that the Soviet Union was in no military position to defend itself against the German army and that any waiting to make peace would simply give the Germans time to take more Soviet territory. His position held sway and the Soviet Union agreed to initiate immediate peace negotiations with the full realization that it was bargaining from a position of terrible weakness. A sizeable minority of Bolsheviks, a group which represented an incipient left opposition within the Party, strongly opposed this position of making peace with Germany at the cost of Russian territory, advocating a continuing defense of the nation and sometimes condemning any peace treaty as a betrayal of the Revolution. Trotsky, as he had in the past, took a position attempting to mediate between oppositions, proposing neither peace nor war. One can surmise that he hoped that playing a waiting game would result in growing militancy in the German army and working class, leading to a German Revolution and an alliance between Soviet Germany and the Soviet Union. As the leader of the delegation to Brest-Litovsk where the treaty was being negotiated, Trotsky did everything to drag out negotiations, at the same time disseminating revolutionary propaganda among the German troops. This dilly-dallying in the end proved Lenin right because the prolongation of negotiations simply led to greater acquisition of Soviet territory by the German army. Trotsky's position and actions at the time were seen as wrong-headed, a mistake but certainly no more than that.

As was asserted before, Trotsky at this time was recognized both nationally and internationally as second only to Lenin in the Soviet leadership. His succession to Lenin's position as undisputed Bolshevik leader seemed assured. Yet as a result of issues both of political tactics and political policy, this apparently assured succession never occurred. Instead, within three years after Lenin's death in January, 1924, Trotsky was already marginal to the Bolshevik mainstream and on a path toward national and international vilification within the Soviet-led, worldwide Marxist movement. For his sympathizers among Marxists, such as Isaac Deutscher, his revolutionary credentials remain impeccable to this day. To these sympathizers, Trotsky's downfall is not seen as due to a result of his own actions. It is admitted that he made small mistakes at key historical moments and that he suffered from temperamental arrogance (understandable and even apparently justifiable in a genius), but the primary cause of Trotsky's fall is seen as a result of the implacable plodding manipulations of a very second-rate Stalin.

While we think there is some truth in all of these interpretations, it is more significant for Marxist analysis to discover the political policies that led to Trotsky's downfall, and to try to evaluate and sum up their political significance. This is no easy matter for a political figure who was steeped in Marxism, wrote and acted widely on the political stage, and demonstrated a broad diversity of political policies at different periods of his life. For example, during the civil war against local counter-revolutionaries and foreign armies intent on destroying the Revolution, a policy that was called War Communism was put into effect. Under conditions of great crisis and threat, the whole nation was militarized under centralized unquestioned command. Trotsky was a foremost proponent and activist in this policy. However, after four years of civil war, an already poor nation was in shambles. Agricultural production was at its lowest level in decades and its small concentrated industrial base produced at levels lower than 1913 while producing mainly military equipment and little in the way of useful products. In these difficult conditions, Lenin advocated a definite step backward in order to rebuild the productive forces, the New Economic Policy (NEP). It emphasized the growth of free market activities while recognizing that guarding against their potential excesses and the danger of resurrection of capitalism demanded the continuation of government control of the major levers of economic activity. Trotsky opposed the initiation of the NEP fearing a capitalist resurrection and instead forwarded the continuation of the totally militarized economy initiated during the Civil War. This type of economy, he suggested, would be a harbinger for a more advanced form of socialism. His opponents, including Lenin, considered War Communism as only necessary during the Civil War. Trotsky here showed himself to be overly doctrinaire with little sensitivity to the actual mood and needs of the country. The people in general were fed up with the extreme deprivation produced by war conditions, morale was at very low level, and there would have been little motivation to produce under military command. NEP was proven the appropriate policy by the degree to which it was embraced and by the swift revival of production and its attendant improvement in living standards. Of course, both Lenin and Trotsky were aware of the contradictory class forces a temporary turn to capitalism would engender. Within little more than half a decade, collectivization in the USSR negated the NEP.

From early in the revolution, a distinct left opposition developed in the Communist Party of the Soviet Union. It began as a small, vocal minority, which opposed what it considered the unnecessary compromises made by the Party, and over the years it consolidated into a semi-permanent bloc. One source of permanent ultra-leftism in the Bolshevik Party came from the history of Russian anarchism. There had always been a substantial anarchist presence in Russia, and many anarchists or anarchist sympathizers became members of the Party after the Revolution. This political outlook introduced a strong 'left' tendency in the Party. Anarchism usually opposes the very idea of a single-party state (if not the very idea of a state) and often rejected Party policies, which it claimed undermined international or national ideals of revolution. A conception of revolutionary purity, most clearly enunciated by anarchism and often appealing to young Marxists, often forms the bedrock of ultra-leftism in Marxist political theory. We do not think it can be underestimated (as it often is) in its effect on revolutionary movements. In the political drama surrounding Trotsky's career and the Trotskyism it spawned, the interplay with ultra-leftism, it seems to us, plays a significant part. The designation 'ism' reflects an entrenched ultra-left theory and practice that, generally, bases policy on principles divorced from concrete conditions and isolates individuals and groups from the class they claim to represent.

It has been often claimed that anarchism (which we dealt with extensively in Chapter Two) has its greatest appeal to peasants in predominantly peasant countries. Peasants are usually small landholders who are insulated from political organization and often hostile to all political authority, a feature common to anarchism. This is certainly the case in Russian revolutionary history where the movement of peasant rebellion from the late nineteenth century took predominantly anarchist forms, especially in individual terrorist attacks on figures in authority. It is significant that Lenin's older brother was executed by the Tsarist regime for his part in a plot to assassinate the Tsar. In Lenin's case, this experience undoubtedly had some effect in consolidating his opposition to anarchism at an early age. When the Bolsheviks took power in 1917, the party of the peasantry rooted in this anarchist tradition, the Social Revolutionary Party, split into a left wing supporting, in the main, the Bolshevik programme and a right wing opposing it. The left Social Revolutionaries, in fact, joined for a time the Bolsheviks in a common governing bloc. This undoubtedly injected anarchist attitudes into a Party in which such currents already existed.

All revolutionary movements have been suffused with what we consider ultra-left tendencies, and it is our contention that this problem has often been treated too lightly. Lenin did consider it enough of a problem to write a pamphlet about it in 1921 called *"Left-Wing" Communism, An Infantile Disorder*. In the pamphlet, however, he considered it mainly a product of youthful exuberance, one which demanded vigilance and education on the part of the Party, but one which he thought would slowly but inexorably disappear with revolutionary progress. We think that the deep-seated hostility to all authority and the tendency to substitute revolutionary purity for an analysis of concrete conditions are found not only in anarchism pure and simple or only in peasant societies, but constitute a broader and more permanent problem to which revolutionary Marxism is far from immune.

In the Soviet case, we have mentioned the issues faced at Brest-Litovsk where the seeming left wing of Bolshevism along with left Social Revolutionaries opposed peace with Germany and strongly endorsed the spreading of revolutionary war. Since the possibility of winning such wars was nil (in fact, such an attempt had failed miserably in Poland), the demand to expand beyond Soviet frontiers is a good example of the substitution of revolutionary purity for the realistic appraisal of events. Trotsky tried to stay on the fence in this situation when there was no fence to stand on, demonstrating a tendency to be against realism or for adventurism at the same time. We shall see later that this adventurist predisposition, in the context of continuing Party and national crises, led Trotsky to a fatal relationship with an opposition that can be characterized as ultra-left. The question of left opposition is not necessarily identical with ultra-leftism. Luxemburg and Kautsky, for example, took leftist positions in a party that was slipping into revisionism.

The fatal relationship with ultra-leftism in the CPSU was not a straight line in Trotsky's case making him subject to a criticism that he wavered indecisively between left and right. We have already mentioned Trotsky's endorsement of the militarization of labour after the Civil War and his opposition to the NEP, a position that may be seen as left; that is, move quickly into socialism rather than detour back to some forms of petty capitalism. This inconsistency was also demonstrated by his actions in two other major issues in the early years of the Revolution: the Kronstadt revolt and the battle over the question of factions in the Party. The response to the Kronstadt revolt was something else again. Kronstadt was a naval base outside of Petrograd (renamed Leningrad later by the Soviet regime), which was noted for its revolutionary militancy. In March, 1921, after the Soviet victory in the Civil War and on the eve of the New Economic Policy, the sailors of Kronstadt staged an insurrection against the Soviet government. It was forcefully put down with Trotsky taking a leading role. The violent suppression of the Kronstadt revolt has been seen by anarchism and by some Marxists as proof of the basic counter-revolutionary nature of the Bolshevik regime, and as the beginning of the demise of socialism in Russia.

On the question of factionalism, Trotsky in this period is unequivocal in his support for party unity and in his rejection of oppositional groupings within the Party. As noted before, the Bolsheviks came to power in alliance with the left wing of the Social Revolutionary Party. The anarchism of the latter party and its active opposition to Bolshevik policy during the alliance led to a break with the Social Revolutionaries and to the monopolization of power by the newly named Communist Party. One of the consequences of this monopoly was that major political opposition began to occur within the Party rather than outside it. And the most vocal opposition to Party policy often took a left form proclaiming excesses of party centralization, lack of inner-party democracy, or claims of betrayal of working-class interests or needs. As discussed in the chapter on Lenin, his attempted solution to problems of party unity and democracy was the principle and practice of democratic centralism. While the theory of democratic centralism is meant to resolve the contradictions that arise between wide-ranging discussion of policy and effective implementation of policy decisions, its application is always difficult, especially so in a society still replete with past class, ethnic, and gender divisions engendering new ones in the hectic and unprecedented process of forced industrialization of a predominantly peasant society. The Russian Communist Party was initiated with the intent to foster open debate and almost obligatory input from all its members while at the same time demanding unified commitment to the implementation of Party programmes. But the reality of the Russian experience was quite different from Party intentions since the revolution, especially in the difficulties faced by the Soviet Union, was confronted with perpetual crises demanding immediate decisions with little time for discussion. In these circumstances, it would be expected that swift unity and effective administration would take priority over wide discussion and debate. Moreover, with new members flocking to a party in power, there was little time for training of new recruits. In this atmosphere, there was a slow evolution toward obedience to Party dictates taking the place of independent understanding and truly voluntary commitment to Party programme.

The trend toward overcentralization and toward minimizing debate over policy in the name of unity has been common to all Leninist parties. Whether this is intrinsic to the organizing principles of Leninist party formation or whether it is due to unusual circumstances faced by twentieth-century revolutions, or to mistaken policies taken by such parties, are questions that are at the very heart of the viability of Leninism as a revolutionary endeavor. We will forward our views on these questions in the concluding chapter since we are here focusing upon Trotsky's response to this matter. When opposition arose within the Party after its accession to power, Trotsky was unequivocal in his support for swift punitive action against what was called factionalism. Thus, when other Parties initially in alliance with the Bolsheviks were banned and then oppositional groups within the Party were also banned, Trotsky was in the forefront of support for these actions. Significantly, in his last testament summing up what he considered the strengths and weaknesses of Party leaders, Lenin attributed the major fault of Trotsky to be a tendency to be over administrative; that is, to not listen to the views of others and to neglect the need for continual discussion and political education of Party members in the making and execution of policy.

Another aspect of Leninist party organization, which differs from standard democratic forms, is its emphasis on the combining of the legislative and administrative functions of governing. Those who legislate are also made responsible for the implementation of policy, a responsibility that is supposed to cut down on bureaucracy. After full debate in Party conferences, in which all are more or less obliged to state their views, a majority vote determines policy, a policy that is to be executed by some of these same debaters who may have stated oppositional views about some of the policies. They are assumed to administer these policies with unity of purpose. In the first years of the Revolution, it may be said that something very close to this theoretical ideal did take place in the Soviet Communist Party. The slow, and some would say inexorable, move toward the lessening of debate and the tightening of decision at the Party center began early, and moves in that direction had Trotsky's endorsement. In 1922, in a letter to the congress, Lenin argued that the Central Committee should be enlarged to as many as one hundred members to reduce the influence of small groups and overcome the potential split caused by the already existing rift between Stalin and Trotsky. In addition, Lenin said, the state planning commission should be invested with "legislative force," a position he linked to Trotsky.

It was the left opposition to Party policy that arose and became the focus of the problem of factionalism, which Trotsky initially opposed as detrimental to party unity. At first defined as a mere tolerable difference of opinion, this opposition over time became defined as an unacceptable faction to be prohibited. Factionalism was seen not as opposition in individuals, but as the coalescence of opinion among groups, groups which were then perceived as threatening party unity. The battle against this opposition became the basis upon which a policy was implemented, which banned all factionalism within the Communist Party. It is important to recognize that the idea of party unity applied to the Party alone as it is clearly recognized that the society at large is suffused with ideas across a broad spectrum of opinion; the lack of unity within the Party can lead to the consolidation of what are considered backward ideas in the wider society. The basic question here is when is difference within the Party an acceptable difference of opinion and when does it represent an unacceptable grouping of pernicious influence? And when does rejection of difference become a sign of thoughtless encrustation of over-centralized authority? There are no easy answers to these questions, but certain trends in answering them arose in the Bolshevik experience. That body of opinion, which was defined and often defined itself as more revolutionary, as more to the left of prevailing Party opinion, was the most continuing and semi-permanent opposition. First seen as a healthy corrective to conservative tendencies, it had already become so much of a problem even while Lenin was still alive that he wrote the pamphlet about it calling such opposition wrongheaded and "infantile." When later it was banned as a factional anti-Party group, Trotsky supported the ban. Later still, however, he became the de facto leader of this opposition, so much so that opposition from the left has become almost synonymous with Trotskyism.

The Russian Revolution, at least the way it was interpreted by Trotsky and other Marxists, was haunted by images of the great French Revolution of the late eighteenth century. His most striking image was that of Thermidor (the French Revolution introduced Roman names for months as a humanist reaction against a Christian medieval tradition), a time when progressive forces were overthrown and reaction set in. Trotsky's fear of a Thermidor in the Russian Revolution was so great that he saw the Soviet system under Stalin in the later 1920s as already clear evidence of the triumph of reaction. We think this blanket interpretation is somewhat simplistic since Soviet history in the first decade of the Revolution appears to us to be a series of twists and turns by a regime living in uncharted waters and facing unprecedented crises. Thus, as mentioned before, when the new society came out of the Civil War at the beginning of the 1920s and found itself in almost total economic collapse with productive levels even lower than that of 1913, the Soviet government introduced fundamentally capitalist measures in the country. The NEP was not a concession to socialist theory and was not seen as anything more than a stopgap measure, but it was enough to set in motion a left opposition, which proclaimed that socialism was being betrayed. The NEP proved to be a transient phenomenon in the regime's major thrust toward a collective and planned economy, but almost total rejection of the NEP among the 'left' opposition continued throughout the process. This kind of occurrence, a step backward considered necessary in specific circumstances and an opposition to it in the name of revolutionary principles, is common in Soviet (and probably all revolutionary) experience.

Since, as we know, the sustaining of a revolution appears far more difficult than was once imagined, it cannot be assumed that all left opposition is automatically wrong-headed or ultra-leftist. Only a very careful analysis of particular issues, their overall context, and how they fit into a general trend either toward revolutionary development or toward capitalist restoration can make such a judgment, far from an easy thing to do. It is also necessary to delve into the history of particular individuals and groups to decide whether a particular pattern is progressive or not. The analysis of leftist tendencies is particularly complicated when a party is devolving towards revisionism.

Be that as it may, left opposition was a continuing presence in Soviet history and Trotsky's involvement with it is part and parcel of the problem of understanding Trotsky's political role in the history of the CPSU as well as the Trotskyism, which he engendered. As we have already mentioned, at least until Lenin died in 1924, Trotsky was in the main a Party loyalist who opposed the "left" in the Kronstadt revolt against the regime (revolt with a distinctively left series of demands), and strongly accepted the prohibition of other parties and factions within the Communist Party. And the struggle over Lenin's succession drew Trotsky increasingly into opposition. In practical political terms, Trotsky lost the battle for primacy in the Bolshevik Party and Stalin was victorious. This defeat occurred in spite of the fact that Lenin's "last testament," in summing up his views of the Party leadership, saw these two men as the Party's most "outstanding leaders" at the same time suggesting that Stalin be removed from his position as Party Secretary – because of his record of rude behavior, he should be replaced by a member who was "more tolerant, more loyal, more polite and more considerate to the comrades, less capricious, etc." In 1924, Trotsky was then in an extremely strong position to assume the top leadership in the Soviet Revolution. By 1927, however, this same Trotsky was thrown out of the Party in enforced exile and was officially vilified by Soviet opinion as one of the most dangerous enemies of that Revolution. How and why did such a dramatic turn of events occur?

E. H. Carr in *The Interregnum*, Volume Four of his monumental history of the Soviet Revolution, explains Stalin's victory and Trotsky's defeat mainly in terms of the former's greater "political sense and acumen" as well as Trotsky's isolation from the Party's rank and file. Undoubtedly, it seems to us, there is some truth to this interpretation. No one, least of all Trotsky, who maintained a rather arrogant disdain for Stalin's abilities, considered that Stalin would become the ultimate leader of the Bolshevik Party. Stalin was seen as a rather dull and colorless bureaucrat surrounded by a panoply of vital and imaginative intellectual lights, with Trotsky without question burning the brightest. In hindsight, it can be seen that of all the twentieth century revolutions, the Soviet leadership perhaps possessed the greatest number of talented and sometimes non-Russian intellectuals. Stalin's apparent intellectual inferiority, which Trotsky later uses to demean the backwardness of Stalin's regime, does not get at the crux of an explanation of Trotsky's downfall.

Because of his pre-revolutionary rejection of Lenin's central position on party organization and the distrust this created against him in the Bolshevik Party, Trotsky, even in his heyday of national and international eminence, had a uniquely marginal position in the Party. He did little to overcome that marginality since he was, as Isaac Deutscher, his most sympathetic biographer, points out, overly impressed with his own intellectual abilities. This meant that his political style tended to re-enforce his marginality. We would surmise that he possibly was overly impressed with his own revolutionary purity, which also increased this problem. It is highly significant for our argument that Trotsky's later attack on the Soviet regime under Stalin was expressed mainly in leftist terms seldom accusing the regime of being too leftist. The opposition by Trotsky to what he considered the betrayal of socialism in the Soviet Union rests not a nuanced critique of its various forms of opportunism but on what he regarded as the fundamentally reactionary nature of the party leadership. What is even more peculiar is that throughout his period of opposition, Trotsky still characterized the Soviet Union as a worker's state, but one led by a reactionary bureaucracy.

Even though Trotsky stayed clear of formal association with the left opposition of the 1920s, his own opposition became more and more integrated with that of the earlier form. In the end he became the de facto leader of what remained of that opposition, so much so that the very name of Trotsky and left opposition became coterminous. Given the fertility and originality of his ideas, the Trotskyism that was a consolidation of those ideas, which is almost all that we now know of as Trotskyism, still maintains a firm connection to his central ideas. It is to these ideas which we must turn below. Next, however, we consider Stalin's place in the development of revisionism in the Soviet Union.

Stalin and Revisionism

ISAAC DEUTSCHER'S BOOK *Stalin: A Political Biography* introduces Stalin as coming from a peasant background. Also unlike most early Bolsheviks, he was not Russian. His nationality and first language were Georgian. As his family descended into poverty, young Stalin attended an ecclesiastical school in Gori, a region undergoing a local, oil-driven industrialization. Stalin was drawn into Georgian and working class politics. In 1901 he joined the newly-formed Russian Social Democratic Labour Party and was active in working class agitation and organizing demonstrations. He was arrested and sent into exile on more than one occasion. Unlike many top Bolshevik leaders, Stalin remained in Russia and did not go abroad. His class background and identification from an oppressed nation, as well as his personal history of revolutionary activism in Georgia, provided Stalin with considerable cachet in a party committed to the interests of the exploited.

In the interpretation of the Chinese Communist Party under Mao Zedong, revisionism in the USSR follows Stalin's death with the movement towards peaceful coexistence and the doctrine of the peaceful evolution towards socialism. In our view, the seeds of revisionism were rooted decades before 1956 under Stalin. Stalin had supported Lenin's conception of the party from the time he entered the RSDLP, but there were important differences. In Stalin's view, there was a particularly wide gap between the spontaneous peoples' movements and the development of theory. The theory of socialism is not only worked up by intellectuals independently of the spontaneous movement, it is "in spite of that movement" and correcting it ("A Letter from Kutais," 1904). The formulation suggests that the relationship between party and class is essentially a one-way street. At that time, however, Stalin wanted to have it both ways. It is "self-evident," he said, "that the spontaneous working class movement will proceed along [the] beaten path and submit to bourgeois ideology." However, eventually through its sufferings and "long wanderings ... the spontaneous movement" will eventually "come into its own, ... break with bourgeois ideology and strive for the social revolution" on its own without the aid of Social-Democracy "because 'the working class spontaneously gravitates towards socialism'" (quoting Lenin). Social democracy only accelerates the inevitable victory of the proletariat.

Deutscher quotes Stalin as asserting that, "Unity of views on program, tactic and organization forms the basis on which our party is being built. If the unity of views crumbles, the party, too, crumbles." He argues that Stalin was insisting "on the need for absolute uniformity of views *inside* the party" (italics are ours). With Stalin, the erosion of inner-party discussion and disagreement goes beyond the need for dealing with immediate practicalities and assumes the status of the principle of unity at any cost. Along with the unquestioned acceptance of productivism – the assumption that material conditions would be more or less automatically reflected in ideology – these are the early seeds of revisionism in the USSR.

On 6 February, 1923, Lenin wrote *Better Less but Better*, described by Carr as "a fierce uninhibited attack on the People's Commissariat of Workers' and Peasants' Inspection," which Stalin had headed from its beginning in 1920. The article was widely interpreted as critical of Stalin. Lenin warned about bureaucracy in both the Soviet institutions and in the party, a critique also aimed, Carr says, at the office of the General Secretary (Stalin). Nevertheless, at the Twelfth Party Congress in 1923, Stalin was named one of a triumvirate at the top of the Party, a group that did not include Trotsky (who was still a Politburo member). Trotsky was quickly under attack as the assumed leader of the left faction within the Party. The Thirteenth Congress met in early 1924, just after Lenin's death. Carr says that Stalin left nothing to chance. The conference was carefully planned down to the important task of delegate selection. In Stalin's speeches on party organization, Trotsky was for the first time explicitly identified as the head of the left opposition. By May, Party purges were followed by a large influx of new members, the "Lenin recruitment." The essential criterion for new membership was proletarian class origin, a decision that reflects the positivist notion that class determines ideology. A few months after Lenin died, Stalin published a major pamphlet called *The Foundations of Leninism* (April 1924) in which he presented an interpretation of Lenin's theories that presented Marxism-Leninism as a set of dogmatic, uncontextualized 'truths.' The pamphlet was aimed, above all, at teaching the new Party members basic principles as interpreted by Stalin, putting the ideological cart before the membership horse. Stalin's immediate "Lenin Recruitment" of members based on their working class credentials breeds the automatic loyalty of untutored careerism and furthers revisionism, which is difficult to stop in its cumulative consequences.

At first, Trotsky was criticized by Stalin and Bukharin, among others, for opposing the worker-peasant alliance and the NEP, and his demand for rapid industrialization. After his expulsion and exile in 1927, however, the CPSU reversed its policy and moved to collectivize agriculture and develop heavy industry through state planning under the doctrine of socialism in one country. By 1928, the change in policy was said by Stalin to be an offensive against the capitalist elements in the countryside ("The Right Danger in the CPSU"): "[T]here are people in the ranks of our Party," Stalin said, who oppose rapid industrialization and collectivization. They were, "perhaps without themselves realising it," adapting "our socialist construction to the tastes and requirements of the 'Soviet' bourgeoisie." A victory for the right, he says, strengthens capitalism and weakens the proletarian democracy, "increasing the chances of the restoration of capitalism," which had emerged under the NEP. Stalin defined the danger of capitalist restoration as arising only from already existing capitalism, and he named Bukharin as the principal leader of the right deviation. He wrote: "Until now, we Marxist-Leninists were of the opinion that between the capitalists of town and country, on the one hand, and the working class, on the other, there is an *irreconcilable* antagonism of interests. That is what the Marxist theory of the class struggle rests on." The rapid and militarized liquidation of the Kulaks and collectivization of the middle peasants followed. At the same time, the social-fascist line against social democracy was adopted by the Comintern. Fernando Claudin defines the move to collectivization as 'ultra-left.' In our view, the move to cooperative farming was socially progressive, but the Soviet practice of collectivization was precipitous, overly administrative and militarized, and represented some of the worst aspects of top-down social change in the face of entrenched popular opposition.

The move to revisionism in the USSR was consolidated in 1936 in the new Constitution of the Soviet Union. By 1936, Stalin's *Report Delivered at the Extraordinary Eighth Congress of Soviets of the USSR* (25 November) claimed that the last vestiges of capitalism had been eliminated in the USSR. Capitalism had been banished entirely from industry, and the kulaks, "an agricultural capitalist class," had been eliminated. With them had gone most of the middle peasants, who had existed in the NEP as "a boundless ocean of small individual peasant farms with backward, mediaeval technical equipment." By 1936 most farms in the USSR were either collectively or state-owned. "Thus the complete victory of the Socialist system in all spheres of the national economy is now a fact," Stalin claimed

As a result of these changes in ownership and productive forces, Stalin said, "the class structure of our society has also changed." All the exploiting classes – landlords, kulaks, capitalists, merchants – had been eliminated. The means of production had been expropriated from the capitalists and handed over to the working class and the people as a whole, represented by the "fully formed multinational Socialist state." For the USSR, socialism, the first stage of communism, "is something already achieved and won." The new constitution of the USSR was designed to reflect that two classes, the workers and the peasants, were declared to be in power. "[A] constitution is needed for the purpose of consolidating a social order desired by, and beneficial to, the working people." Classes were defined in terms of legal relationship to the means of production. Factories and farms were state and not privately owned; hence, there was no capitalist class left in the USSR. There was no notion that the control over productive forces, accompanied by great material privilege and power, could become the basis for a new capitalist class in embryo.

Following Stalin's death in 1953 and the more obvious revelation of revisionism in the Soviet Union, Mao summed up Stalin's place in history in an article for the *People's Daily* (1956). Mao argued, in a period when the two countries were still formally allied but the split between them was churning beneath surface politics, that Stalin had "creatively applied and developed Marxism-Leninism." Stalin, he said, had defended Leninism from Trotsky and Zinoviev, "brought about the triumph of socialism in the Soviet Union and created the conditions for the victory of the Soviet Union in the war against Hitler." These were victories of "the Soviet people" and reflected the interests of the international working class and progressive people. In addition, Stalin was being condemned by all reactionary forces, through which means they sought to attack Marxism-Leninism. To defend Stalin was to defend the entire movement; to condemn him was to undermine it.

Mao did not defend Stalin uncritically, however. For Mao, Stalin "committed several gross errors." He "erroneously exaggerated his own role and counterposed his individual authority to the collective leadership, and as a result certain of his actions were opposed to certain fundamental Marxist-Leninist concepts he himself had propagated." Leadership is essential, Mao argues, but "when any leader of the Party or the state places himself over and above the Party and the masses, instead of in their midst, when he alienates himself from the masses," he can "not avoid making unrealistic and erroneous decisions on certain important matters." Consequently, "Stalin fell victim to subjectivism and one-sidedness and divorced himself from objective reality and from the masses."

Mao attributes Stalin's errors to the "cult of the individual," which was denounced by the Twentieth Congress of the USSR in the movement to criticize Stalin shortly after his death. The cult of the individual, Mao says, is rooted in the long history of exploiting classes and the "patriarchism" of the "small-producer economy." In short, it was a hangover of feudalism and bourgeois individualism. This cult of personality, particularly as it was exaggerated during the Cultural Revolution, was an Achilles heel of the Chinese Revolution, as well,

More significantly, Stalin "violated the Party's system of democratic centralism and the principle of combining collective leadership with individual responsibility." Among Stalin's "serious mistakes" Mao noted that "he broadened the scope of the suppression of counter-revolution." Mao did not condemn the Hitler-Stalin pact outright, but it was an error, he said: Stalin had "lacked the necessary vigilance on the eve of the anti-fascist war." In socialist economic policies, Stalin "failed to pay proper attention to the further development of agriculture and the material welfare of peasantry." Finally, Mao criticized Stalin for giving "wrong advice" to "the international communist movement." Mao said that, "Stalin put forward a formula that in different revolutionary periods the main blow should be so directed as to isolate the middle-of-the-road social and political forces of the time." This formula, however, should not be applied dogmatically. At times, isolating middle forces may be correct, but not in all circumstances. Mao argued that the correct tactic was to identify, isolate, and direct the main blow at the "chief enemy" while uniting with (and struggling against) middle forces. They should at least be neutralized and "efforts should be made to shift them from their position of neutrality to one of alliance."

Given how strikingly concrete and to the point is Mao's evaluation of Stalin's political actions, we are puzzled by the fact that in another context, he asserts that Stalin is 70% good and 30% bad. We would not usually accept mere percentages in a problem like this, but we must remember that Mao was known and appreciated in a peasant country for his folksiness. Here as with much else political, we would submit that this mild critique of Stalin might be seen as essential since it was made when the Soviet Union under Khrushchev had become a definite counter-revolutionary danger to the very existence of socialist China.

In 1951, Enver Hoxha, the Albanian leader, met Stalin in Moscow and, among other matters, addressed the problems of agriculture in Albania, as outlined in "Stalin's Place in History." The agricultural sector in Albania, Hoxha said, was not sufficiently productive "for the population, raw materials for industry or for expanding export resources." Hoxha believed that collectivization was the means to pull agriculture out of its backwardness, which was necessary for developing large-scale production, but he wanted advice about taking "cautious steps" in setting up new cooperatives. He reported that Stalin had advised:

> "You should not rush things in setting up other agricultural cooperatives. Try to strengthen the cooperatives you have, but you must see to it that the yields of crops in these cooperatives are high," he said. "In this way," he went on, "the members will be satisfied with the good results of the production in the cooperative, and the other peasants will see this and will want to become collectivized, too.
>
> "As long as the peasants are not convinced of the superiority of the collective property you have no way to increase the number of cooperatives. If the existing cooperatives prove beneficial to the peasants, then the other peasants will also follow you, too."

Given the great emphasis given to negating Stalin and the Soviet Union, which he led, in almost the whole spectrum of Western political commentary, it might be surprising that we have given his activities rather short shrift in this book. We have done this purposely since we consider that, in Marxist terms, the problem of revisionism is the most central issue in a discussion of Soviet history, and it is that discussion which is largely left out of conventional thought on the matter. Instead, a reiteration of Stalin, the great tyrant, has filled the void. Only if this thing called 'Stalinism' adds some significant elements (positive or negative) to Marxist theory does it deserve to be called an 'ism.' Even one of the strongest critics of Stalin, Isaac Deutscher, following Trotsky sympathetically, proclaims that an intellectual clog like Stalin can add little but tyranny to the human experience. For Marxism, what is significant for the Stalin period is not only how he, in attempting to deal with unforeseen and overwhelming difficulties, ultimately forwarded the positivist impetus (what Mao later called productivism) that still haunts the Marxist revolutionary project, but how his policies built the foundation for a new form of revisionism during the development of socialism. On the other hand, we have given Trotsky and Trotskyism more elaborate treatment because they represent what we consider an issue too lightly touched upon even by Lenin and Mao, the issue of ultra-leftism. We also consider that our treatment of this issue is one of the major contributions of the present work. Trotsky's truncated theory of the Soviet experience is nevertheless an important cog in the understanding of problems for the contemporary left.

Trotsky and Trotskyism

TWO FUNDAMENTAL internal problems faced the fledgling Soviet Union, problems that, in the end, were not resolved. The first involved those problems stemming from the technical backwardness of the society. Traditional Marxism, as we have stated, had postulated that socialism would be generated in the most advanced industrial conditions of mature capitalism, that time when production bears the fruit of highly sophisticated technology. It was postulated that only a proletarianized society already producing the enormous abundance of developed technology would introduce socialism. On the basis of these ideas, the Menshevik opponents of Lenin had argued that the revolution, which had displaced the Tsar in Russia, could not move to socialism but must first go through a process of capitalist development. Lenin countered this view with his thesis that the new era of monopoly capitalism and imperialism had changed the way in which socialist revolutions may happen. In the modern conditions of world imperialism, he argued, it was the backward imperialized societies, integrated into a world where they were super-exploited, which had become the loci of revolutionary transformation. Lenin called this a theory of the weakest link. On this basis, he could justify the view that Russia could and would have a revolution that would move immediately into a socialist transition. Even with this shift in theoretical and practical emphasis, Lenin still assumed that this transition could not be consummated by Russia alone. Right up until his death, Lenin saw the Russian Revolution as socialist, but since its backwardness necessitated that Soviet Russia must get technical and other assistance from the advanced countries, it would mainly be a catalyst for revolution in the more advanced capitalist nations, especially Germany.

The Marxism of early twentieth century Europe was explicit and direct about revolution in the periphery. A backward society in revolutionary change would be nationalist and intrinsically bourgeois in direction and consequences. Carr sums up this outlook very well when he says in *Socialism in One Country* that "The revolution which they made in Russia was conceived by them not primarily as a Russian revolution, but as a first step in a European or world-wide revolution; as an exclusively Russian phenomenon, it had for them no meaning, no validity, no chance for survival."

Thus, at that time, the outlook that saw the Bolshevik experience as a catalyst to wider revolution was fundamental not only to Russian, but to all of Marxism. It was a position never once questioned by Lenin, and enshrined in everything said and written about the matter, Bolshevik and Menshevik alike. The formation of the Communist International in 1919, two years after the October Revolution, bringing together all revolutionary Marxist parties in many countries to support and help foment revolution everywhere, attested to the view that Russia was the first among many revolutions and that it could not survive alone, given its backwardness. There was a high expectation at the time that the German defeat in the Great War would lead to a weakening of the German ruling class and an upsurge of working-class militancy. Revolutionary militancy and possibly even a revolutionary situation did arise in Germany in the first years after the war, but capitalism was not overthrown. By the mid-1920s the revolutionary impetus was much attenuated, and capitalism appeared to be relatively stabilized.

This situation presented the first great socialist revolution with a dilemma, a dilemma of such magnitude that it remains significant for Marxism to this day. What was seen as unique to the Russian experience, a socialist revolution in a technically underdeveloped country, became the general experience of all subsequent revolutions. All revolutions following the Russian in the twentieth century occurred in backward societies, in some cases in even poorer circumstances. While the Russian Revolution did become a stimulus to revolutions elsewhere, the elsewhere has not been the advanced capitalist world, but the impoverished and technically undeveloped one.

The response to the failure of the anticipated revolution in Germany defined the first and perhaps the most lasting difference between the outlook of Trotsky and that of Stalin. In the mid-twenties, the Soviet Union embarked upon a policy of what it called "socialism in one country." This policy involved the acceptance of the brute fact that the now isolated and still backward Soviet Union must face the problem of building socialism alone. This meant that it had to go through the pangs of industrialization turning a massive peasant population into a modern technically developed workforce, and that it had to do this in a socialist way without the stimulus of the extreme poverty and insecurity that marked this process in nineteenth century capitalist industrialization. Trotsky opposed this view on two counts, the first that he considered the problem insurmountable and the second that it was a betrayal of the Marxist principle of internationalism. Throughout his exile, he reiterated that socialism in one country would appeal too much to Russian national sentiment so that the Soviet Union would turn inward to its own problems first and would lose the stimulus to assist other countries in revolutionary transformation. The fact that this turn undoubtedly occurred did little to minimize the consequences of Trotsky's opposition, an opposition that made him an enemy of the only country attempting a socialist transition, a transition fraught with inner difficulty and outer hostility from an already rich capitalist world. Like his earlier centrism, with his theory of a workers' state with reactionary leadership, Trotsky tries to have it both ways – sympathy with the revolution; opposition to what he called the bureaucracy. In a world in which being anti-Soviet translated into being pro-imperialist, a particularly difficult conundrum was posed for Marxists and progressives.

History is not a determined and lawful process, not for Marxism or any social theory. It holds surprises for those who wish to embed it in solid certainty no matter how pure the motives. Both the Menshevism and all ensuing social democracy and Trotsky and the Trotskyism, which evolved from his thought and action, suffer from the attempt to maintain theoretical purity in the face of stubborn fact. In claiming this, we are not denying the importance of internationalism in Marxist theory; nor are we denying that serious nationalist errors were committed in the Soviet Union's long engagement with almost purely internal concerns. The similarity with social democracy is striking. More than small mistakes have been made on this front where the almost complete integration with national patriotism and chauvinism became the order of the day. Moreover, at its worst, social democracy became an instrument of bourgeois dominance. At the present time when the major revolutionary projects of the twentieth century have been aborted, social democracy can take an "I told you so" attitude toward all future attempts of socialist revolutions in poor countries (especially when poor countries are still the major loci of revolutionary militancy).

It is obvious from the above that we consider that the Soviet Union, like all revolutions that followed it, had no choice but to attempt the hard road to industrialization with little or no help (in fact only opposition) from rich developed countries. Trotsky's antagonism to the very idea of socialism in one country, while articulated with all the theoretical drama of which he was well capable, was, to our mind, a major step in making Trotskyism into a movement possessing highly revolutionary rhetoric usually out of step with practical necessities. We must reiterate here that we are not claiming by this assertion that Stalin's regime was always on the right course and Trotsky was always on the wrong one since it is obvious that Stalin took many fundamentally wrong turns throughout, proven most clearly by the ultimate collapse of the Soviet Union. The major question for Trotskyism in this context is whether his specific opposition to socialism in one country, a position that is one of the cornerstones of both Trotsky's response to Soviet experience and of almost all ensuing Trotskyism, is a progressive position.

Two factors are often noted in viewing early Soviet experience. One is the fact that not only did it have to industrialize without outside assistance, but that there was no blueprint for socialist industrialization in a predominantly peasant country. A traditional peasant society in its labour activities follows the dictates of nature; it is the seasons, the weather, and the soil that determines when the work is done and how much to do. Work is extremely heavy in planting, growing, and harvesting in the warmer months and much lighter in winter months, perhaps more so in cold Russian conditions. Industrial work is much different from the labour of traditional peasant agriculture. It is routine, repetitive, and ongoing. The transformation of agricultural peasantry into industrial workers has never been easy and has always been resisted by the rural (and often romanticized) tradition. This great change took over fifty years in nineteenth century capitalism, and it occurred there with outrageous exploitation and wretchedness imposed on the new urban proletariat population, often with a tremendous disruption of traditional more or less stable agricultural conditions (witness the enforced English enclosure of small landholding in the countryside). What Marx called primary accumulation, the construction of machine production, which is the precondition for industrialization, was a process suffused with blood and tears. The Soviet system was faced with this enormous task to be done in breakneck speed for fear of attack by superior advanced capitalism and without the spur of competitive wages and fear of unemployment. That is, the commitment to a socialist economy was undertaken through a highly tyrannical industrialization process suffused with and in part sustained by the humane promise of a better life for all. A new kind of working class had to be forged by creating a technical basis for progressively better standards of living, but the fruits of this labour, usually promised in an undefined future, were not forthcoming for the working masses in what amounted to be a Soviet-style primitive accumulation.

The opposition to the Soviet Union by capitalism was symptomatic of capitalism's greatest fear: the fear of the very idea of socialism, even when such socialism was occurring in a weak and relatively harmless country like Russia. The scope and intensity of this hostility to the Soviet revolution was unprecedented. This antipathy is demonstrated in the first instance by the invasion of the infant Soviet Union by armies from 14 capitalist countries as soon as the First World War ended. Then, when the economic crisis of the post-war depression occurred in the West in the 1920s in Germany and in the rest of the capitalist world in the '30s, there arose in Germany and Italy, with sympathy from ruling classes elsewhere, the most virulently anti-socialist forces under the rubric of fascism. As early as 1922, Mussolini's black shirts marched on Rome and fascism secured its first triumph. Although the attempted socialist revolution in Germany after the First World War failed and the wave of working class militancy following that war subsided, the ruling classes of all advanced capitalist countries were deeply threatened by the possibility of revolutionary change. Standing as a material force and ideological symbol of that threat was the Soviet Union. While conventional scholarly and popular opinion usually dates the overt conflict between Soviet socialism (called communism in the West) and capitalism as a post-Second World War phenomenon, the 'cold war,' the real beginning of that conflict is more appropriately after the First War and the initiation of the Soviet Union. Only in this way can we more clearly understand the nature and significance of the rise of fascism, a system which had, as its first and major goal, the destruction of Soviet socialism.

Fascism was not, as is commonly believed, a political system that is unique to the nations of Italy and Germany. While taking full power in these latter nations, it was widely popular in all the advanced capitalist nation and, one might add, is still manifested in various forms up to this day. While the crimes of German fascism are almost always principally associated with anti-Semitism and the Jewish holocaust, we do not think that anti-Semitism is fascism's central defining characteristic. It did play a major role in German Nazism, but it was very secondary in Mussolini's Italy, and did not exist in Japan's brand of fascism. Only by understanding what is common to all of fascism – its appeal to capital and its relentless hostility to working-class organization and socialism – can we understand the nature of the beast.

Fascism promises and delivers one overwhelming important gift to any capitalist class. Being fundamentally anti-socialist, in fact hostile to egalitarian ideologies in general, it guarantees to that class that it will destroy any actual or potential independent political status to the working classes. When all is said and done, this is the meaning of the anti-socialism found in all fascist movements. In the deepening economic crisis in Germany in the 1920s and in the worldwide crisis of the depression in the 1930s, strong movements for socialist transformation arose in varying scope and intensity in various capitalist countries. While it may be questioned whether a revolutionary situation existed in any country, there is no doubt that ruling classes perceived a revolutionary danger. Enter fascism to fill the breach. Creating an atmosphere of national paranoia, jingoism, and the demand for military conquest, fascism deflects and explains away any crisis by creating false enemies and false causes – at that time trade unions, Bolshevism (socialism), and Jews; in our time feminism, Islam, blacks, and immigrants, among others. At its most acute as in Nazi Germany, it openly jettisons all the hard-fought gains made in the past and even democracy itself, all in the name of Aryan superiority and national purity. It promised and delivered prosperity by military expansion and conquest as long as such conquest was successful.

In all of the artistic and cultural critique of historical fascism in recent times, the whole period is subsumed by the centrality of the Jewish holocaust. This is so much the case that one commentator claimed that there is now a "holocaust industry"; the relentless turning out of cultural commentary where all other holocausts are seldom mentioned and where we are to understand Nazism only by equating it with anti-Semitism. In the very well-done movie about the Jewish holocaust, *Schindler's List*, it is highly significant that the inmate population presented in the concentration camps gave no sense that there was anyone else besides Jews in the camps – no socialists or communists or trade unionists or gays or Roma. Yet when Hitler came to power, it was mainly leaders on the left who were the first to be picked up and sent to concentration camps. With these acts, Hitler fulfilled the pledge, which brought him ruling-class financial support, a pledge that was the fulcrum that defined Nazi and fascist policy everywhere. It is for this reason that the Marxist interpretation of fascism sees it as capitalism showing its most extreme features, usually under conditions of crisis. This interpretation differs significantly from the widely-touted belief that capitalism and democracy are inextricably bound together, an interpretation that does not confront the basic fact that capitalism's connection to democracy appears more a matter of convenience than principle. Under conditions where there are real or perceived threats to the rule of capital, capitalism appears quite ready to either jettison democracy, or as is the case today in many capitalist countries, to dismantle central parts of the democratic process. What defines fascism or fascist tendencies is the attempt by capital to destroy the actual or potential possibility of working-class power and, in so doing, solidify the domination of capital.

During the revolutionary period in the Soviet Union, the regime was seen by literally all the media mills of capitalism as perhaps the greatest horror in history. For capitalism everywhere, the very existence of a socialist alternative was anathema; it had to be destroyed both as a real historical fact and as an ideal for humanity's future. Only capitalism must be accepted not only as the goal, but even the end of history. The overwhelming hostility of advanced capitalism, possessing industrial and military might far beyond that of the Soviet Union, was the continuing threat to the viability of the first great socialist experiment. Along with the obstacles presented by internal technical and cultural backwardness, the anti-Sovietism of capitalist societies goes a long way in explaining the course of Soviet programme and policy.

It is in this latter context that the Trotsky-Stalin conflict, a conflict that raged throughout Marxism in the 1920s and '30s, must be understood. If this context is not kept in mind, it is all too easy to see the conflict as one between personalities alone or as often a question of which of the contestants was right or wrong on specific policy questions at specific times. For example, it seems to us in hindsight (which we know is often easy) that Trotsky was more prescient about the danger of fascism when he called for a united front with social democracy to meet that menace; he was therefore right in criticizing the Soviet Union and the Communist International position of calling social democracy "social fascist," in consequence splitting the left and facilitating the fascist conquest of power. Rather, the meaning of Trotsky's role must be seen in the more general context of Soviet difficulties and of the way in which he became defined and defined himself (whether he realized it or not) not as a help in overcoming such difficulties, but as a continual carper living outside the realities of Soviet life. In this way, he appeared to be exacerbating those difficulties. With this in view, it becomes possible to see the connection between ultra-leftism and Trotsky.

Analysts of Trotsky's defeat and vanquishment vary greatly in their interpretation of these events. Sympathizers of Trotsky such as Isaac Deutscher see his downfall as a great historic tragedy. Some variation of this theme dominates almost all standard Western thought on the matter. For Deutscher, Trotsky is seen as a noble revolutionary figure standing head and shoulders above his contemporaries, brought down by the low manipulation of others. In this interpretation, Trotsky is a grand idealist and revolutionary innovator ultimately defeated by the plodding, dull, bureaucratic maneuverings of a man of petty stature like Stalin. In left-wing intellectual life, this would be an interpretation that, more or less, remains standard.

In Carr's historical analysis of the early Soviet Union, however, he does not indulge in lofty imagery as he looks at the struggle and defeat of Trotsky in straight political terms. That is, Carr discusses each major policy decision during that time and demonstrates how and sometimes why the positions of Trotsky lost and those of Stalin won. Carr concludes that Trotsky lacked the political acumen possessed by Stalin mainly because he maintained a lofty disdain for the details of political organizing and day-to-day gathering of support. Trotsky throughout, says Carr, was out of synch with political necessities. We think that, as far as it goes, this interpretation is manifestly true. But it does not answer the question of how he was out of synch in Marxist terms. Carr's recognition of Trotsky's separation from day-to-day politicking demands a deeper analysis of the ideological terms, which Trotsky represented in the process. Trotsky was first and foremost a man of the highest intellectual talent, an intellectual who valued these talents, it appears, often above all else; one who would, as the saying goes, "not suffer fools easily." He was also, as we mentioned before, a Marxist intellectual much in command of the powerful tools of Marxist analysis. These qualities, in Trotsky's hands, tended to meet crisis and difficulties with demonstrations of theoretical purity, a purity often divorced from practical necessities. These qualities lead to ultra-left mistakes, mistakes that ultra-leftism denies by again covering them with the lexicon of Marxism.

Although Trotsky was undoubtedly a great leader, orator, planner, and even administrator, he spent most of his political life at odds with Bolshevik policies and governance. Prior to the Revolution, he wrote and acted as perhaps the most striking opponent of the Bolsheviks and aligned himself primarily with the opposition Mensheviks. While an independent member of the Menshevik faction, he also opposed its conservative reformism since, throughout his career, Trotsky almost always couched his opposition in the most revolutionary terms. His attack on Lenin's conception of a party at that time was in terms of its alleged elitism whereas Trotsky considered that his own conception accorded with egalitarian principles rooted in the revolutionary working class. It is that class, he proclaimed, which will make the revolution and will need at most the guidance of outside leadership. That class does not need a professional band of leaders who, he said, will always stand above that class, and in the end will substitute bureaucracy for the working class' raw revolutionary energy. Lenin branded this position as amateurish, as leading without dedication or focus; and Trotsky later agreed with Lenin's critique by joining the Bolsheviks in 1917. We think, however, that Trotsky's opposition reflects more than simply irresponsibility. Whether as rejection of the party before the Revolution, appealing to the spontaneous energy of the masses as a counterweight to the very idea of a vanguard party or after the Revolution appealing to this same energy to oppose the existing Bolshevik Party in power, both cases have a distinctly ultra-left flavor. At the end, Trotsky's ultra-leftism took the form of defense of Lenin, at the same time rejecting any party that had been built on Lenin's principles. This became the hallmark of Trotskyism up to the present day: its continual opposition to Leninist parties while proclaiming itself Leninist. It can do this only by proclaiming that such parties, particularly when they are in power, are not representative of the 'real' working class, but are no more than elite bureaucracies.

Marxism is the most powerful tool of social and political analysis for understanding contemporary events. At its best, it is most prescient in foreseeing the unfolding development of capitalist society. It should not be surprising, therefore, if Trotsky, fully steeped in a Marxist mode of thought, should often demonstrate sparks of prescience; and this can occur at the same time that his major political tendencies remain ultra-left in consequence. This paradox often lies at the heart of ultra-leftism. The question of ultra-leftism, however, is complicated. For example, when Trotsky was first in exile, great economic and political crises were occurring in Germany and Trotsky foresaw their consequences.

In the late 1920s, deep depression descended on Germany, which had been defeated in the First World War and forced to pay huge reparations as a result of its defeat. Even before the Great Depression hit the rest of the Western world, Germany was also hit with galloping inflation, which literally wiped out the middle class. Echoes of revolution were again heard throughout the nation. Germany at this time possessed and industrial working class with a long history of militancy and was led by the largest socialist and communist parties ever seen in advanced capitalism. Had there been some unity between these two parties, there was some real possibility of blocking the Nazi accession to power. Instead, the International Communist Movement (the Comintern) led by the Soviet Party branded its socialist rivals as no better than fascists (in fact, as we mentioned, called them social fascists) and rejected any attempt at a common front against Nazism. In that conjuncture, the Comintern's policy was clearly ultra-left in its consequences. By this time, revisionism in the Soviet Communist Party was congealing. Russian national interest dominated both theoretical principle and effective analysis of concrete social conditions, in the USSR and abroad. In our view, such a situation leads to inconsistent politics, leaning towards right-wing tendencies but sometimes taking ultra-left swings depending on short-term, national needs. The USSR did reverse its policy on social fascism after Hitler had come to power in Germany, but only temporarily, and two other abrupt policy reversals occurred between 1939 and 1941.

The Comintern incorrectly prophesized that the economic collapse would precipitate a political crisis and an imminent working class revolution, making social democracy apparently counter-revolutionary. The ultra-left, social-fascist policy gravely split the working-class movement in the West and helped lead to Hitler's ascendancy. Trotsky from afar saw this problem most acutely, foresaw that the ruling class would jettison bourgeois democracy, where necessary, and turn to fascism. He warned of the dire consequences to follow and strongly urged a united front against fascism by all anti-fascist parties. His correct analysis in this case went unheard since it contradicted the Comintern's positivist interpretation of historical necessity. It was interpreted in the Soviet Union simply as sniping by an already defined enemy.

Overall, however, Trotsky's correct analysis of fascism was embedded in a series of ultra-left posturings, and the political movement he spawned, Trotskyism, has been suffused with ultra-leftism to the present day. For example, first he predicted that the New Economic Policy would not only fail, but that it would enthrone a new rural bourgeoisie. This would, he said, block the road to rural collectivization, a prediction proved false by the huge campaign of collectivization in the late twenties. He also strongly criticized the slow pace of industrialization in the 1920s, predicting dire consequences. The rapid pace of Soviet industrialization in the 1930s against a backdrop of worldwide depression and the increasing threat of fascism directed mainly against the Soviet Union again showed Trotsky to be dramatic, but wrong about the economic possibilities of Soviet development, articulating his criticism in the most revolutionary language.

Trotsky could not accommodate an analysis that might conceive the danger of counterrevolution as a slow process inherent, it appears, in all socialist revolutions (especially in backward societies, which have been the loci of all modern revolutions). For this kind of analysis, he had to see the Soviet Union not chiefly as a stimulus to revolution in the advanced industrial societies, but as a forerunner to revolutions in societies mired in imperialist oppression and kept perpetually underdeveloped. He would have had to accept the need for what Samir Amin has called a process of "delinking," of breaking with the imperialist stranglehold and forging a relatively independent process of development (itself full of new unforeseen problems). Stalin's acceptance of the idea of building socialism in the Soviet Union alone, called "socialism in one country" was then a more realistic response to conditions facing the country. This position was relentlessly attacked by Trotsky as itself a sign of reaction in the Soviet Union.

Trotsky along with Stalin and Lenin accepted one essentially nineteenth century problematic, and one which was later transcended by Mao Zedong. Lenin had defined socialism as Soviet power plus electrification. Implicit in this definition is the absence of class and class conflict in socialist society. There may have been recognition of remnants of older classes or backward ideologies within socialism, but as long as the working class has assumed state power and that state controls the "commanding heights" (Lenin) of the economy, this definition assumes an almost automatic transition to a classless society. Trotsky maintained this position to the end. Throughout his life, he conceived of Stalin's regime as a bureaucratic excrescence sitting atop an already solid socialist body. This corrupt and small tyranny was always in danger of joining what was left of the bourgeoisie along with rural kulaks to bring about a Thermidorean restoration of capitalism. His use of the word Thermidor in the twenties to warn of counterrevolution in the Soviet Union was the hallmark of Trotsky's analysis. In the original Thermidor, Napoleon's military coup reversed many of the radical and democratic aspects of the French Revolution, and ensconced a reactionary dictatorship. In Trotsky's view, Stalin and the party apparatchiks surrounding him had risen above party and class to become a dominating elite. To Trotsky, a working class in control of the means of production is always in a real position to overthrow the bureaucracy and solidify an already socialist society. From this body of ideas easily flows the later prediction made by Isaac Deutscher, a major defender of Trotsky in the post-Second World War years, that the rise of working-class living standards in the Soviet Union would lead the Soviet bureaucracy to lose hold of state power, and the nation would return to full proletarian rule.

This denial of any fundamental class analysis in socialist transition has had negative consequences for revolutionary Marxism. It has meant that the problems, which have arisen in the transition, have been interpreted in such wrong-headed ways that attempts to deal with them have often exacerbated the problems and even paved the way for capitalist restoration. This appears to be the case in the Soviet Union in the thirties, as was elaborated in the above discussion of Stalin. With Trotsky, he never veered from the view that bureaucracy alone was the major obstacle to a smooth transition to a classless society, and the view has been a mainstay of Trotskyist ideology to the present day. Moreover, this view usually does not view the bureaucracy as having the potential to become a new bourgeoisie, a view that could have linkage to a Marxist analysis. Instead, the bureaucracy is simply a sickly appendage on a healthy body. Cut off the appendage and there will be smooth sailing.

A fundamental characteristic of an ultra-left approach is its unrealistic optimism about the working class, what has been called left spontaneism. This aspect seems to apply to Trotsky and to subsequent Trotskyism. Throughout his career in exile, his conception of the Soviet regime rests on the assumption of an inherent revolutionary zeal among the Soviet working class, which will at any day erupt and overthrow its bureaucratic masters. This assumption, it seems to us, explains why he rejected the obvious idea that the working class was no more the master of its fate and that a new class may be in the process of taking power. This romanticization of the working class also may explain why Trotskyism has often had a great appeal among idealist young. It explains as well the easy connection that Trotskyists have had with the recent upsurge of anarchism in both the new left of the 1960s and 1970s and with contemporary youth rebellions. While Trotskyism in theory embraces the idea of a Leninist party, its comfortable relationship with anarchism in practice seems more central to its activities.

In spite of its tendency to itself splinter into smaller sects in conflicts over small doctrinal differences, Trotskyism retains definite features connecting it to its founder. First is its assumed dedication to a Leninism purer than the party of Stalin and therefore purer than all existing parties, which do not blankedly reject the experience of the USSR under Stalin. Thus, there is a rejection of all existing parties as supposed repositories of Stalinist, anti-democratic bureaucracies. Finally is the appeal to the revolutionary militancy of the masses to overthrow these bureaucracies. These positions whether taken polemically or with gentle persuasion have put Trotskyism into opposition with almost all post-Soviet socialist revolutions. In never getting beyond the bogeyman of Stalinism, Trotskyism becomes rooted in a perpetual anachronism from which it appears it cannot extract itself. The perpetual ultra-left dilemma that Trotskyism reflects is the categorical rejection of all post-Stalin socialist experience. This problem was certainly complex in the post-1945 cold war era, the dominance of the USSR over its satellite countries in Eastern Europe revealed a new form of 'social' imperialism. In our view, however, contextually, not all imperialisms should be treated alike in all circumstances. The hyper aggressiveness of German and Italian fascism necessitated an anti-fascist alliance among progressive forces and bourgeois democrats world-wide. Following the Second World War, the Soviet Union played a significant role in the international struggle within so-called third world nations against American imperialism. This aid was not the socialist internationalism to which both Trotsky and Lenin would have aspired, but it deserved critical support at the time. Marxists were caught in a bind because condemnation of the Soviet Union played into the hands of Western imperialism. It is characteristic of ultra-leftism that this contingent nuance is lost in the demand for revolutionary purity and the rejection of compromise.

At this late date, it does not appear surprising that Trotsky's response to his exile and to his almost total estrangement from the Soviet regime would be articulated in leftist terms. To himself, Trotsky was always a quintessential revolutionary Marxist. As a regime which had spurned him, he could not see it as anything but a betrayal of Marxism, as a counterrevolutionary turn to the right. He himself, as we have said, referred to the regime as "the revolution betrayed," but it is his interpretation of how and why the betrayal had occurred, which defines Trotsky's role in revolutionary history and puts its stamp on the Trotskyism that evolved with and after his life. Trotsky's attempt to create a fourth international to oppose the Comintern was doomed from the start to insignificance. In hindsight, it is not difficult to create new 'parties,' whether Trotskyist or supposedly communist, or attract, for a time, a coterie of like-minded members. Such political groupings have a tendency to split over issues of doctrine and moral high-mindedness.

Trotsky's analysis of the worm in the Bolshevik Revolution remained mired in personality. Fundamental to Trotsky's interpretation of events is his perception of the place of Stalin in the whole Soviet experience. So important is Stalin in Trotsky's view that often Stalin's very personality is seen to personify the very essence of counterrevolution. It might be said that without Stalin, there is no Trotskyism, but as a Marxist, he could not avow that Stalin alone is the problem for this would signify the disavowal of wider social factors as the basic motive force of history. The issue of social class tends to disappear from Trotsky's analysis to be replaced by the concept of bureaucracy. To repeat, the bureaucracy was seen, however, as an excrescence, as a foreign element in a still healthy revolutionary society. We have surmised that this formulation was necessary in order to defend a revolution in which Trotsky was himself a central figure, at the same time opposing almost everything that the revolution had become. He had little to add to the question of class problems facing a socialist society in transition beyond the potential danger posed by a rural petty bourgeoisie. The Soviet regime, to Trotsky, became a strange amalgam for a Marxist – a worker's state ruled by a (temporary) administrative tyranny called Stalinism. Significantly this conception of the Soviet Union has become part and parcel of conventional wisdom whether from the left or from the right. The end of Stalin and his bureaucracy should, according to Trotsky, generate a flowering of the revolutionary essence of that society. Of course, as we now know, this did not happen, and a Marxist understanding of why not cannot be elaborated without an understanding of the next development of revolutionary Marxism in the Chinese experience.

The problems involved with the initiation of Trotskyism, we would contend, dog it up to the present day. Trotskyism like anarchism, has a long and checkered history and we do not intend to do a detailed history of this variegated subject. What muddies the waters somewhat is the fact that there have been many Trotskyisms since there have been many groups in many places often in contention with each other, yet identifying with its central viewpoint. Our view, however, is that this outlook, regardless of its variegated forms, is uniquely connected to Trotsky's original conflict with Stalin and his interpretation of this conflict, and that all subsequent Trotskyisms continue to do battle with the ghost of this conflict, a ghost that is only vanquished by transcending the very terms with which that battle has been fought.

While we are uncertain about what is a positive direction right now, we are more fairly confident about certain negative lessons from the experience of the Soviet Union. The latter include opposition to the idea of 'Stalinism' in its strictly individualistic, tyrannical terms since this makes no Marxist sense. Trotsky's condemnation of the Soviet Union as a distorted workers' state is not correct. (Trotsky was approached with the idea that the Soviet state under Stalin represented a new ruling class and rejected this conception, suggesting that Trotsky, without the later advance by Mao, cannot be seen as simply overwhelmed by an objective Alp). Rather, Trotsky himself was completely personalistic on Stalin, which we see as not a small mistake.

Conclusion

WE ARE LEFT with Stalin as an initiator of revisionist directions with the Lenin recruitment, but with revisionism as a process not consolidated until later with the mid-thirties constitution. Without class analysis and with a lockstep party, the purges become the only response to internal opposition and are reflected in the paranoid atmosphere of the period. The zigs and zags of Soviet policy become the result of both objective conditions facing this new and economically poor revolution and of budding revisionism. Trotsky's potshots, sometimes hitting the mark, reflect an overly personalistic theory of what was going on, but should also be seen in the context of all other opportunistic undermining of the Soviet experiment at the time; that is, in the face of worldwide opposition and rejection of this first revolution, Trotsky's type of opposition plays into reactionary channels.

Between the NEP and 1941, many of the specifically socialist policies implemented after the Revolution had been erased or eroded, including the loss of many rights specific to women, changes in education, and the turn to nationalism. Material incentives were expanded as socialist consciousness waned. While socialism implies distribution according to the principle, to each according to her or his work, these reversals were not theorized as temporary moves away from socialism with a conception of how they would themselves be reversed as the conditions for socialism were built. Instead they were normalized in Soviet Marxism. Second, the rudimentary class analysis of the 1936 Constitution failed to address the specific circumstances and contradictions of the socialist transition. What was required was an analysis of the contradictions of socialist construction, such as between town and country, between the intelligentsia and workers (mental and manual labour), and between centralization and internal party democracy. Third, despite the existence for many decades after 1956 of the socialist economic shell (central planning, state ownership, the denial of inheritance rights etc.), central control, as in one-person-management, coupled with the special prerogatives of income and power created a relatively permanent class-in-embryo that was able quickly to convert public to private ownership when the USSR collapsed in 1989.

Finally, it was crucial to address the handling of contradictions between the party and the working classes. Not least to consider is the dilemma that party policy designed to reflect the most advanced proletarian consciousness is typically in advance of the consciousness of most of the people. This gap cannot be addressed solely by formal socialist propaganda or mere administrative tools, which easily become manipulative and repressive. The key is the relationship that has been established between local leadership and the people, but in the history of the USSR, this relationship had not just withered, but had been largely emptied of any real content and become consistently one-sided. Consequently, the Party experienced a long-term erosion of its legitimacy that made possible the easy transition in 1989 to private capitalism and the semblance of bourgeois politics. By that time, revisionism in the USSR had been entrenched for decades. In this circumstance, no genuine return to socialism was possible. The only question was how long the socialist shell could be preserved before the burgeoning capitalist class threw off the shackles that hindered its consolidation as a ruling economic and political class.

When Trotsky and Luxembourg rejected the Leninist theory of the party, they were at one with the whole Marxist world (and Trotsky changed his mind on this at the right time). But Trotsky's theory of 'Stalinism' as Asian despotism came at the wrong time and he never changed his mind. Moreover, even if the Soviet Union was ineluctably moving into revisionism, it was still the first great revolution in uncharted fields, still the major opposition and major socialist example in the face of overwhelming Western capitalist power, and potentially a bulwark against burgeoning fascism. Trotsky added a chorus from the left to the fascist and the traditional capitalist opposition to the Soviet Union. In so doing his leftist credentials and his leftist language forces us, I think, to classify the Trotskyism that he originated as essentially ultra-left while realizing that the long time frame of Trotskyist existence would indicate some straight opportunist vacillations as well. It is on these grounds that Trotskyism has been seen as forever splintering, at the same time opposing existing revolutions as Stalinist. Finally with the re-growth of anarchism in recent times, we find Trotskyist groups finding their natural bedfellows.

To repeat in conclusion, the early Trotsky was a left-wing Menshevik prior to the Soviet Revolution, and a theorist and intellectual of the first order. While he condemned reformism, he was still aligned with what must be labeled a right opportunist political position. He joined the Bolsheviks on the eve of the Revolution, and the clarity of demands and the solidity of the Party brought Trotsky's talents to the fore. His gifts in oratory, writing, and his administrative abilities led him to the front ranks of the Bolshevik Party, second only to Lenin. After Lenin's death, the baggage of his Menshevik past, his disdain for intra-party politics, and his opposition to the NEP resulted in Stalin's accession to power and to Trotsky's political demise. His inexorable movement into de facto leadership of the left opposition was the final stroke against him, a defeat that he increasingly interpreted in what we consider personalist and non-Marxist terms. Moreover, his intellectual gifts, however unintentional, were of great assistance in the ideological assault by conventional bourgeois thought against the Soviet

Union. The idea that the Soviet Union up to Stalin's death and beyond was little more than a Stalinist tyranny was certainly much assisted by the ideas of Trotsky. After Trotsky's death, his ideas, even when couched in a Marxist rubric, have been a means of opposing and criticizing all subsequent socialist revolutions on the altar of anti-Stalinism. Ironically, with the sinking of almost all of existing socialist societies into revisionism or outright capitalism, Trotskyism continues as a movement, or a series of movements, which proclaims its purity as a Leninist heritage still carping against the bogeyman of Stalinism. History is indeed often wondrous in its surprises and permutations.

CHAPTER SIX

Mao and Marxism

IN THE WEST has arisen a view about the Chinese Revolution and the place of Mao Zedong within it which we believe clouds rather than clarifies the significance of Mao and his place in revolutionary history. Much of this cloudiness is implicit in the usage, common to almost all points of view including those of contemporary Marxists, of the term "Maoism" to refer to Mao's historical record. In conventional anti-Marxist Western thought, Maoism is used as an epithet suggesting that Mao deserves a place in the pantheon of the worst of historical despots such as Hitler, Stalin, and Genghis Khan. In Western Marxist circles Maoism has been used as a positive term by ultra-leftists who in the 1970s and '80s, created immediate Leninist groups they called "parties" with little connection to actual circumstances, and it was used as a negative term by social democrats of various stripes who used it as an epithet to condemn or avoid talking about Leninism. We find all this strange since Chinese thought during the socialist period used the term "Mao's thought." This may appear to be a very small point but the adding of an 'ism' to the political contributions of a major historical figure suggests that his/her life involved some significant and unique addition to contemporary experience. While recognizing that Mao was a great revolutionary leader, we think that the greatness is not of the order of Marx or Lenin. Therefore, the use of the 'ism' is a sign of something else going on in the political arena, something we think is not very progressive in its consequences. The present chapter hopes to articulate the problems surrounding this strange dualism of 'thought' from 'ism.'

There is much ambiguity and division within contemporary Marxism in the evaluation of the contribution of Mao Zedong to revolutionary thought and action. Evaluation of Mao becomes even more troublesome, especially for those outside China, by the fact that, while he died in 1976, translation of his written work stops in 1958 and his activities in later life lack firm documentary basis for evaluation. To add greater cloudiness to the problem, the Chinese themselves have made major changes in their interpretation of Mao's life and work. The once seemingly simple evaluation of Mao and of the Chinese Revolution so prevalent in Western progressive thought in the late 1960s and early '70s has changed, under the impetus of recent Chinese events, to great perplexity.

The biographical details of Mao's life are rather sketchy compared, say, with those of Marx or Lenin, but they are now fairly well established at least until official biography takes over, and his significance as a public figure often outweighs everything else. His life and his thought both originate in the cauldron of the most revolutionary period in Chinese history, and his own thought became so intertwined with, if not generative of, the success of the Chinese Revolution that the Revolution and his thought often appear and are presented as almost one and the same thing.

Mao was born in 1892 the son of a well-to-do peasant – such prosperity in China at the time being defined by some minimal economic security and the ownership of enough land and tools to hire extra farmhands. His father was a working farmer himself, not a non-working landlord, but his wealth permitted the son to go to school and become literate. This economic background was more stringent than most of China's early communist leaders who, like Zhou Enlai for example, usually came from landlord or officials' families, but it was still privilege by Chinese standards. Even for this most indigent of China's early leaders, it confirms Lenin's cogent observation that Marxism is first introduced to working classes by people external to those classes. In China, the simple fact of reading and writing at that time put one in a far more fortunate condition than the vast majority of the population.

Early Revolutionary Theory and Practice

ALL OF MAO'S biographers mention the concurrence of his own life's activities with the significant events affecting China in this century. This along with the fact that he never studied abroad (as did many Chinese intellectuals at the time) gives his whole style and political outlook a particular rootedness. It also gives Mao's Marxism a cast, which responded to the unique problems of China's history. While still very young in 1911, Mao lived through the final termination of the Manchu monarchy, a domination of China by a foreign minority, which had lasted four centuries. At the same time, he was witness to the steady intervention into China of the new, more dynamic, and more powerful forces of Western imperialism. The explosion of national protest against such penetration by the May Fourth Movement in 1919 found Mao in the middle of the movement. Thus, his early experience as someone fully immersed in the dense cultural milieu that is China and having encountered the threat to it from external power made Mao, and Chinese Marxism in general, extremely sensitive to the connection between national independence and socialist revolution. This is now fairly taken for granted but was not so easily accepted in Europe at the time when many Marxists (Rosa Luxembourg for one) considered nationalism and Marxism as eternally contradictory ideologies.

The holocaust of the First World War and its aftermath were a watershed in contemporary history and they were especially significant in the formation of specific ideas, which became so firmly implanted in Mao that he never wavered from them for the rest of his life. It was then that he became a Marxist and a Marxist of a distinctly Leninist stamp. For a young progressive intellectual living in old China at that time, the issue of making China modern and developed was the first order of the day. China had no tradition of liberal capitalism; instead, what was known of capitalism was its completely negative side, its imperialist depredations, the carving up of China by various Western capitalist powers.

The revolutionary Marxist interpretation of the First World War as a voracious conflict between equally imperialist plunderers fell on sympathetic ears in China. Even Sun Yat Sen, the first great hero of modern Chinese nationalism, although no Marxist himself, was quite responsive to this interpretation of the Great War. The other Marxist interpretation of the war, the reformist one, which advocated to the working class of its own nation that its own militarism was progressive and that of its enemy expansionist, had little credibility in China. None of the reforms that gave foundation to such an interpretation had happened there. To speak of liberal capitalist development for China or of a slow evolutionary accretion of working class reforms leading inevitably to socialism had very little meaning in a country where neither of these processes had ever occurred and where Western imperialism appeared to be a major factor in restricting their appearance. Thus for Mao, as has been true for Marxists in the underdeveloped world ever since, the revolutionary interpretation of Marxism, which later has been associated with Leninism, was quite simply and naturally the only Marxism.

And it was at this time, by his own account, that Mao became a Marxist. He had, also by his own account, up to that time been a somewhat sentimental dreamer, a lover of old Chinese novels with a penchant for those about bandits and rebels. He was certainly full of indignation about the rampant injustices around him, but until his readings of Marxist works and his meeting with some of the first Marxist scholars and intellectuals (especially when working in the library in Peking University), this indignation did not take systematic theoretical form. The Chinese intellectual tradition had more in common with elite theory than class theory. The main differentiating factor was whether you belonged to the elite of officials or the mass of peasants. Applying Marxism to China necessitated a different analysis of Chinese political economy; for example, applying the designation 'feudal' to traditional China is problematic, although the term is more applicable to Japan. Feudalism refers to the existence of a local and regional ruling class that is in significant ways independent of central authority. Marx had briefly theorized an Asiatic mode of production, parallel to ancient slavery and feudalism, characterized by political despotism and the extraction of surplus from relatively independent village communities. In these terms, class conflict took place between peasants and the agents of central authority.

Under pressure from Western imperialism in the nineteenth and early twentieth centuries, the Chinese class structure was being transformed. The peasantry became increasingly differentiated, markets expanded, and landlordism became a significant factor in the countryside. The emergence of warlordism in the countryside had feudal connotations. From a rudimentary class structure, China was becoming a more complex class society, which made it ripe for Marxist analysis. Furthermore, class conflict in the form of peasant rebellion was endemic to Chinese history, the most recent a massive and almost successful one in central China in the mid-nineteenth century (the Taiping Rebellion). All that seemed missing, according to Mao, was the theoretical understanding of this conflict and the application of the theory to the tasks of the day. Marxism appeared to be the only theory offering a solution to the problems China faced.

The existence of Marxism as a theory to explain and respond to Chinese conditions was paralleled by an event outside of China, which was certainly equally as important in Mao's embracing of Marxism. This was the first practical success of Marxist theory in action: the victory of the Bolshevik Revolution in Russia. Up until that victory, Marxism was no more than a theory – a theory that perhaps explained the world better than other theories, but still a theory not proven by experience. Now in Russia, Marxism had been validated by its success in application to a concrete set of circumstances. This is what makes the Russian Revolution not only a watershed in twentieth century history, but perhaps the great watershed in the theory that interpreted and made that revolution. When Mao Zedong and the small band of progressive Chinese met to form the Communist Party of China in Shanghai in 1921, the revolution in Russia was the beacon and stimulator for its own thought and activities. The very fact that they called their party "communist," a name that was not used for such parties until the Russian Bolsheviks renamed their party in 1919, was symptomatic of this close alliance.

Not only had the Russian revolutionaries renamed their party a communist party; they had also in 1919 been instrumental in forming a federation of kindred parties into a new international organization – the Third International (Comintern). This development marks the great division between the Marxism of the Second International with its dedication to reform of capitalism through parliamentary processes and that of the Third International with its emphasis on the need for insurrectionary overthrow of capitalism (with reform being accepted as a tactical moment in the process). As has already been indicated, for Mao, under China's conditions there could be no other choice but revolutionary Marxism (leaving aside the question of which Marxism appears more or less valid on its own terms). Moreover, there were more specific features of this Marxism, which bore the imprint of Lenin's thought since he was the major impetus behind the success of the Russian Revolution. These features form the bedrock of Mao's Marxism and remained a core of principles for almost sixty years of revolutionary life. They are the reasons why he always considered himself not only a revolutionary Marxist, but a Marxist-Leninist. In discussing, as we do later, the specific changes and new emphasis Mao brought to Marxism, it is important to remember this bedrock of ideas.

The most fundamental assumption of the Marxism of Lenin, so fundamental that it remained implicit and unspoken, was that social theory should prove itself primarily in action rather than contemplation. Lenin was a Marxist who took seriously Marx's oft-quoted thesis on Feuerbach that the purpose of theory is not just to interpret the world but to change it. The dedication to this purpose gives Lenin's Marxism and Mao's, which followed him, a singularly political direction. Lenin's methodological position on social theory stresses that the passive observation of social classes cannot but elicit partial truth. The testing of theory by its intervention into ongoing social experience becomes an indispensable necessity. The very common critique of Marxism that it tends to freeze history into a solidified dogma, a critique that does indeed apply to some Marxists, cannot apply to Lenin or Mao. Lenin's attack on what he called the economism and spontaneism of Russian Menshevism represents an attack on the attempt to revivify and deepen this major methodological position. If humanity is an historical animal, an animal who can change and become different through the discovery of knowledge through experience, then experience itself is the crucible for confirming theoretical knowledge. There is little that is purely academic in Lenin and even less in Mao. The basis of this is not the obvious fact that they were practicing politicians rather than university scholars, but because they believed that Marxism as social theory could not develop outside the din and smoke of everyday political battle. Even those studies by Lenin such as *Imperialism* or *State and Revolution*, which did not appear to be directed to immediate political needs, were written both to attack contemporary political enemies and to prepare the way for future action.

In Mao's case, this methodological stricture is even more completely adhered to. His writings have such a singularly political bent, usually taking up with immediate and practical needs that, while they are suffused with general Marxist theory, their style is ordinary and even homiletic. Even more abstract treatises like "On Practice" or "On Contradiction," written later and in quieter times, still maintain this down-to-earth quality. More to the point, the analytic investigation of the class structure of Hunan done in the middle 1920s was written with an eye to direct action by and with the peasantry in the immediate present. The reason why in Mao one finds little, for example, of Marxist economic analysis of value and surplus value is because these more long-range categories were taken as given, and they were not so clearly useful in the battles of the moment. These economic categories, so relevant for explaining both prosperity and impending crisis in capitalist society, could remain unexamined in the permanent crisis that was China. Thus, the even greater 'political' emphasis of Mao's Marxism evolves both from what he considered central to Marxism and from the objective conditions demanding action for the validation of those ideas.

Another equally significant aspect of Lenin's development of Marxism, which was implicitly accepted by Mao, was the type of leadership considered necessary for a socialist revolution. When Mao and the small body of militants met in 1921, they may have been quite naive, as Mao himself later admitted, about defining the contours of a revolutionary programme for China, but they were not at all doubtful about the nature of the leadership for that revolution. It must be a party of the Bolshevik type, demanding full revolutionary commitment from its members, tightly organized and disciplined, and unified by a body of principles and policies. Given the absence of a liberal tradition in China, it is doubtful whether any opposing conception of a party, based on more Menshevik ideas of loose commitment, loose organization, and internal ideological diversity was raised even as a theoretical alternative.

This dedication to a centralized party was due not only to the fact that revolutionary efficiency under conditions of repressive authoritarianism demanded it, but because both Lenin and Mao believed that the ethos and ideology of such a party represent the microcosm of a socialist future. They rejected all preexisting types of parties, again, not only because they ultimately could not be effective in transforming society, but because such parties created and recreated leadership, which embodied all the older values – elitism, careerism, backroom decision-making, privilege-seeking – which a real revolution must fight against. There is much skepticism on this point, especially after the debacles of the later twentieth century when so many of these parties of a Leninist type were far from rejecting these older values (indeed they could usually be characterized by them). This all important fact notwithstanding (and it was Mao whose later life became extremely involved in countering this troublesome fact), the *theoretical* conception of such a party is formulated as an attempt to discover, maintain, and deepen new values, those representing a rising revolutionary class.

Mao took very seriously the idea that such a party must not only be centralist in programme and action, but democratic in spirit and conduct. The latter would appear to be extremely difficult in an overwhelmingly traditional country steeped in customs of unquestioned respect for status and authority, but there is little doubt about the seriousness of the intent to build such an attitude and outlook. It also seems clear that the overall success of this party through the anti-Japanese struggle to the early years of the Revolution in mobilizing long and deep support among the masses of Chinese people could not have been done without the Party communicating such a spirit in its relation with the people. Guerilla warfare requires a close connection between revolutionaries and the people. What later came to be called the "spirit of Yenan" appears to have been real and represents the success in initiating a close, reciprocal relationship between leadership and populace in areas where revolutionary activity was effectively established. Sustaining this relationship through the various stages of the socialist transition proved to be a difficult problem. In addition, as to how well the ethos of democracy took hold in the internal workings of the Party – that is probably another matter. Many Chinese would be the first to admit that democratic operations are not the norm in the Party, but little is said about how much this has always been so.

Although there would be much debate in China today about Mao's overall role in creating an undemocratic climate in the Chinese Party, especially during his last decades, there is some evidence that Mao was aware of this problem and might have done something to counter it. During the Cultural Revolution, Mao has been quoted as being dissatisfied with being treated as a Buddha. What has been called the cult of the personality was, it appears, distasteful to Mao in his later years. At one time he even complained about the unwillingness of party members to speak freely in his presence. These bits of information would indicate some commitment to egalitarian conduct, or at least a dissatisfaction with its absence. That there was a cult of personality surrounding Mao is clear. The argument that such an Emperor cult is unavoidable in a traditional society does not excuse the failure actively to confront it. Worse was the use of this cult for political purposes. Westerners know more about Mao's personal life now than they did in the later twentieth century; from wanting to highlight Mao's achievements, Western biographers became more interested in the sometimes sordid details of his private life. But, more importantly, they provide bits of information about inner-Party workings and nothing more. In addition, in the case of the Chinese Revolution, there is a great paucity of hard documentary evidence about the operations of the Party. When the Chinese present the history of the Party, it is done at the very general level by presenting ideological disputes and their resolution without giving the specific debates that went into these disputes. Whether there was a full airing of the various positions on the dispute, whether the atmosphere was one of intrigue and manipulation, or whether the results were by collective or by authoritative ruling are simply impossible to know. It is upon information like this that one must depend on coming to conclusions about Mao's potential contribution to deepening Marxist knowledge on this all important issue.

The difference in the Russian case is very revealing on this matter of inner party democracy. Even the greatest opponents of Lenin and all that he stood for would probably admit that the internal workings of his party were full of the storm and stress, of forthcoming debate and straightforward airing of views. The evidence found in clearly documented presentations of these debates completely bears out these views. It is rarely said even by non-Marxist scholars that Lenin forced his views on his party or that he was followed as a result of fraud or threat of force.

In fact, what at first glance creates suspicion about a change in the Soviet Union to authoritarian rule in the Stalin era is absence of concrete information about how the Soviet Party then operated.

The same suspicion exists during the whole period of Mao's leadership of the Chinese Party, and following the Cultural Revolutionary period, such suspicion turned to downright distrust among many Chinese. What can be said, however, about differences between the Chinese and Russian case is the much greater weight of a customary, non-democratic tradition in the former. If Mao was committed to truly democratic norms in the Chinese Party, he must have faced overwhelming obstacles in a society with thousands of years of sanctified obedience to a single authority.

It must be concluded, then, that Mao did not appear to develop Marxist ideas about party organization beyond Lenin's. Neither has anyone else, however, and given the lack of party development truly representing ideas of democratic centralism (if anything, most existing Leninist parties demonstrate a marked divergence from such ideas), this absence remains a very great problem in contemporary Marxism. It is to Mao's credit, in opposition to all those parties, which claim that everything is always going swimmingly, that he recognized this problem and tried to do something about it at the end of his life. That attempt, which initiated over a decade of turmoil in China, is very significant for Marxism, but more about that later in this chapter.

Contributions to Marxism

IT IS IN HIS RESPONSE to the demands of Chinese events and possibilities that Mao Zedong made his major contribution to Marxism. Official histories in China often present Mao's ideas as if they sprung full-grown from 1921 onward; such glorifications do not help in understanding the way ideas really develop. It is obvious in Mao's remark about the amateurishness of the first communists in China that his own ideas were no more than embryonic at that time. Again, sadly, there is little information about the origin of specific ideas and how they were refined in the face of opposition and with greater experience. What we do know is that Mao's ideas had a long struggle before becoming the authoritative ones in the Chinese Party. Until 1935 in the midst of the Long March, when Mao became undisputed Party leader, he fought an uphill battle against both internal Chinese opposition and that of the Communist International based in Moscow. The reason for this opposition lies in the nature of revolutionary Marxism's understanding of the Russian Revolution and its significance for revolution elsewhere.

The major critique made by the Second International of the victory of the Bolsheviks in Russia, the critique of Karl Kautsky and Julius Martov, was that it was not a real revolution, and if it was, it could not last since it had occurred in the wrong place at the wrong time. They based this critique on what they considered to be completely in line with the original ideas of Marx and Engels that socialism could take power and fully evolve toward a communist future only in societies at the pinnacles of capitalist development. Since they assumed that societies without advanced productive forces and without an industrial working class mastering such forces could not initiate a socialist experiment, so this critique saw the Marxist role in pre-revolutionary Russia to be one of stimulation of that society in its development of capitalism, not socialism. Lenin's recognition that a socialist regime could take power in backward Russia was therefore a great break with prevailing orthodoxy. It was such a break that Lenin himself was quite tentative in the theoretical meaning of the revolution he did so much to inspire. Right up to the end of his life in 1924 he still considered the Russian Revolution as a catalyst for revolution in the more advanced countries and he considered these latter revolutions to be indispensable in their potential assistance to the Soviet one. Although he never went so far as to deny the possibility of socialism maintaining itself in one backward country, his own thought was certainly open to question on this matter. Thus, while Lenin's theory of uneven development under imperialist conditions was an attempt to explain why revolution came to backward Russia first, it remained in his hands a theory of a special case. The generalization of the case to a theory of revolution for a whole epoch was left for Mao.

The fact that Russia was a predominantly peasant country in the pre-1917 period had not been neglected in Lenin's formulation of a political programme. He saw the hope of revolutionary insurrection as an alliance between the peasantry and the industrial working class. Even though the latter was a small minority in the coalition, it was still considered the leading element. According to Lenin, the dominance of a proletariat was what assures the revolution of its socialist direction. This remains the case even when the party of that class is recruited originally from disaffected members of the middle and ruling classes. Thus, Marxist control over this alliance of classes through a unified body representing the new rising class is indispensable, even if that class is a minority as it was in Russia and was even more the case in China.

The needs of the peasantry in Russia and in societies similar in class composition, according to this view, must be met by a programme of land reform, which breaks down large feudal estates and slakes the peasant thirst for land. This part of the programme, however, was frankly acknowledged to be a response to the 'backward' demands of the peasantry, since it would produce a countryside full of small, profit-minded farmers. This outcome would especially be the case when technically advanced estates had to be broken down, but Lenin considered the land hunger of the peasantry to be fully legitimate at that time. Intrinsic to this view, however, is the perceived transitional nature of this alliance; the hope, if not the probability, that socialist revolution would bring a rather swift transformation of the peasantry into a modern, literate, industrialized working class. The tremendous growth of farm machinery resulting from industrialization would lead to the regrowth of large-scale farming, this time operated by a new, advanced, cooperative, and cooperating class. Lenin's reliance upon the future technical assistance to be granted by revolution in the more developed countries of the West – Germany was at that time in turmoil and revolution seemed imminent – was one of the reasons for this optimism. Even when the New Economic Policy had to reintroduce and reinvigorate a small peasant economy in war-ravaged Russia, the policy was avowed to be a step backward and of short-lived duration. To the Russian revolutionary, the peasantry still appeared steeped in what Marx had called "the rural idiocy" and was an extremely undependable ally. It is quite possible that precipitous agricultural collectivization in 1929 was rooted in the continuation of this attitude.

Although the proletariat of Russia was a minority seen literally to be drowning in a peasant sea, it was still that minority that essentially took power through the Bolshevik Party in the October Revolution. Lenin's whole policy from his return from exile in April 1917 until the success of the insurrection was to win over the working class of Petrograd, then organized into soviets, to a revolutionary programme. As soon as that programme controlled the majority of the representatives in the soviets then the Bolshevik Party, along with the working class of Petrograd, initiated and was quickly victorious in the overthrow of the Menshevik-led Provisional Government. What is significant in this event is that this was an essentially urban, industrial working class insurrection. Much has been made in hindsight about the fact that the Russian working class at the time was often little more than one generation from the countryside, but this appeared to have little effect on the relative divergence in political attitude between the working class and the peasantry; although some of the peasantry was also organized into soviets, many in a country as vast as Russia were not members of soviets and, more importantly, these soviets were not at any time prior to October led by a revolutionary Marxist programme. It can thus be said of the Russian Revolution that it was victorious because it took cognizance of the needs of the peasantry and therefore won its mutual support (especially due to the seriousness with which the Bolshevik Party implemented land reform), but the peasantry was a relatively secondary element in the popular insurrection.

We have reiterated these well-known facts about the Russian Revolution as a backdrop to an understanding of Mao Zedong's and the Chinese Revolution's initiation of a new direction in Marxist theory and practice. For Mao, the peasantry becomes not a secondary factor but a primary and active voice in the revolutionary process. He remained fundamentally Marxist in his commitment to the leading role of a Marxist Party but the peasantry of China became the major force in carrying out the revolutionary programme. This viewpoint was introduced against overwhelming odds both in his own Party and more especially in the Communist International but ultimately proved its validity and vindicated Mao. Even today, however, many people apparently adhering to a Marxist-Leninist outlook still consider that Mao was not really a Marxist, but a mere peasant revolutionary. The reason for this continuing critique resides in the strength of the traditional belief that a peasantry cannot be a leading revolutionary class.

Throughout the 1920s, the viewpoint of the Russian Revolution was the viewpoint of Chinese Marxism transplanted to Chinese circumstances. There it met with failure after failure. The working class of China, that infinitesimal minority living in cities, was supposed to carry out a quick and successful insurrection and draw the backward countryside into the revolutionary maelstrom. As a member of the Communist Party much impressed with the Soviet experience and influenced by its advisors, Mao took part in a number of fruitless attempts at urban insurrection in the 1920s. It is hard to know exactly when he recognized the bankruptcy of these attempts but we do know that by the late '20s he was the leader of a policy that was at odds with the prevailing one in his own Party.

In 1928, one year after the disastrous decimation of the Communist Party of China by Chiang Kai-shek's repression in Shanghai, Mao had set up a rural base for revolutionary activities in his native province of Hunan (actually on the border of neighboring Kiangsi Province). Although he called this a soviet base area, it differed from Russian soviets in important respects and it is these differences which indicate a new emphasis in Marxist theory. First of all, the construction of a relatively stable area controlled by revolutionary power, yet still existing in a nation whose government was hostile to revolutionary change (or usually hostile to any change at all), reflects an entirely new conception of the way revolutionary transformation was to take place. Instead of achieving power in an insurrectionary moment by toppling the existing regime through a mass upsurge, here was a movement that saw accession to power as a long process. The assault upon the barricades, the imagery of revolution which had dominated popular thought and action from the French Revolution to the Russian Revolution, is seen as unnecessary, if not downright adventurous. The disastrous attempts during the 1920s by the Chinese Party to rouse the urban working class and take and maintain power in Chinese cities had led Mao to jettison this old method. For him, the countryside became the focus for long-term social transformation, the lever for the conquest of nationwide power.

In conceiving this new more processual approach to revolution, Mao also had to articulate a much larger strategy for relations between revolutionary leadership and the populace at large. In the close interplay between leaders and led necessitated by all living and working together for a long period of time, the simple construction of sloganry to rouse people to action is not enough. Consonant with a deep Chinese affinity for questions of moral conduct, leadership had to prove itself worthy by building respect and legitimacy in everyday affairs. In the building of base areas and more significantly in maintaining them, issues of economic, military, political, and moral concern become highly intertwined and extremely dense. The much discussed and much misunderstood process of criticism of and self-criticism by the leadership during the Chinese Revolution often connected to massive movements, which were originally aimed at increasing mutual respect between the leadership and the people, was undoubtedly part and parcel of this new long-term view. Mao was instrumental in introducing this factor to modern Marxism even though it must now be admitted that the precise ingredients that go into the correct usage of criticism-self-criticism are now much open to doubt (especially after the obvious misuse of the practice during the Cultural Revolution).

For Mao, the peasantry became the prime movers in the revolutionary transformation of China. No more was an alliance by the working class with the peasantry a temporary or secondary phenomenon. At every step in the long years of taking power in China and in transforming the society afterwards, policy affecting the peasantry took centre stage. The revolutionary army that fought a long civil, national, and then civil war again was an overwhelmingly peasant army. The reforms leading to overthrowing landlordism, redistributing land, and then later to cooperatives and communes were the most significant reforms in the revolutionary process. When this was done most successfully, it demonstrated the application of Marxist theory at its best, combining firm commitment to the future with a clear and flexible grasp of problems of the present. As the next chapter demonstrates concretely, however, the theory of revolutionary transformation and the actual applications of policy are equally thorny if not intractable problems.

The reliance on the peasantry as the major force in making a socialist revolution represents more than a shift in mode of class alliances. It also signifies a whole shift in the location of such a revolution. Marxism arose as a theory by and for a proletariat in an urban industrial environment. The first successful revolution utilizing the theory occurred with the industrial proletariat as the main force but in a surrounding backward environment. Lenin considered the backwardness of Russia to be a stimulus for revolution (in his theory of uneven development and the idea of weakest link breaking the chain), but it was still a revolution dominated by an urban proletariat. Moreover, although the revolution in Russia was considered untimely, it was prophesied to be the catalyst for revolution in the advanced countries, which in turn would help backward Russia advance into the industrial age. This manner of thinking both explained the Russian Revolution and kept intact Marx's original ideas about transformation being a result of the most advanced state of industrialization led by a fully developed working class. Later, when the hoped-for and expected revolution in the West did not occur, Soviet thinking introduced the idea of socialism in one country, but even this was still seen as a response to an unfortunate necessity.

With Mao and the Chinese Revolution, backwardness is still something to be transformed, to be prodded and pushed into technical development. Moreover, the idea system, which conceived of the world in terms of class conflict with the proletariat as its vanguard, remains at the centre of his thought, which is why Mao is no Narodnik or rural populist, but remains firmly wedded to a Marxist viewpoint. But the peasantry and backwardness are not given short shrift. His famous statement that the Chinese peasantry are like a blank sheet of paper upon which beautiful characters can be written indicates the intensity of his belief in that class. That they are not, in fact, blank sheets may represent a significant misrepresentation by Mao. This notion makes the movement through revolutionary stages much less problematic than they proved to be. In his viewpoint, however, backward nations and backward classes become the galvanizing forces for revolutionary change.

At the theoretical level, this shift represents a deepening of the understanding of imperialism in the modern world. Lenin's recognition that capitalism in its monopoly stage carves up and retards the development of the underdeveloped world becomes for Mao the realization that socialism itself will be generated out of a battle against imperialism by the most oppressed section of the underdeveloped world. For Marx, capitalism is still a progressive force, which in conquering the world sets in motion new and expanding techniques of production. The rising bourgeoisie are the agents of that change and represent progress. Now with imperialism, development of a capitalist nature led by a local and independent bourgeoisie becomes impossible because the strongest of the native elite become completely dependent on external and all powerful imperialism for their existence. In the Chinese context, Mao called this comprador class "bureaucrat capitalists" and saw the Koumintang, from 1927 onwards, as the political representatives of that class. Capitalist development for China and for all underdeveloped countries becomes impossible under imperialism; only a clean break with capitalism through an anti-imperialist and socialist revolution can clear the path for progressive transformation of society. These ideas became standard stock-in-trade for revolutionary Marxism in the 1970s, but they gained ascendancy and demonstrated their validity through Mao's articulation and application of them.

Mao is perhaps best known for his contribution to the military side of revolution with his development of the techniques of guerrilla warfare. Since partisan warfare of an irregular nature has a long history, it cannot be said that he originated the idea. But he did deepen it and extend it much beyond anything before. The fact that a force, which in sheer numbers and military strength was weak, could defeat a much superior army, is a feat that could occur only with the application of careful planning, planning much beyond numbers of soldiers and ordinance. In Mao, the military aspect of warfare is intrinsically related to questions of politics, economics, and ideology. Guerrilla warfare cannot succeed by the mere stimulus of a band of brave men as advocated by anarchism (and by a later theory of "Focoism" emanating from the Cuban revolution). It can succeed only by building long-range support of the people through careful attention to their needs and their outlooks. This means that the guerrilla army itself had to be politicized in order that it be clearly distinguished from the traditional predatory armies of China. The image of successful guerrilla warfare as one of an army swimming in a peasant sea is still a popular image for movements of a similar type throughout the world, although their number and significance have been largely negated in the present.

The protracted nature of guerrilla warfare also had an effect on the idea of revolution itself. One victory does not a revolution make. Each victory is a prelude to even more battles, to future defeats as preludes to greater victories. Revolution is no more the preparation for one final cataclysm ushering in a totally new system, which peacefully unfolds towards the future. Revolution is a process of continual movement, of struggle, resolutions, and new struggles. Since for Mao, revolution was not only military deeds and economic reform but the construction of new ideological outlooks, so the struggle with old ideas is as important as the struggle with material forces. There can never be any rest in the revolutionary process since rest is often a symptom of potential decay. Mao's now famous aphorism that "unity is relative, but struggle is absolute" perhaps best sums up this processual outlook.

In his successful application of these ideas about the centrality of backward nations, the revolutionary potential of the peasantry, and the elaboration of the strategy and tactics of guerrilla warfare, Mao Zedong contributed a legacy so rich and significant that they remain vital to revolutionary Marxism today. That is, when one speaks about Marxism as a revolutionary theory, these ideas are often commonly accepted. The many successful revolutions that occurred and persisted for a time in underdeveloped parts of the world inevitably embody the crux of Mao's ideas. While Mao's legacy with regard to making a socialist revolution remains relatively accurate under the conditions of late imperialism, the same cannot be said for his ideas about maintaining the revolution. Here the limits of his theories become problematic in ways which are not at all clear since they hit at a reality that has thus far remained hard and impenetrable. They are especially problematic among the presently unresolved dilemmas of modern Marxism.

Mao's attempts to solve the problem of maintaining a socialist revolution in a wretchedly poor peasant nation still surrounded by highly advanced capitalist states necessarily involved two impetuses, one foreign and one domestic. As to the former, since Lenin, the foreign policy of socialist states had attempted to maintain the uneasy balance between coexistence with more powerful enemies and inspiration for revolution elsewhere. The overwhelming demands of economic development stimulated a more purely national policy in China where long-range peace and stability appear a necessity. Under Mao, the demands of international solidarity with rising revolution (as well as maintaining internal vigor) stimulated a policy of limited internationalism, tempered by concern about Russian revisionism.

Except for the central significance of the peasantry specific to the Chinese Revolution already mentioned above, the prestige and influence of the Soviet Union still made it the major model for development when the Communists took full power in China in 1949. Thus, the problems emanating from the need to develop socialism in a backward country encircled by much more technically advanced enemies were met in ways similar to, if not directly copied from, Soviet policies. In foreign policy this meant an accent on peaceful coexistence between different social systems and attempts to assist revolutionary movements where feasible; and in domestic policy it meant that economic development would emphasize the growth of heavy industry (a policy which has always been more or less inconsistent with the immediate needs of the peasantry). What is most distinctive about Mao's post-revolutionary activities appears to devolve from his growing disaffection from the Soviet model. And it is in the result of this disaffection that Mao's work is most surrounded with controversy.

In foreign policy, the Soviet position was based on the premise that the world was divided into a weak struggling and ever growing socialist camp headed by the Soviet Union and a much stronger but evanescent capitalist camp. Accordingly, China, the largest and most populous country ever to join the socialist camp was seen and saw itself as adding great weight to the cause of world-wide socialism. Moreover, while still engaged in revolutionary militancy, China took seriously the revolutionary side of foreign policy, the need to assist the upsurge of revolutionary activity elsewhere. In the tension between maintaining its own stability by building interdependence with capitalist states and enhancing revolution abroad, for a time revolutionary China seemed to emphasize the latter. To have offered and given the kind of aid in personnel and equipment to North Korea in the early 1950s when the Chinese economy was still in shambles after so many years of upheaval and foreign depredation is clear example of Chinese predispositions. China's Red Army became a proxy for direct Soviet intervention and, hence, direct conflict between the world's two super-powers. At the time, China was dependent on Soviet aid and a small army of economic advisors, and was still under the spell of Soviet industrialization.

Revisionism and Capitalism

AS HAS BEEN mentioned before, China's revolution took place in the context of a movement for national liberation by a semi-colonialized country, and it was this context that diverged from Soviet experience. For the Soviet Union, backward countries had become opportunities for weakening enemies with whom the Soviet Union fundamentally identified (for their level of industrialization was a target to be reached), whereas for the Chinese (through Mao, their greatest spokesman), backwardness was considered the fundamental condition for new types of development. While being no romanticizer of backwardness itself (no Marxist ever is), Mao still fully accepted the centrality of the underdeveloped world for revolutionary advance. Thus he categorically embraced the revolutionary potential demonstrated there and considered China's assistance to revolution in underdeveloped countries to be the central plank of China's foreign policy. In this difference lay the seeds of a great hiatus between Soviet and Chinese foreign policy. This would later develop into Mao's conception of three worlds rather than two worlds, a product of the complete split between Soviet and Chinese outlooks in the 1960s and up to Mao's death.

The problem of maintaining a revolutionary direction for a socialist society was one directly confronted by Mao and it was the one in which he made his last important innovation in Marxism. Since Chinese policy itself now considers much that Mao said and did on this problem to be either dubious or downright wrong, these later contributions are now clouded in controversy. The difficulties encountered by these problems bring us into the centre of the dilemmas of modern Marxism. The significance of Mao here lies less in the ways in which he failed to resolve these dilemmas (since they remain formidable indeed against the acts of any individual or group) than in the fact that he boldly faced the issues and refused to hide from the difficulties when it would have been so easy for him to do so. Mao recognized as no one else before him that a socialist regime could come to power by revolutionary means (that is, by popular insurrection) only to be subverted by counterrevolutionary forces internal to the socialist society itself. The Soviet Union, said Mao, while instituting a genuine socialist revolution in 1917, had by the mid-1950s become a society that had reinstated a new type of capitalist regime, despite the maintenance of the economic shell of government planning, state ownership, and the absence of legal, bourgeois classes. Marxism had always considered that backward political currents could be concealed under the cover of its ideas; now Mao had proclaimed that a whole society could return to capitalism while still calling itself socialist. This disaster, according to Mao, is the complete triumph of revisionism in a once-socialist society. As a fully counter-revolutionary society with no healthy forces in power, only a new revolution can set it again on a progressive path.

The idea that a revolutionary regime has a high degree of militancy only in its first generation and that time itself wears away revolutionary purity is one of the most common conceptions of non-Marxist social science. Michel's iron law of oligarchy, Pareto's circulation of elites, and the sociological convergence theory developed during the Cold War, all share the idea that a real programme for social equality in any society may have its revolutionary moment, but must be eroded by more recalcitrant and permanent social forces. The evidence for such theories was overwhelming and the institutionalization of inequality in Soviet Russia was defined as another telling example of their validity. Unlike the Russians themselves who continued to maintain that encrusted inequality remains temporary, Mao saw contemporary Soviet society for what it was and attempted to understand it on terms which were still Marxist – terms of class, class conflict, and class transcendence.

For Mao, the realization that the Soviet Union had developed into just another class society came slowly. Thus, throughout the 1950s in the first decade after full revolutionary power, the Russian model for economic development remained, despite significant variations in peasant policy, the prime example for China's future. After Stalin's death, however, and with Khrushchev's not-so-secret speech to the Russian Party Congress in 1956 in which all past difficulties, mistakes, and crimes were laid personally at Stalin's feet, Mao came to fundamentally different conclusions about the state of the Soviet Union. These conclusions are summed up in a series of polemics in the early 1960s attacking Soviet theories and policies.

In these polemics, Mao proclaimed that the Soviet revolution had been derailed by conservative forces taking full power in Russia and that capitalism, this time with a state monopoly in control, had been restored in the Soviet Union. At one stroke, Mao reinstated within Marxism the idea that history is not a determined unilinear series of stages but is an activity of conscious social agents. If a socialist revolution can fail, then history can move backwards as well as forwards. Moreover, since, to Mao, Marxism represents the first attempt to move history through the planned agency of a scientific theory, then the question of why a revolutionary society becomes aborted can only be answered by confronting the ideas and rationalization of self-conscious Marxist leadership. Lenin's dictum that there can be no revolution without highly articulated revolutionary theory takes the converse form in Mao that there can be no destruction of a revolution without incorrect social theory. This latter social theory advanced by the Soviet Union to justify its slide back into an exploitative society may still call itself Marxist, but to Mao it is nothing but a distortion of Marxism; that is, revisionism.

Mao's initial attack on Soviet theory is quite similar to Lenin's earlier opposition to what he considered the revisionism of the Second International. The Soviet Union had proclaimed that peaceful coexistence between states was a fundamental rather than tactical policy for socialist states. To this Mao reiterated Lenin's position that warlike behavior was intrinsic to advanced monopoly capitalism and imperialism, and that coexistence may be contingently necessary but can be no more than temporary. Mao recognized the important dimension that nuclear weapons added to the significance of war, but did not see that this changed the bellicose proclivities of monopoly capitalism. Peaceful coexistence in Russia, then, meant no more than a fig leaf to cover Soviet collusion with existing capitalist states.

A similar argument was advanced by Mao with regard to Russia's seemingly new version of the idea of peaceful transition to socialism. Since, according to the Soviet Union, the threat of nuclear war must make war unthinkable, so it must also make revolutionary insurrection unthinkable since the latter may foment wider nuclear, world-destroying conflict. For Mao as for Lenin, a ruling capitalist class cannot and will not accept the consequences of democratic procedures if those procedures threaten its rule. Only revolutionary overthrow can finally decide the fate of capitalist rule as had been the case in both Russia in 1917 and China in 1949. This need was even more pressing, according to Mao, in the underdeveloped societies, which were long suffering under the yoke of colonial oppression. To caution these countries against popular resistance and to forward the position, as did the Soviet Union, that a peaceful transition to socialism was possible was no less than a complete betrayal of Marxist principles. It led to support for backward social forces and to a continuation of all the ills and injustices that beset those societies.

Recognizing the intrinsic connection between domestic and foreign policy in any society, Mao considered that a restoration of capitalism in an advanced industrial society like Russia must go hand in hand with an aggressive and expansionist foreign policy. It was on this basis that he classified the Soviet Union as a superpower along with the United States and formulated his now well-known theory of three worlds. This theory, which became the cornerstone of Chinese foreign policy, is subject to much controversy, especially with regard to whether it can be considered a socialist outlook at all. Moreover, it is somewhat debatable whether the form that the theory now takes in China can be completely attributed to Mao or whether it represents one of the basic alterations in his outlook, which have occurred in China since his death.

Leaving aside this all important and, at present, unanswerable question, a few remarks about the nature of the theory of three worlds may be made. To see the third world (the world of Western colonialism) as the center of revolutionary revolt fighting both for national liberation from superpower domination and for socialist construction follows the path already successfully trodden by China and all the other successful revolutions in this century. It is in line with the whole shift in Marxist theory to the significance of the underdeveloped world as the locus of revolutionary change. It can also be seen that, as a political metaphor, as an image classifying types of states and their interrelationships in the contemporary world, the theory of three worlds has an originality which captured the changes that have occurred with the rise of Soviet power as a conservative force and the tottering of America as the central power in the world. However, the treating of whole states as classes, as for example, the first and second worlds as *all* capitalist versus the third world as *all* proletarian is an error all too easy to make since a conception of worlds made up of states tends to ignore the presence of classes within states. The same problem occurs when all third-world states and their governments are seen as uniformly progressive against the onslaught of the great powers. When such states, many of whom remain tied to older imperialism, are dogmatically given an independence they are supposedly preserving, then the theory leads to utter absurdity. It is the ease with which this theory of three worlds jettisons all class analysis which makes it so questionable from a Marxist standpoint, whether it leads in an adventurist direction or in the direction of the present Chinese regime. Since the essence of the theory must be attributed to Mao, it remains the most dubious part of his legacy. The actual explanation of it in his political biography is still much clouded in the still inadequately explored last part of his life.

To Mao the most subtle form of revisionist ideas was its justification of conceptions, which denied the class nature of socialist regimes themselves. Does the fact that a socialist regime overthrows older exploiting classes and introduces public control of the productive apparatus mean that classes no more exist within such regimes? Under Stalin, Soviet thought answered this question in the affirmative leaving it in the very difficult position of explaining obvious problems of corruption, crime, and inequality as an exclusive result of remnants of older classes or of the intervention of external enemies. Moreover, since remaining backward productive forces are so overwhelming in these regimes, the supervention of all problems becomes dependent on technical development alone. Working class control over the productive apparatus is taken for granted, and its leadership has only the problem of economic and technical development. Mao refused to deny the obvious fact that the actual development of the Soviet Union into a major world power did not resolve its problems; it seemed rather to exacerbate them. Thus he came to the important conclusion that a theory, which uncritically accepted that a regime is socialist because it legally institutionalized public control and saw all its problems as merely economic ones, is a false theory in line with the positivism that this book has so often mentioned. Marxism is not a theory which mechanically juxtaposes the relationship between economic and ideological factors with the former basic and the latter secondary. For a monolithic Communist Party such as the CPSU to proclaim such a theory is to deny the problems of its own ideological conflict, conflict which is inevitable in a society still replete with contending forces. This denial is then hidden behind the idea that the state of higher communist harmony is assured by its continued unquestioned rule. Only backward technological conditions, claims revisionist theory, are hindering the automatic transition to communism.

Mao frontally attacked this theory of productive forces in socialist regimes as a distortion of Marxism, as no more than an ideological justification for privileged and corrupt leadership. The theory, said Mao, had been completely codified by a new bourgeois ruling class in Russia, and the same ideas were being articulated by leading elements in China. So great was their influence within the Chinese Party and high government positions that the danger of such capitalist restoration there was extremely great. Taking the view that socialism was already guaranteed by formal legal public ownership of the means of production and that technical backwardness alone was the reason for all other problems, much Chinese leadership around Mao considered that campaigns to raise ideological levels were a waste of time and that China should get on with the job of modernization (as had the Soviet Union already). By the early 1960s, it appears that this outlook had gained ascendance in the Communist Party of China, such ascendance that Mao considered only the most radical measures could be used to counter it. It is likely that Mao's anti-revisionist position was in a minority in the Party leaving him with no other option but appeal to popular response to this threat to revolutionary advance in the country. Thus, Mao utilized his great prestige to initiate the Cultural Revolution, ten years of popular ferment meant to purge and cleanse communist leadership by deepening ordinary peoples' engagement with politics. In the context of this great internal struggle, the problem of ultra-leftism surfaced among Party members who were closely allied with Mao. That this effort failed is evidenced by the policies of the present regime, policies which represent the same body of ideas which Mao's Cultural Revolution meant to attack and supervene.

Given its failure, there is no doubt that some of what went wrong in the Cultural Revolution must be laid at Mao's feet. Given the overwhelming problems he faced and which, it appears, socialist revolution in backward societies especially face, it is difficult, however, to charge Mao alone with lack of their resolution. The problems confronted by China are among the great unsolved problems of the world today. Seen in these terms, Mao's last failure must be seen as a noble one since he was the first to really confront the present crisis in Marxism. This crisis raises questions about the nature of democracy in communist parties *after* they take power, about the growth of class contradictions in socialist societies (demanding a class analysis of socialist society), and about the contradictions of economic development in societies like the Soviet Union (which were not socialist but neither were they capitalist in the traditional way). Upon answers to these questions lies the fate of Marxism as social theory. Mao's greatest contribution to Marxism may ultimately rest less in the failure to answer such questions than in his boldness to raise them in the first place.

Conclusion

THUS, IT MAY BE concluded that the ambiguity surrounding Mao Zedong's final thought and action is the ambiguity surrounding Marxism itself. To take revolutionary power in a backward country seems easier than to maintain it. Both the causes of a failed revolution and the nature of its political economy are unprecedented problems, the surprises of history. Given that socialist revolutions do not yet appear probable in advanced capitalist societies and that the vast underdeveloped world, which is its cradle, also does not appear to be ripe for Marxist insurrection, it is upon the resolution of these problems that rests the future of Marxism.

The following chapter, which details the history of struggle in one Chinese village, demonstrates the great fault line that emerges between revolutionary principles and the concrete practices meant to forward socialist transition in specific times and places. One local story does not adequately reflect the experience of a country as diverse and culturally rich as China, but it does highlight some of the key problems of socialist transition in a particularly specific and stark manner.

CHAPTER SEVEN

Rural Revolution in China – Problems and Prospects

THERE HAS BEEN a tendency in Marxism and in Western scholarship in general to assume that all forms of pre-capitalist societies beyond the simple, tribal stage are similar to that found in pre-bourgeois, feudal Europe. China typically consisted of a multitude of villages with families or lineages farming land pretty much as they liked while owing allegiance to a faraway emperor who officially owned the whole kingdom, which was managed by agents who represented him. On the face of it, the European and the Chinese systems have important similarities. In both cases, the majority of people worked in agriculture on land on which the producers were customarily fixed. Surplus was extracted through a variety of means, including taxation, which supported the King/Emperor as well as a small elite class that lived off the surplus product, consisting of hereditary aristocrats in Europe and appointed officials in China. In both systems, peasants revolted periodically, principally when the degree of surplus extraction was too burdensome and greatly exceeded the customary amounts. In Europe, regional and central authority prevailed; in China, revolts might be linked to changes in dynasties. In neither case was the mode of production changed.

When looking at the traditional social structure and ideology of China, however, we see that it differs in significant ways from European feudalism, to the point where Chinese scholars do not refer to the mode of production in China as feudal. Unlike Europe, China did not have a fixed landed aristocracy that controlled land in perpetuity, land which in general was worked by a serfdom obliged to live on and work that land in a state of manifest exploitation. The European fiefdom was an organic and legally-bound class system.

Politically, except in periods of regional warfare in China, when local warlords competed for power over the central authority, China was singularly monolithic in the structure of its political system. European feudalism was decentered, and local aristocrats competed among themselves for power and also waged a struggle with central authority. Not until the modern era and the rise of commercial capitalism was full-fledged national sovereignty attained in most European territories. In China, the traditional system of singular power persisted through many centuries and dynasties. It did not develop, over this time, a consistent and permanent system of landlordism through which a hereditary aristocracy controlled the land.

In China, landlordism at the local level was a process that varied greatly both geographically and historically. Generally, the majority of cultivators lived in villages organized along lineage lines. China may have possessed one grand landlord as well as an official class that, through taxation, could exploit the producers, but the producers themselves exercised a degree of independence and also had the possibility of becoming landlords if they accumulated enough land to hire and exploit the landless or small holders of land. The vicissitudes of history made landlordism a variable and unpredictable phenomenon in the Chinese context. Nevertheless, landlordism never became the dominant mode of surplus extraction in traditional China. Landlordism developed on a significant scale in some parts of China only after the intrusion of Western imperialism in the 1840s, and it expanded under the Kuomintang in the early twentieth century. As we shall see in our exploration of one Chinese village in contemporary times, the complex situation of the persistence of traditional modes of farming with some landlordism affected the policies of the socialist regime quite differently from what would have occurred in a typical European feudal village.

Keeping these differences in mind, there are still some features that define a pre-capitalist, feudal or traditional mode of production. It is a productive system where labour is tied to the land producing, with simple tools, not for a market but mainly for subsistence, with surplus being taken by a dominant leisured class with its head in the imperial court and utilized primarily for consumption and ostentatious display. It is because of this state of affairs that such modes of production are not dynamic, highly productive systems of wealth accumulation. As we shall see in looking at Chinese history, for long periods Chinese civilization was a more dynamic and more productive system at a time when Europe was a stagnant feudal backwater. The centralized political system in China, which maintained control over production for long-distance trade, was partly responsible for this difference. And this could occur without China ever going through a full-fledged bourgeois revolution, although as in any pre-capitalist economic form, there were political and economic limitations that prevented industrialization.

One of the major goals of the Chinese revolution was the complete destruction of the basic structural and ideological characteristics of traditionalism, defined by the Communist Party of China (CCP) as feudalism. Landlordism in any feudal or traditional sense was extirpated along with technically simple means of production associated with this productive form. And we think it can be said that, in this form, it shall not return. As well, illiteracy was almost wiped out (to return again with contemporary capitalism) and women were freed from bondage to male controllers of property.

The absence of a thoroughgoing bourgeois revolution in China as a precursor to socialism bequeathed to China not only industrial backwardness; it also meant that much of the traditional ideology stemming from the past was often left untouched and uncriticized. Moreover, as one would expect, this kind of ideological alp affected not only the wider populace but as well the advanced party, which led the revolution. We would surmise that the capacity of a socialist project to carry through to a classless future depends very much on the capacity of the new regime to inculcate a new set of values into the population at large, what Che Guevara called producing a "new socialist man" (sic). This transformation will also be necessary in a bourgeois society, but a bourgeois revolution may make the transition to socialism potentially easier by erasing both the traditional social structure and its sustaining practices and ideologies (although older ideas persist in different guises for a long time). Mao recognized this very well when he attempted to put politics in command of the socialist process. The problem that arises in this context revolves around the question of which kind of legitimacy is the dominant force within the transition. Is it the traditional ideology that has been the encrusted vision of Chinese history, the newer heretofore untested viewpoint of the future socialist society, or the worldwide capitalist viewpoints that suffuse much that is called modernity?

We think that the kind of legitimacy found in Chinese traditionalism may have had significance in dealing with a central question confronting the Chinese socialist transition. That question has to do with the failure of socialist values and practices to be institutionalized by the Communist Party in its internal workings and its relationships with the people and, consequently, the absence of internalized socialist values among most of the Chinese people, to the point that the break with socialism occurred very quickly, with little opposition and apparently little regret. The following analysis will point out how this process of delegitimation occurred in one Chinese village, and how traditional ideas and the structure of Chinese village agriculture played their part.

Traditional Social Structure

IN IMPERIAL or traditional China, centralized political power dominated the social structure. The long history of imperial power, which was punctuated by periods of social and political turmoil leading to dynasty changes, created a major divide between officialdom and the people. According to conventional scholars, peasant rebellions were caused by landless peasants, and the revolts were aimed at the emperor who supposedly represented the interests of the landlord class. Qin Hui has examined all major historical uprisings started from the one led by Chen Sheng and Wu Guang, which eventually led to the overthrow of the first dynasty (Qin 2012). Most uprisings in China involved independent cultivators having small landholdings, not landless peasants. The cultivators rebelled not because they had no land to till, but because of the heavy levies that they could not afford. This phenomenon often happened during the late years of a dynasty, when corruption was rampant from top to bottom and across the vast empire.

Some scholars and politicians often place blame on the Qin dynasty for implementing a nationwide imperial bureaucracy (Liang 2010). Few have pointed out that the regime of tyranny started long before the first dynasty. Qin Shi-huang, the first emperor of Qin Dynasty, was actually the thirtieth king of Qin Kingdom under the Zhou Dynasty and the thirty-ninth generation since the death of the founder of Qin, Qin Feizi in 858 B.C. Had other states conquered China, such as Qi, a powerful rival of Qin in Shandong province, China would still have developed a similar form of imperial tyranny. According to Xie, the tyrannical kingdoms evolved from a system of chiefdom, from which a single authority derived. The dynastic system did not arise from tribal alliances, which often led to some kind of political mechanism entailing decentered power somewhat more similar to a feudal alignment in which central power was checked by regional power bases (Xie 2002). Traditional modes of production, whether feudal or imperial, do not separate political and economic power. Exploitation of the agricultural labouring classes is inseparable from the military power to enforce the extraction of surplus, although custom, religion, and family ties play important, routine parts.

Throughout Chinese imperial history, political power squeezed the surplus from agriculture and also from commerce. The latter impeded the development of industries. Any new business opportunities, such as iron and salt, would end up as a monopoly exercised by the imperial court. Routine economic transactions at the local level were mostly barter in nature. Villagers who engaged in trade other than farming often kept their land for life's necessities. It is significant to point out that the imperial court maintained a relatively low level of taxation, but the levies collected by local officials were often unbearable. Not surprisingly, extravagant consumption by the state and its local agents went hand in hand with the meager consumption of the people. In this sense, exploitation in China could not, in a practical sense, be laid solely at the feet of the imperial court. Local elites also lived off the surplus. If rebellions were, nevertheless, directed at imperial power, this situation reflects the importance of the direct chain of authority stretching from the local officials to the Emperor.

Since B.C.134 during the Han dynasty, local officials made recommendations of selected people (male, of course) to higher-level authorities or the imperial court. These people would be appointed to office after examinations, called *cha ju*. The examination system of selecting officials since the Sui dynasty (600 A.D.) had virtually eliminated any possibility of local influence because the selection of officials was entirely dependent upon these examinations, a system called *keju*. The imperial bureaucracy, however, stopped at the county level. With limited hands, the local magistrate relied on the village elite (who often had passed the official examinations). The elite generally controlled an average size of land, although the amount of land varied with some possessing more than others. The village elite, either gentry or patriarch, often acted informally but were the real leaders in the village. The village elite helped the magistrate to collect taxes and, in return, was endorsed to manage the village. The educated elite was also often granted tax exemption by the government.

The formal tax was low in traditional China, and the official compensation for the magistrate was also low. Thus, local officials often sought other ways of making additional money, which implies some degree of exploitation at the local elite level, through any number of means. That's why a wealthy merchant would rather see his son enroll in school in order to pass the imperial exams and become an official. This appointment was a more secure way to not only make more money, but also protect the wealth obtained through commercial exploitation.

Aristocrats as a class were eliminated when Qin defeated six other states by 221 B.C. Thus, there was no longer an independent class in the middle between the emperor and the people. The local elites and provincial officials were directly tied to imperial power. While the emperor ruled the country ultimately through force, the legitimacy of the regime rested on long-standing customs and traditions, including acceptance of the principle of imperial rule.

The elite class (also referred to as gentry by Fei Hsiao-tung), for the most part, passed various imperial exams and was not necessarily associated with above-average land ownership. Officialdom often related to knowledge of Chinese classics, representing an educated elite with learning and high-brow tastes defining its high status. Because the titles and privileges of the gentry were not hereditary, they had only some limited opportunity to pass on their positions directly to their offspring. As for a large land-holding family, while the land accumulated was limited to a certain degree due to the similar farming tools and farming techniques, the land would be divided equally among male heirs, unlike the Europeans who passed their land only to first sons, diminishing in China the possibility of successive expansion of land ownership. Without the intervention of external factors, such as political or military power, it was typical that a majority of peasants were independent cultivators at any given historical period, and no hereditary class, similar to Russian kulaks, could arise.

In traditional China, any trade other than agriculture was not as safe as farming because a guarantee of food supply was a prerequisite for doing any small business. Carpenters or masons also tilled their farm land, and specialization did not lead to further industrial development other than providing complementary income. A market economy was never fully developed.

The idea of a market carried different meanings in Chinese history. Skinner claims that, at a standard rural market in China, "what the household produced but did not consume was normally sold here, and what it consumed but did not produce was normally bought here" (Skinner 1964: 6). This description is not strictly true in traditional China. Rather, sellers were cultivators who generally produced the same products as did the buyers. Consequently, the products they possessed often had only seasonal differences. Buyers at one market fair may end up being the sellers at the next market fair. The crucial point is that market exchange did not result in specialization, which was concomitant with the division of the agricultural economy; on the contrary, this kind of specialization actually strengthened the natural, traditional economy.

The ultimate 'ownership' of land was in the hands of the imperial court. Regardless of the land size and the owner, the land was at the disposal of the state (Wang 2000). According to traditional ideology, people just 'rented' the land from the state. Nevertheless, it was viewed and treated as ancestral land. A male occupier of land had no ultimate right of execution (or 'ownership') of the ancestral land, which customarily belonged to his family members including the deceased of the past generations and descendants of future generations. According to the traditional beliefs, he is just a link that connects all the members of the lineage. The afterworld is not much different from this world. The ancestral land guaranteed the well-being of both worlds. Land transfers were seldom made through market transactions. Even if it happened to go through the market, land would not be concentrated, which is different from the belief of some scholars who claim that private ownership and market transactions automatically lead to land concentration and capitalism (Wen 2009). We will use Ma village later to examine this question.

Late Qing and Early Republican China (to the 1930s)

THE INTRUSION into China of Western imperialism, especially after the Second Opium War of 1863, began to change agriculture with the introduction of more widespread commercialization of land for agricultural production and early industrialization, which began in textile and mechanical flour mills. As more and more trade developed with the West from the south, Japan from the east, and Russia from the north, China was gradually changing. Typical of the experience of the advent of imperialism in traditional societies, more and more villagers moved to the city, and the coastal rural areas were more and more involved in international trade.

In a vast country such as China, natural environments vary tremendously. Under the imperial system, grain and tribute were sent to the capital in the north of China through canals, rivers, and along post paths. Following the 1860s, the geopolitical map changed due to the unprecedented transformations from the West sweeping China from the south to the north and from coast to inland. Chinese authoritarian regimes and agrarian culture were seriously challenged thereafter.

Several scholars documented the transformation of the Chinese society in a number of areas, including Lin Yueh-hwa, C. K. Yang, Fei Hsiao-tung, and Martin C. Yang. Their work covers Guangdong and Fujian in the south, Jiangsu in east China, and Shandong in north China. These classic studies document the gradual erosion and breakdown of the centuries-old agrarian life under the influence of Western commercialization and industrialization.

The changes that occurred in Chinese agriculture in this transitional period, through the republican revolution and Kuomintang China, were not identical in the various regions of China, which experienced increasing differentiation of landholding and the mode of surplus extraction. In periods of political turmoil, it is more difficult to maintain centralized authority over the countryside. In general, more intermediary groups appear between the peasantry and the central government, leading to more exploitation developing as a local focus. Meanwhile, agricultural differentiation accompanied the growing commercialization of agriculture. Non-traditional concepts of land ownership, occupancy rights, and alienation from the land were imposed or emerged. The result was a growing distinction among the peasantry in which the amount of land owned and the type of land assumed increasing importance, as well as the relationship among village residents. It is important to note that, despite this differentiation, villages were still rooted in lineage relationships and loyalties often affecting the emerging landlord-tenant relationships, which were more developed in some parts of China than others. To discuss the effects of these changes in one area of China, we examine the transformation of Ma village in Shandong.

Ma village in the Traditional Era

IN 1404, the second year of the Reign of the Yong-le Emperor (1402–1424), Ma An and his wife surnamed Wang immigrated from Sichuan's Li-zhou (now Guang-yuan) municipality of southwestern China to Shandong's Ye county (now Lai-zhou) municipality of north China. After propagating for more than six centuries, the Ma's now had 161 households with a population of 432 in Ma village as of March 2010. The Ma's, through the waxing and waning of the Ming, Qing, early Republican, Nationalist (KMT), and socialist periods, are now in their thirtieth generation. For six centuries, the history of Ma village was not interrupted in its basic organization, making it a good social unit to be analyzed.[1]

Given the documented variations in the transformation of Chinese agriculture under pressure from Western commercialization and limited industrialization, and since Ma village is situated in the north but close to the coast, we probably could say that Ma village is in the middle of the spectrum, which has quantitative variations from villages in other parts of China and possibly qualitative differences on the question of whether landlordism had become a dominant mode during the Kuomintang period.

In Ma village in 1949, there were two types of land: about 750 *mu* of rich, relatively flat and ancestral land in the village centre and 750 *mu* of poor land on the hillsides surrounding the village.

(1) Rich Land

For the holders of the rich land, householders traditionally would not sell the land but would rather pass on their land to the next generation. It was the Chinese belief that, when a person passed away, he and she would enter the "other world" in which the deceased needed spiritual and material supports from the living descendants; therefore, the more male siblings you had, the more guarantee of security in the afterlife. Land, as the most important piece of property, was not only for grain production, but also critical for human reproduction. For a family without a son, having only daughters or no children at all, the only way to carry on the family root was through adoption *guoji* (literally, come over and continue). A young male from relatives either on the paternal or maternal side would be transferred to become the adopted son who would then carry the surname of Ma.[2] Thus he would be able to pay respect to the ancestors and make appropriate offerings. The rich land was considered the family's life line, which was not for sale unless the family was in a desperate situation, for instance, when there was no money to bury a deceased parent. Since there were no sellers, there were also no sales, and land accumulation was impossible given these circumstances.

Ancestral land transfer from one family to another was not through a market transaction, but rather through kinship connections. To have a market transaction, the buyer and the seller must both act for a transaction to be executed. From a buyer's perspective, with limited money-making opportunities, it was highly unlikely that an individual would have additional resources to purchase flat land from another village. From the seller's perspective, they would not sell their land. As a result, landholding was relatively stable and rich land was not put on sale. Since level land was not part of any market circulation in this traditional society, there was little land centralization. Large scale land accumulation through dramatic societal change did occur, however, on the occasion of political confiscation or military occupation.

(2) Poor Land

Poor land in Ma Village consisted of less-productive, hillside land. It was not deemed ancestral land and was subject to changes in ownership. Plots of poor land on the hills often changed hands through market transactions. Nevertheless, social conditions and customary practices prevented only a few owners from amassing large amounts of land. In short, even if there were market transactions, land accumulation was very difficult; thus, there was little tendency toward polarization. Since cultivators had similar farm tools, it was difficult to accumulate great amounts of money. If one was lucky and made money, most likely he would buy land and consequently could afford more sons but, in general, the only land for sale was the relatively poor, hillside land. It was possible, within a generation, to accumulate land to some extent. With the next generation, however, the rules of inheritance would result in the sons again becoming average owner-cultivators. For six centuries, then, land centralization was not achieved even on the hilly land.

In a word, only poor land (hillside) was bought and sold through the market. Rich (ancestral) land traditionally was held by the family through lineage inheritance. In either case, land accumulation was almost impossible. This information should shed some light on land reform in Ma Village, which was not primarily about landlords and landless peasants. Rich peasants, landlords, and even some middle peasants believed that taking the land and giving it to the poor would violate property rights. As we will see, the majority of the middle peasants were alienated by communal policies against commercial marketing.

Ma Village and Land Reform

TABLE 1 shows the distribution of land at the time of land reform in Ma Village, which was liberated prior to 1949. At first glance, as of 1945, the Ma village census indicated that there were two landlord and seven rich peasant families. How could this have happened given the traditional barriers to land accumulation in the village? Where did the landlords and rich peasants obtain their land? It is possible to trace the development of land holdings over time in the village, beginning in 1925.

Table 1 Land Distribution and Yields in 1945

	Unit	Subtotal	Poor Peasants	Middle Peasants	Rich Peasants	Landlord
Households	Household	145	39	97	7	2
Population	People	595	154	390	33	18
Arable Land	Mu	1650	195	925	140	390
Annual Yield	Jin	395108	34958	201240	41910	117000
Grain per capita	Jin	664	227	516	1270	6500
Beggars	Households	6	6			
Full time Hired labour		2	2			
Yield per Mu	Jin/Mu	240	180	218	300	300

In March, 1925, Ma An's descendants took down the village temple, which was a three-room thatched house with crude soil bricks, and built a tile-roofed house with marble and granite. At the same time, a stele was erected to trace the origins of the Ma lineage. The inscription on the back listed all fundraisers' names with specific amounts of money donated. This list has provided a first-hand record, which reflects the economic status of the Ma family in 1925.

The complete rebuilding of the village temple cost silver dollar 869 *yuan* and copper coin of 2822.7 *qianwen* or *guan*. Not only did the Mas in Ma village contribute money, but also the Mas who had migrated from Ma village contributed from three other villages. There were 167 households that made contributions. The largest amount came from Ma Chun-jing with silver dollars of 400 *yuan* and copper coins of 2100 *qianwen*, followed by Ma Rui-guang, with silver dollars of 172 and copper coins of 56 *qianwen*. The least contributions were made by Ma Dai-feng and Ma Tong-jing with copper coins of 0.5 *qianwen*, an obvious token contribution, proving that even the poor felt obliged to partake in the building of the temple. The family temple was such an important affair that every single one of the Ma descendants made contributions, regardless of their economic background. This list roughly reflected the distribution of wealth at the time.

In 1946, land reform was carried out in Ma village, and all families were classified into different households as indicated in the table above: landlord, rich peasant, middle peasant, and poor peasant. Once designated in one of the classes, the family class origin was so important that it affected virtually all villagers' lives for more than thirty years until the importance of class origin was officially abolished in 1978. The classification was based on landholdings in 1945, exactly 20 years or one generation after 1925. History has facilitated a perfect case for us to compare and analyze the relationship between economic distribution and family classification.

The donors are ranked based on the amount donated starting from the largest, Chun-jing and Rui-guang. They are followed by seven heads of families who contributed from 5 to 40 silver dollar *yuan*.[3] Not surprisingly, the two largest donation families in 1925 were classified in 1945 as landlord families, together with other donators on top of the list who were defined as rich peasant families. Where did the wealth of these families come from? What was the background of the two landlord families and seven rich peasant families? And where did these families obtain their wealth?

Considering first the two landlord families, Chun-jing was one of three brothers with their respective childhood names of Shun-jing, Chun-jing, and Bao-jing (big cow, second cow, and third cow). Shun-jing was the first to go to the northeast, without having much luck. Bao-jing gave his try, and left wearing his mother's pants. Bao-jing's family was so poor that they were buried in debt. As a matter of fact, sorghum on the granite roller was not even fully ground until the creditors picked it up and left. Thriving in Harbin, Bao-jing owned fire-powered grinding mills in Mudanjiang and Mohe, where many Ma villagers later joined him. While Bao-jing was doing business far from home, Chun-jing stayed home looking after family affairs. The second landlord family, Ma Rui-guang, was not as rich as the three brothers. He was a retail merchant and owned stores that dealt with building materials in Beijing.

Examining the background of the seven rich peasant families,[4] it can be seen that they were long-time, major peasant families. For example, Jun-qi opened and owned a carpentry shop in northeastern China and he sent home money from which a peanut oil mill was opened in the village. Relatives in the village worked in or ran the mill. (Jun-fu was doing the chores and Jun-lu was running the business). It can be seen from the family backgrounds that rich peasant families also reached their class position by migrating to Qingdao, the region's most commercialized coastal city or to Manchuria or the Northeast where trade was opened with industrialized Japan.[5] Thus the classification of rich peasant was not always consistent.[6]

From the above presentation, we can draw the conclusion that the accumulation of excessive landholdings of the landlord and rich peasant families were brought about through the influx of funds from commerce rather than from farming. In other words, land accumulation in Ma Village was not due to the exploitation of grain surplus within agriculture itself; it was from surplus obtained outside the village from commerce and industrialization, linked to urban migration. As the table indicates, only two members of the village were classified as full-time labourers. The figures, however, do not reveal part-time employment of village members. Absentee owners whose land is nevertheless productive must have had arrangements with other family members to work the land. Nevertheless, the main source of capital for accumulation and investment in the village came from external exploitation. The chief difficulty preventing accumulation of wealth in agriculture was the relatively low productivity of farming at the time.

With 35% of the villagers living outside the village, 543 *mu* of land was available for sale, as the total arable land at the time was 1573.29 *mu*. The census of Ma village dated December 25, 1951 included detailed statistics on each household including the number of family members, the size of the house, and the size of land. Among the population of 1087, there were 375 former villagers (35%) who had left the village and migrated to the cities. In a very short period in the pre-Revolution decades, land centralization was begun not through exploitation of inner village farming, but rather through money coming from outside. Villagers were no longer restricted to hilly land sales, but started selling ancestral land and were able to migrate to the cities. The newly formed landlords were not landlords in the traditional sense of an elite who stayed in the village and hired landless peasants. They were merchant, absentee landlords whose land was worked through lineage relationships.

Ma villagers also took advantage of opportunities in northeastern China that resulted from the intrusion of Western imperialism and the introduction of capitalism in trade and production. Some of the villagers who left the village accumulated wealth from commerce and sent home money to start a business or to purchase land from those who left the village and would not return.

With the influx of funds from the cities and emigration out of the village, the speed and extent of polarization of land ownership were astonishing during the Kuomintang era. Within a few decades through trade and investment in flour mills, Bao-jing sent home money to purchase lots of land and built a two-story building with marble, granite, and redwood. From the amount of money he donated to the village temple in 1925, it was easy to tell he was a wealthy man.

The 1945 statistics also show that in Ma village, owner-cultivators made up the majority of the village population (97 of 145 households – about 67%). This situation is typical in north China, where landlordism was not well developed. It is important to note, however, that this class division was different elsewhere in China. In the Yangtze delta of southern China, for example, rural society was characterized by many absentee landlords and tenant-peasants. Based on some Marxist theory, revolutionary potential might appear to be greater in the south than the north, as it was rooted in class conflict between tenants and landlords; but revolution did not succeed in the former where landlordism was more developed. Obviously, factors other than class conflict intervened at that time, such as war dislocation and the great military strength of the KMT, for example, which demanded different tactics in that particular region. The Long March relocated the revolution from the south to the north because conditions were more propitious away from the seat of Kuomintang power.

According to Liu, landlords acted as a buffer between the peasants and central officialdom in the south, whereas there was an unmediated conflict between peasants and central authority (officialdom) in northern China. More specifically, in the Yangzi delta, tenants paid rent to the landlords, from whom in turn the government collected taxes; thus, taxation was an affair between the government and the landlords. The state is not only a tax extractor, but also a mediator between landlords and tenants: "The small tenant-composed communities bore no tax responsibilities to the state and therefore no violent confrontations between the state and rural communities over taxation occurred in this area" (Liu 2007: 164). Because, traditionally, tenants had no tax obligations to the state, a community composed predominantly of tenants did not deal directly with the state in the realm of taxation, the most important area of state and rural society relations. "Intensified struggles against corrupt village heads, against exorbitant taxes, and ultimately, against the oppressive state, became the major political drama on the North China plain" (Liu 2007: 188). In terms of class analysis, the conflict between tenants and landlords is over rent. For long periods of time generally in traditional societies, the extraction of surplus through rent (and other means) proceeds with minimal (although always implied) coercion. On the other hand, in the right circumstances, tenants can be politicized and come to see local surplus extraction as exploitation. It may not be the general political economy of the situation, which is the telling point, but the strength, legitimacy, and rootedness of alternative authority that make the incipient class struggle into a political force. The Communist Party had little strength or legitimacy in the south and retreated north in the face of entrenched Kuomintang control.

From Land Reform to Commune

IN MA VILLAGE in 1945, a majority of the households (66.7%) were middle peasant families, or independent cultivators, while less than one third of the households (26.9%) were poor peasant families. The Communist Party strategy was to mobilize the poor peasant families against the landlord and rich peasant families, take the land of the latter and distribute it to the former, while the middle peasant families neither gained nor lost any land.

The land reform in Ma village was led by the Communist Party in 1946 and the land of those families having hired labour and landholdings above the village average were classified as landlord or rich peasant families. Their land was confiscated and given to the families with landholding below the village average who were classified as poor peasants. And families having land about average were considered middle peasant families who did not gain or lose land during the campaign. Thus, during land reform, the land of the rich was taken away and distributed to the poor, while the landholding of the middle peasants remained intact; they simply watched as the land reform unfolded. Land reform not only divided up the land, but also the houses, utensils, and farm tools. Class struggle was politicized so that the village was divided along two lines; that is, between the poor peasant families and landlords and rich peasant families. As the most exploited group in the village and the least privileged, the poor peasants were assumed to be the most solid allies of the revolution. While the middle peasants were considered potentially reliable allies, the new government relied mostly on the poor peasants, not just in local leadership roles, but including the recruitment of new urban employees and drafting new soldiers from poor peasant families. All people were registered in the village and, with the exception of those recruited or drafted, were not allowed to move out of it. In Ma village at least, and we assume many other villages in China, the method of imposing criteria for benefits and targeted regulations did not have the effect of building strong support for the revolution among middle peasants.

The aim of land reform was more than only redistribution. The long-term objective was to proletarianize the agricultural workforce, centralize land, and introduce modern but collective production methods. The Communist Party viewed lineage relationships and customary practices as inimical to their long-term goals. Since all Ma villagers were connected by family ties, the government combined Ma village with Li village and called in the poor peasants from Li Village to lead the land reform. As a result, the leader from Li village became the party secretary of Ma Village. Party Secretary Li's house was eventually built on Ma's traditional territory, and Li's mother obtained a house from Ma Bao-jing, the richest landlord family. Land reform involves social, political, and economic goals. Ancestral land was not simply taken from the large landholders; it was redistributed to people who were not ancestral to the village. As always, the way changes were carried out matters about as much as the actual redistribution: from rich to poor. In retrospect, the Communist Party had adopted different policies towards urban capitalists and rural landlords and rich peasants. The government adopted the policy of redemption for urban industries, offering compensation instead of deprivation in the expropriation of capitalist enterprises. But a direct deprivation was enforced on the landlords and rich peasants. This policy had a long-term impact. Land reform had made landlords and rich peasants into enemies of the revolution, which was a necessary and unavoidable consequence. More importantly, to the extent that the way land reform was carried out also alienated the majority of the middle peasants, it had sown the seeds for discontent and delegitimacy by underestimating the strength of peoples' allegiance to the traditional landholding system, by integrating separate lineages, and by demonstrating preferential treatment for formerly poor peasants on the grounds that class background made them the most reliable revolutionaries. Existing local-level leadership was bypassed. In this context, traditional anti-government sentiments were reinforced. The majority of middle peasants did not benefit from land reform and felt some grievance in the way the reforms were carried out. However, this was just the beginning. The relatively successful deprivation of the land from the landlords and rich peasants was the first step in the collectivization campaign.

Land reform was intended to make all families into independent, middle-peasant cultivators. The tendency for small-scale cultivators to begin a process of re-polarization and new concentration of wealth and resources was checked by policies that restricted the buying and the selling of land. Of course, there continued to exist some differences in the amount of land and other forms of productive property owned by each family. As the revolutionary government followed the Soviet model of investment in heavy industries, however, middle-peasant production was insufficient to support the need for increased production to sustain the urban industrialization that was underway in China.

The need to industrialize China had been haunting the Chinese elite for more than a century, ever since Western powers invaded Qing's China. In one sense, Chinese, regardless of being Nationalists on the right or Communists on the left, sought to catch up to the industrial development of the West. While the Nationalists finally aligned with the US and the West, the Communist Party aligned with the Soviet bloc. It should be noted that land reform was also implemented in Taiwan, similar to movements that occurred elsewhere. However, economic development in Taiwan was more successful than in other Third World countries. The success of Taiwanese industrialization was inseparable from the US policy of containing socialism while financially supporting development in strategic countries, which included South Korea. In China, the Communist Party adopted soviet-style industrialization through state-owned enterprises. It was a model that put productive forces in command and required substantial support from the countryside.

To ensure the supply of grain to the cities, in 1954 the government implemented unified sales and purchase programmes across the country, which required that all grains had to be sold to the state to support urban industrialization. Since the land was divided equally in the hands of independent cultivators, dealing with each individual family was both expensive and inefficient. The government had difficulties purchasing enough grain to support the urban population. Hence, villages were called upon to organize co-ops in 1955-56, a more advanced form of social ownership that would begin the process of centralization of land and allow for more productive agricultural techniques. Change though successive stages was precipitous. In 1957, villages were reorganized into communes. In 1958, all agricultural regions in the whole country were collectivized into communes, to which the villagers donated all the grain and all the cooking utensils as well.

In 1953, prior to the introduction of co-ops, seven mutual aid groups were organized in Ma village with 40 families of 182 people, and in 1954, it increased to nine groups with 57 families and 256 people. This change was relatively easy, since communal activities existed throughout lineage groups especially during the harvest and planting seasons. However, in 1955, the first Preliminary Co-op was established with 16 families representing 72 people, including both Mas and Lis. Co-ops were introduced partially as a means to increase the production of grain to be bought by the state and used to support industrialization. From the point of view of the middle peasant, the Government offered a guaranteed purchase of grain, but the guarantee was also a monopoly. The Soviet experience suggests that industrialization can entail the disproportionate extraction of surplus from peasants. The benefits of industrialization are supposed to flow back to rural areas in the form of advanced technology, making agriculture more productive, and in the exchange for manufactured consumer goods, improving the quality of daily life. On the other hand, if the standard of living is unchanged or, indeed, worsened, then the rural/urban contradictions in society can become more severe and government policies become sources of resentment and division.

In the early Preliminary Co-ops, distribution was based on the size of land originally contributed to the co-op, a system that advantages those who had owned more. In the Advanced Co-ops, distribution was based solely on work points because land was all collectively owned. In 1956, an Advanced Co-op was established including all families except landlord and rich peasant families, a total of 618 people. In 1957, every family was obliged to enter the Co-op. In 1958, 48 villages in Liang Guo were established as one single Commune, creating Liang–guo Commune, with about 30,000 people. The move to communes took place following the political and economic break with the Soviet Union (the Sino-Soviet Split) and the implementation of the Great Leap Forward. China moved from land reform to advanced co-ops in seven years, and then to communes in two.

Cooking instruments were turned over to the commune in an effort to break down the traditional household roles, since women and men were both expected to work for the commune. There were three public cafeterias in the then-called Ma Brigade. Foods were offered free of charge; sometimes, commune members would come back to eat again if better food was cooked. The public cafeteria appeared to be a great leap beyond household production but, as an experiment, it did not last long.

A more serious situation arose in the effort to establish a commune-wide accounting system for production and also for allocation. The political pressure on local party leadership to report great increases in production, both agricultural and industrial, masked extreme shortage of both, the results of which contributed to three years of famine, unexpected in the socialist period. The years of natural disaster were not a minor factor here. China has periodic natural crises, but it was assumed that a socialist society would develop policies that would mitigate the worst effects of these disasters. The policies of the Great Leap, however, actually exacerbated the disaster. Three reasons related to public policies caused the famine: one factor was waste during the harvest season, which relates directly to peasant resistance to the commune. The public cafeteria, which related directly to state policy, was also wasteful. Second, the disproportionate grain tax and enforced sale of grain met with peasant resistance to production quotas and removed too much of what was grown from the village. Third, villagers no longer had any standby grain stored for leaner years, which was the traditional practice, because all the extra supply had been confiscated by the commune. When famine struck, there was no local store of grain that could be distributed, and the expectation that supply could be brought into a drought area from a more productive region was nullified by the widespread nature of the disaster. Seventeen people died of hunger in 1960 in Ma village alone. No one was born in 1960 and 1961 since women could not get pregnant.

The cafeterias were abolished in 1961. In general, things began to improve in 1962. On February 23, 1962, the central government issued a directive, "Regarding Changing the Commune as the Basic Accounting Unit." Ma Brigade was divided into four teams and each team became a separate accounting unit in which each member participated in the collective work, and distribution was mostly based on work points. In addition, the number of family members was also taken into consideration when distributing grain and vegetables. Families with fewer labourers but more children would incur debt to the team and pay back in the future when their kids grew up.

The scaling back of the commune movement from commune to production teams was a compromise between traditional and socialist ideology. In Ma village, different lineage branches developed around the village temple, which had been the residence of Ma An and Wang, the first couple. Different geographical areas then were occupied by more closely-related families. When the village was divided up geographically into four teams, each team was mainly formed by four or five close families. In Team II, for example, there were 42 households in 1958 with 189 people. Among them, Ma Yu-huan's descendants had 8 households with 43 people, about 20% of Team II. The geographic division of the four teams, in a way, had institutionalized the earlier communal tradition. As well, team leaders were elected by the team members from below, not from above, as was the case for the brigade party secretary and the brigade leader. Despite the social intention of the commune movement to replace traditional lines of loyalty, to a large extent socialist communalization had led to the reinforcement of lineage; that is, lineage connections persisted and, with them, other aspects of traditional ideology.

After the three-year famine, the central government maintained its policy of requiring grain production in the countryside to be sold to the state. Many changes were introduced during the co-op and commune periods. Through the combination of long-time leveling of land, the introduction of organic and chemical fertilizers, scientific seedlings and planting, mechanized irrigation, and the use of pesticides, grain production steadily increased after 1962. Grain yield per mu grew from 280 *jin* in 1949 to 665 *jin* in 1975. However, given the restrictions on crop sales and on production, villagers did not have sufficient food until 1972. Throughout the communal period, grain was rationed and production beyond this amount was sold by law to the government at the price fixed by the state. The county government determined what to plant and how much *mu* to plant. Commune members felt that the benefits of the modernization of agriculture were not flowing back to the producers.

In 1972, under the directive from the Liang-guo Commune to which Ma village belonged, villages exchanged and consolidated small plots of land with each other in order to work on the larger plot, which was the consequence of the move to collective farming. Before communalization, hilly land was owned by nearby villagers from Zhang village, Ma village, Upper Yang village, Shang Po, Li village, Liu village, Qiu village, Shi village, Ma Hui village, and Lu village. Overall, total land exchanged was 602.81 *mu* with 204 plots. Each plot had an average of 2.95 *mu*. In other words, the six-hundred some *mu* of land was owned by more than 200 families. As a result, Ma Brigade had taken in 124 plots with a total of 384.71 *mu* and given up an equivalent amount to other villages.[7] The fact that different owners from different villages were on the same bigger plot showed that the land was sold many times; thus the distribution was mixed with different village names; that is, different family names.

One of the difficulties of central planning of agriculture comes from balancing the directives of central planning, which specifies demand, and the specific conditions of different locales, which affect supply. Regardless of different local conditions, each brigade would have to grow grain following the directives from the central government. For example, hilly lands in Ma village were better suited for growing fruit rather than grain, yet the authorities at county levels and above determined what kind of grain to produce and how much land to plant. The question of diversification of agricultural production is bound up with local knowledge and leadership, but agricultural decisions were centralized beyond the power of the team leaders. On the other hand, diversification can also bring up the question of the existence of local markets where surplus products could be sold or exchanged. Demand for the latter practice arises easily in peasant communities.

Landlord and rich peasants had been targeted in land reform, and they were integrated into the co-op only gradually. Middle peasants, similarly, were obliged to join – it was not voluntary. It may be argued that there was resentment against the state government for taking the land from the landlords and rich peasant families and giving them to the poor, especially in the circumstance in which not all families shared a single family lineage. It must be reiterated that, in the case of Ma village, the original funds used to buy the land was not accumulated from exploitation within the village and, as noted, the government did not purchase the land with a redemption policy, similar to the one which had been adopted in the city. In fact, while the Great Leap Forward is acknowledged to have been precipitous and to have had seriously deleterious, ultra-left consequences, its failure discredited what was potentially an important socialist policy of transforming industrialization and diversifying economic development to the benefit of rural rather than urban areas. Its failure strengthened political calls for market relations in the countryside and concentrated urban industrialization.

According to our view, the move to advanced cooperatives and communes was too rapid. The change was not based on the build-up of necessary ideological and economic preconditions. The two systems, cooperative and private (middle peasant) agriculture could have co-existed. The government might have organized the poor, supported the peasants in the election of their own leaders, and supported the poor peasant associations with better seeds, new planting techniques, etcetera, to raise grain production. The co-op would then set examples for the middle peasants. Meanwhile, the government could introduce more social programmes with national support, such as bare-foot doctors and public schools, in the existing co-operative, which would have made them more attractive to join. As a revolutionary government, the government could provide material and ideological support for collective roaders. The peasants might have had their own right to join and withdraw from their organizations. The government's job would be to show that, through the collective ownership of the means of production, they could have increased their standard of living. This gradualist argument is reflected in what Engels says in *The Peasant Question in France and Germany*:

> [I]t is just as evident that when we are in possession of state power, we shall not even think of forcibly expropriating the small peasants (regardless of whether with or without compensation), as we shall have to

do in the case of the big landowners. Our task relative to the small peasant consists, in the first place, in effecting a transition of his private enterprise and private possession to cooperative ones, not forcibly but by dint of example and the proffer of social assistance for this purpose. And then, of course, we shall have ample means of showing to the small peasant prospective advantages that must be obvious to him.... We, of course, are decidedly on the side of the small peasant; we shall do everything at all permissible to make his lot more bearable, to facilitate his transition to the cooperative should he decide to do so, and even to make it possible for him to remain on his small holding for a protracted length of time to think the matter over, should he still be unable to bring himself to this decision. (Engels: 468)

Engels assumed that a socialist revolution would occur in an advanced capitalist country. He did not contemplate, nor did anyone before Lenin face the problems of a socialist revolution in a non-industrialized country, which would require industrial development without a long period of 'primitive' accumulation, the creation of an industrial proletariat, and the substantial erosion of traditional customs and practices. By moving rapidly to communalization, Chinese practices certainly followed the example of Soviet Russia. The partial retreat back to production-team accounting in 1962 and, therefore, brigade level (village and lineage) production suggests the move to full communes was precipitous. Nevertheless, the structure of a commune system continued to exist in China until it was broken up in 1983 during the early years of the Deng era. It could also be noted that egalitarianism also had roots in Chinese traditions. Share and share alike was often the slogan of peasant rebels, such as the Tai Ping Rebellion.

Industrial Workshops (1956--1982)

THE CHINESE population began to grow in the 1950s and, with the increased grain production after 1962, population growth was unprecedented. With the restriction of internal migration from rural areas to urban centers, population in the countryside grew, requiring an increased ration of grain. Meanwhile, the state continued to be the sole buyer of grain products. Small-scale local markets existed in rural areas. In fact, the scale of these markets waxed and waned depending on political policy changes and local factors. Usually, various forms of unofficial exchange occurred at the village level.

In general, markets are understood in Marxism to be capitalist forms of distribution that, over time, tend to exacerbate class differences. As inequalities grow between peasant families in the village, between villages, between regions and so on, vested interests are developed for whom extending their privileges become a priority. In the long run, these economic changes and the development of class polarization would be reflected in politics and in policy (line) struggles in the state. The Chinese Communist Party believed that developing a commodity economy through market transactions would automatically lead to capitalism, therefore markets were closed periodically. Strategic produce such as grain and peanuts were prohibited from private trading.

As a result of the increased population, more productive agriculture, and the restriction on markets, village industries were developed to absorb more labour. Rural industrial development had been a goal of the Great Leap Forward, which had attempted to reverse the Soviet-style policy of developing heavy industry at the expense of both light industries and agriculture. The result of Soviet development had been an increase in polarization between rural and urban China, as well as other forms of inequality, such as between manual and mental labour. Economic development in China in the socialist period was rooted in politics – the slogan was to "put politics in command." Consequently, market policies, the sourcing of raw materials, and selling of the products were all restricted. Mobility of villagers was forbidden as well with the issuing of living permits. Farming offered little hope for employing the next generation of young villagers. The CCP understood the key Marxist principle that a market economy was not a tool to realize a socialist economy. At different times and places, however, market mechanisms are acceptable within an overall planned economy with centralized political control. Lenin's New Economic Policy, for example, provided for capitalist development in the countryside. The resulting polarization and establishment of entrenched vested interest in the continuation of the market economy contributed to making the Soviet attempt to collectivize agriculture a highly contested and ultimately violent venture. Whether a market economy would become the origin of a reversion back to capitalist development depended on political struggles within the CCP, as Mao understood.

After developing and expanding a variety of workshops in Ma village, including but not limited to a brush-pen shop and brush shop, the value from workshops in 1972 was 80% compared with farming, and one year later the former was more than the latter. And this was ten years away from 1983 when private farming was restored. The labour transfer from farming to industries was obvious. Work-points provide an objective index measuring the labour distribution. In 1970 for example, the work points from the brigade were as high as 330,959, and 14,893 *yuan* were given to the teams in exchange for the work points. The daily value of an adult labourer per day was 0.45 *yuan* for 10 work points. So villagers from the work-shops would take their work points back to their team to which their family belonged and participate in the distribution of grain, stalks, vegetables, peanuts, etc. The work points of 330,959 were from the following industries (see Table 2):

Table 2 Work Points by Sector (1970)

Sector	Work Points
Blacksmith	16271
Quarry	32473
Workshop	154860
AgriTechTeam	25899
Tractors	8343
Management	75791
Benefits	17322
Total	330959

For Team I, the total working days were 30717.5 (that is, 307175 work points), including work points transferred from the brigade for the commune members who belonged to Team I but worked for the brigade. If we separate these points into two groups, then the labour force working in farming was 39%. We can also compare Team IV, with total work points of 245267.3, including transfer from brigade of 7213, for which the percentage from agriculture was 42%. From this finding, we can see that even in the communal period, the transfer of labour outside of farming was already happening, supporting our position that this historical process did not start after the reform, as many scholars have claimed.

In 1972, the revenue percentage from industries over farming was 80% and industries had become the dominant source of revenue. The growth of village-level industries indicates that market restrictions did not prevent the diversification of the rural economy, and villagers still believed that liberal market relations would bring them greater benefit. The collective enterprises, including the Tire Shop, Pen Shop, Brush Shop, etc., were controlled by the party secretary. Though land and enterprises were collectively owned, decision making and public management were never done collectively. All decisions were made from the top. The appropriate relationship between central authority and local input and control is a difficult tactical question that differs in time and place. Nevertheless, one of the central, unresolved problems of socialism is to devise mechanisms for both, captured in the term democratic centralism. The potential for abuse of control from the top can be checked by internal party mechanisms and by the type of relationship existing between local leaders and village members. Here it must be admitted that, in the Chinese case, democratic processes of discussion and deliberation were not very common.

The main source of inequality lay in the assignment of work, not the distribution of grain. Distribution was based on the number of people and work points. Commune members without working capabilities would get grain from the production team. Vegetables were divided strictly on the number of family members. Given these rules, cadres could not easily abuse power in the distribution process. Team leaders, however, could assign easier or more lucrative work to relatives or friends, though this practice was also limited to a certain extent, because team leaders not only had to work together with the members, but also they were related as they were from the same Ma clan. But the brigade leaders had access to more power and opportunities. When the upper authorities gave a quota to the brigade, such as recruiting new urban workers or drafting soldiers, the brigade leaders, usually the party secretary, would make the decision. The brigade leaders could appoint relatives or friends to the brigade-owned shops where the work was easier than farming. Most of the villagers working in these shops were related to the cadres. In the context of scarcity, what appear to be relatively minor privileges assume an exaggerated importance.

Nevertheless, as was typical for the period of early economic development in other countries, most young villagers were trying to get out of the villages and become city residents. The divide between the city and the country is a typical tendency of capitalist development, as the almost incredible growth of shanty-towns and slums around major cities in the global South demonstrates. Chinese migration policy during the socialist period was designed to prevent this mass migration, which exacerbates the rural/urban division. Nevertheless, these efforts were insufficient, leadership was problematic, and morale among commune members was low, especially in the younger generation. As the divide between town and county is exacerbated, the demand grows in tandem for internal migration, as does discontent with the restrictive migration policies.

Mass Campaigns and Class Struggle

FROM THE PERSPECTIVE of Ma village and, arguably, more generally in China, the CCP did not create or institutionalize elements of local self-governance and did not develop mechanisms for democratic participation in the decision making and management of the commune. Instead, the CCP relied on propaganda and education to inculcate an ethical code of serving the people and self-discipline. Political campaigns were periodically launched to contain corruption and bureaucracy. In a centralized government, the quality of the leadership and the relationships they maintain with local-level leaders and the people are crucial elements of democratic centralism. Most mechanisms of control, however, were maintained within the Party. As inner-party struggles intensified during and after the Great Leap and into the Cultural Revolution, Mao identified the major contradiction of socialist construction to be between party leaders and bureaucrats who were taking a capitalist road and the masses. On the other hand, many peasants did not see things this way. Since the capitalist road was defined, in part, by the existence of markets, villagers were discouraged from growing non-grain, market crops, but this curtailed both their incomes and ambitions. And the benefits of communalization were not perceived as outweighing the potential gains of independent cultivation.

The CCP organized mass campaigns, down to the village level, to popularize the socialist road and identify and combat traditional customs and practices as well as forms of self-interest. At the village level, mass involvement, at best, entailed making Big Character posters, which was an anonymous form of protest pasted on walls and exposing and criticizing the wrongdoings of some cadres. When matters were raised in village meetings, the cadres often would find some scapegoats to deflect responsibility. Under the banner of class struggle, members of the landlord and rich peasant families were once again discriminated against as class enemies. They were an easy ideological target. Emphasis was put on a person's family background, a practice that is questionable in the first place. Sons from this kind of family background could not even find a wife. There were cases in which families exchanged their sons and daughters in order to secure marriages.

Cadres had Party rectification meetings every year, in which they would carry on criticism and self-criticism. In the late 1950s and early 1960s, the campaigns were more effective than they later became. Cadres, after admitting their mistakes, would at first return to their brigade and give back anything they had admitted to during their self-criticism. But as time passed, it became a formality. Both cadres and commune members went through motions in the campaigns and political meetings. The annual Rectification Meeting often became a party for Communist Party members, an occasion to eat better food purchased by brigade funds. Despite such evident anti-socialist practices among the leaders, the Cultural Revolution, for example, barely touched Ma village. By that time, socialist leadership had deteriorated and the typical village orientation was to revert back to the traditional ideology of opposition to all forms of central authority.

Persistence of Lineage Relationships

THE COLLECTIVE SYSTEM had neither transformed nor transcended the family system. When villagers did not have access to the formal channels to get things done, they were forced to use informal means, often involving lineage relationships. Thus, on one hand, a centralized system was in place, which did not address concerns for local input and control, and on the other hand, familism prospered again. Facing authorities from the outside, villagers wove an informal network through family relations, lineage, and marriage that filtered any policies implemented from the top and from outside. We will start from village leaders and party members, who were the pillars of the communist system at the village level (see Appendix). Brigade Head, Ma Jin-you, for example, had five sons and four daughters, and five of them married within the village. Through marriages, Ma Jin-you easily established relationships with five families, and these five families had their own intra-village marriages. A net had been woven and all other relations would have integrated into it. While the formal lineage through male siblings had been suppressed, new types of lineage had formed through marriages. The Brigade Mediator Ma Yu-shan had five children, and three of them married in the village. Some families seemingly had no direct connections, but they often were connected indirectly.

Rural relations were based traditionally on family relations within the village. Facing the commune, a powerful institution in China's history, villagers resorted to a new form of traditional relationship to increase their own power and to deal with outside authority that was not deemed legitimate. Historically, there had never been endogamous marriages in the village. But since the beginning of the co-op movement, marriages occurred more frequently among Mas. Thus a new form of lineage emerged. From 1955-1980, there were 56 marriages within Ma village. Village relations became more and more complex.

The End of Socialist China

SHORTLY AFTER Mao's death and Deng Xiao-ping's assumption of power in 1978, the right-wing of the CCP started to dismantle the dominant planks of the socialist system, although the restoration of capitalist relations of production did not occur overnight. Given the rampant ultra-leftism in the Cultural Revolution, purging any form of opposition in the Party was relatively easy, and left-wing views were silenced or co-opted. In 1983, together with almost all of the brigades, Ma Brigade was broken up. The ruling Party maintained a level of control over agricultural land while it privatized the majority of industrial assets. Land was not returned to individuals but formally leased to individual families.

Like the step towards communalization in 1955 when villagers were organized into co-ops, often against their will, the decisions to break up the communes was made without consulting the villagers. And most of the villagers found new reasons to resent the breakup. The villagers at the eve of the breakup were concerned that the collective was beginning to produce some positive results, such as they had enough to eat, village shops were doing well, and mechanization was gradually being introduced. As the breakup of the communal system proceeded, land redistribution tended to reward politically-connected families. Village industries were handed over to the people who had controlled them; that is, to Party officials and local leaders. Had the villagers anticipated these issues, they would have been more vocal in their concerns at the time of the change in policy.

The fact that China's course could change so abruptly and definitively is a problem demanding much more analysis and discussion. There is no doubt, however, that the turn to capitalist relationships and market forces made some people rich literally overnight. Public assets were privatized and turned over to individual or corporate ownership. From 1979 to 1993 a so-called double-track price system was in effect, an economic policy that maintained certain elements of political control that were dubbed a continuation of "central planning" and, at the same time, allowed market fluctuations. Controls on strategic goods, such as crude oil, coal, grain were gradually reduced. During this process, whoever had political power or had access to power could buy cheaply from the planned quota and sell dear on the market. In this sense, the system was doubly corrupt. Overall, corruption is simply a descriptive term for a system that utilizes any means to secure private advantage. From a socialist point of view, the wholesale expropriation of public assets to individuals, whether they were politically powerful or not, is a form of sanctioned 'corruption.' In a system that is rife with corrupt practices, from top to bottom, 'corruption' technically means going beyond the normal limits of business practices utilizing access to political power to give individuals economic advantages within the emerging market economy.

By 1989, China was already well on the capitalist road and had developed deep connections with Western capital. Believing that, "Regardless of whether a cat is white or black, it is a good cat as long as it can catch a mouse," Deng's strategy was to further develop the economy by tying China intimately with Western capitalism while firmly holding political power in a one-party state. Deng claimed that the development of large-scale capitalism in China was "socialism with Chinese characteristics," which has been jokingly described as "flashing the left signal but turning to the right." In 1992, widespread, nation-wide pro-capitalist business policies were implemented, which is considered by Xueqin Zhu as the "second reform." It was implemented without opposition. By this time, all the old comrades were either dead or too fragile to make any opposition (Zhu 2008).

In 1994, a tax-sharing system between the central and local governments was imposed by which the central government took a majority of the taxes; local governments only received a portion determined by the top and ended up with fewer funds available. Local governments were becoming more and more like business corporations and officials becoming business people. Crony capitalism flourished. A market economy became official, and now government and officials could make money legitimately through capitalism.

In the countryside, after the dismantling of the commune, political control has been gradually loosened, and villagers are left alone in the village. Due to the lack of political participation, public land and collective enterprises have been left in the hands of former team and villager leaders. The subject of ownership ended up in the hands of the cadres who now directly controlled the means of production. While team leaders would divide up the farm implements, village leaders would rent out collectively-owned enterprises and embezzle public funds. From the stand of the township governments, they would rather deal with the same leaders even if they were corrupt, since the township governments would rely on the village heads to carry out the orders from the upper authorities and at the same time take advantage of their own positions for their private interests.

Village Organization Law

AFTER THE COLLECTIVE was broken up, the central government passed the Village Organization Law in 1983. Rural self-governance and village elections were hailed as a promotion of local democracy and the rule of law. However, there is something internally contradictory within the Village Organization Law. According to the law, villagers elect the village head, but the head should report to the township head, who is appointed by upper authority and reports directly to the township party secretary. The village party secretary, of course, reports to the township party secretary. On the other hand, the village secretary is not elected but appointed by the township party secretary. In a word, the elected village head will report to the appointed village party secretary. Of course, the township officials are also appointed by the county government. Despite local elections, the power is actually held by officials from above.

During and after the collective break-up, the sell-out or rent-out of collective-owned enterprises caused public outrage because the selling price and rent were often manipulated by village leaders appointed by upper authorities. Benefits, then, were monopolized by people who had entrenched positions of political power, and other villagers had no participation in the decision making about these transactions. In a close community like Ma village, villagers knew almost everything about each other. While villagers were outraged with the corruption and embezzlement of the village leaders, they also had to pay all sorts of taxes, levies, and fees, which were charged mostly by village, town, and municipal governments. Local governments had come out with all kinds of programmes and plans in the name of economic and social development, such as post offices, schools, and roads. Villagers were forced to pay for these services. From their point of view, they had no input into the services that were to be implemented, how, where, and for whom the services were to be built, and who would benefit from them. When villagers refused to pay, they were harassed by the local security bureau, which is full of temporary hires and local bullies. Access to political power opens many sources for legal exploitation and also for acquiring illicit income, the latter being defined as corruption.

In Ma village the conflict between the villagers and the village leaders backed up by township officials has escalated to an unprecedented level. In 2000, Ma Guo-ti, Ma Jun-yao, Zhao Li-bo, and their supporters refused to pay levies, and accused Ma Xiang-bo, then party secretary, of corruption. They went to the township and asked for an investigation of the accounting books. The township did investigate and then claimed that there were no wrongdoings. The villagers then went on to the county seat, and without any reply within the promised 20 day waiting period, continued with their petition to Yantai, the prefecture seat, and eventually to Jinan, the provincial capital. An official from the provincial Discipline Committee told the villagers that, based on the amount of funds embezzled, in comparison with cadres elsewhere, Ma Xiang-bo was not that bad. Three representatives finally made it to Beijing. The petition was then pushed back to Jinan, and the municipal government finally decided to take some action.

In the autumn of 2003, about thirty villagers went to the provincial capital, Jinan, to protest again. The secretary of Laizhou Discipline Committee, the deputy police chief, and some 20 other police officers went to Jinan and put the villagers in police cars and took them back to Laizhou. Some of them, including Ma Guo-ti and Zhao Li-bo, were detained for twenty days; others including Ma Jun-yao fled the village.

There are numerous similar incidents reported in coastal and suburban areas, where local governments have taken the land from villages and sold the land to developers and given very little to the villagers in return. Villagers were seldom involved in the transactions and were, of course, dissatisfied with the compensation they had received. The conflicts often end in injuries and even deaths. By this time, so-called state ownership and collective ownership are really privatized ownership managed by government officials for private gain.

Village Elections

LOCAL ELECTIONS were organized in Ma village in 2004, when the township realized that the situation was out of control if they continued to support Ma Xiang-bo. Almost half of the villagers refused to obey the party secretary, which had paralyzed public services in the village. When the cadres at the township changed, Ma Xiang-bo lost his connection. The Township then agreed to an election.

In the first election, Ma Xiang-bo was defeated. The second election was held three years later. Before the election, Zhao Liang paid RMB 50 for each vote, and Ma Xiang-bo paid RMB 25, to undecided villagers. Even though Zhao Liang was elected on an anti-corruption platform, he also did not make the accounting books public, as promised in the election campaign, because villagers were questioning the revenue of the contracted land, sales of trees, and the sale of the tire factory.

The township officials are half-hearted with the village elections since they make it difficult to control the elected village leaders. That's why they usually do not follow up after the elections and won't enforce public participation and transparency. Nationwide, villagers were still dissatisfied with the elections and are becoming cynical about elections. According to the Land Administration Law, local authorities must consult with the villagers before selling land. Yet throughout China, whenever there is a business opportunity, there is the same kind of graft, such as in the suburbs where land is valuable because it is close to the city, or the coastal areas, which are often set up as economic zones, and even in the remote areas where there may exist money-making opportunities, such as in mining. Thus, in all these areas, villagers have encountered land grabs backed up by the state apparatus. On the one hand, it could be said that confrontation between the villagers and the government continues. On the other hand, in a world where self-interest rules, the solution is to become a political insider and gain access to the sources of graft; it is not to create a system in which the opportunities for graft are systematically limited. Now villagers can vote, but they have almost no confidence in the local governments.

Land Centralization and Fragmentation

UNDER THE POLITICAL control of the current regime, industrialization gains momentum. As the survey of Ma villagers in March 2010 demonstrated, among a total population of 416 excluding 58 juniors, only 27 villagers under the age of 59 relied totally on farming, 210 people either had small businesses or worked full time and farmed only on the weekend for food, and 60 younger villagers had left the village.

Younger villagers are migrating in larger number to the cities, a pattern typical of capitalist development world-wide, leaving less-able hands in the village. Modern industrialization and commercialization unequivocally play an instrumental role in dramatically accelerating the subversion of the centuries-old lineage system. The combination of a market economy and a market-oriented polity has transformed the rural population from families being in the village to individuals being atomized in the city.

At the same time, more machinery is being used in farming. In 2008, only a third of the corn fields were harvested by combines, which were owned by two families. As of 2014, all fields were irrigated by water pumps. The adoption of coating seeds with pesticide has cut down the labour required for pulling weeds. Wheat and corn harvesting are almost all mechanized. This change has not only increased grain output, but it has also required less labour. Industrialization has finally come, and with it land centralization. But again, market transactions are often superficial. Wheeling and dealing are done through political maneuvering. Political power is used to consolidate the villages so that land can be contracted to capitalists. The use of "capitalism to build socialism" has resulted in the use of "socialism [the one-party state] to build capitalism" (Hinton 1996).

At the same time, the village social network is more and more fragmented. Family members are often living in different places, and they get together only during special festivals. New forms of social network are emerging in the cities, where most young and middle-aged villagers have migrated and lived. As long as there are employment opportunities outside agriculture, the current regime will hold on to power. Nevertheless, after following a capitalist growth-at-all-costs development model, hailed as the "hard truth" by Deng, the Chinese people are paying the social costs for one of the world's largest and fastest-growing economies: an increasing gap between the rich and the poor, rampaging social insecurity, and highly polluted urban environments, among other social problems.

Conclusion

THE MARKET MECHANISM operates differently in China from early, liberal capitalism. The invisible hand is manipulated by political power and the market is often a handmaiden of the state. In other words, political power, whether operating within the laws of capitalist development or through corruption, decides on the allocation of opportunities for wealth-production. Those in power skim the proceeds, acquire benefits themselves, and utilize political power as a means for accumulating economic power. However, the system they are manipulating, the investment they are channeling or providing, are creating a capitalist economy that is tied inextricably to Western capital.

In this sense, China is capitalist in that its economic (and, relatedly, its political) future is bound up with global capitalism. Unlike the neo-liberal regimes in the West, however, China's political barons have a greater say in economic development policies. China is not a capitalist country in the same way as in the West. But political decisions are made in the interests of strengthening the capitalist economy and, therefore, to the advantage of capital.

There are two striking features in Chinese history. One is the long continuing presence of a unified, centralized kingdom and the other is the presence of a rural producing class of individual cultivators tied to the land and politically tied to the kingdom. The socialist revolution attempted to transform, in traditional centralized fashion, the state into a public servant of the people; at the same time it tried to change the individual cultivators into a cooperative body of producers. In both cases, we have seen some success but ultimate failure. The present system of capitalism in China is a product of its history. Using the traditional and centralized state as a means, capital successfully appealed to the deep self-interest that is entrenched in the individual cultivator. This new form of state-directed capitalism, we think, is an unstable and transient form. With the crises inevitable to capitalism, we would expect that this form of capitalism, where the depredations of capitalism are seen as stemming from government action, will not last. Public profit making will always have the whiff of corruption. As big capital grows in China, the question becomes more pressing whether it is better to retain the centralized government including its controls on investment and labour, or abandon it and the fiction of "socialism with Chinese characteristics." Only when capitalism takes on its more modern form of formally separating the state from the private economy will China join the ranks of the legally entrenched corruption of "democratic" capitalism.

CHAPTER EIGHT

Marxism and Feminism

MARXISM HAS OFTEN been considered limited in it relative silence about what has, by Marxists, been called the 'woman question.' The growth and more elaborated forms of modern feminism have criticized the Marxist approach to the oppression of women as something of an afterthought, as something tacked on after the central problem of class exploitation is taken care of. While we think that some of modern feminism has taken a fully reformist approach to the problem, one that perceives that women's emancipation can take place without essentially changing the capitalist class system, we do think that the feminist response has some validity. While all modern revolutions made progressive strides in liberating women from feudal and other traditional forms of oppression, and also in female literacy and entrance into the wider workforce, there remains still the sense that these strides were quite secondary to the main need for industrialization with women being liberated to help production, leaving many patriarchal attitudes and institutions intact. All one has to do is look at who runs almost all major economic and political institutions to see that patriarchy has been alive and well in the process of socialist transition.

Socialist Theory and the "Woman Question"

THE EMANCIPATION of women is a crucial aspect of progressive and Marxist politics. A wide array of theorists have agreed on the need to emancipate women, including social liberals, Utopian and Marxian socialists, and even some *avant-garde* artists. Friedrich Engels developed an historical theory of women's oppression in *The Origin of the Family, Private Property, and the State*. Engels wrote that, at an early point in history (primitive communism), women had substantial power in society and were held in high esteem. Consistent with his materialism, Engels linked this high status with the important economic role women occupied at that time. However, with the development of private property, which was under the control of men, women suffered an "historical defeat." In the agricultural and traditional societies that subsequently developed, men initiated the full oppression of women, treating women as property under patriarchal domination.

The subjection of women continued under capitalist relations of production. By the late nineteenth century, liberal and socialist women were fully engaged in the struggle for emancipation, and a powerful women's movement had emerged. The goal of the movement was to secure legal and political rights for women within bourgeois democracy. While socialists in this movement certainly agreed that women must fight for their political emancipation, the main issue in the 'woman question' was the potential contradiction between the struggle for women's equality within capitalism and the struggle for socialism. If the current foundation of women's oppression was capitalism, should women cease to struggle for their own liberation and put all their energies into joining with men to bring about the socialist revolution? This policy implied not fighting for specifically women's issues – against violence in the home, for example – because it would distract from the class struggle and break the class solidarity between working class women and men. Lenin pointed out, for example, that social democrats in Austria had campaigned for electoral rights for men, but postponed the struggle for women's rights until a later date. After the revolution was victorious, they claimed, there would be plenty of time to address other forms of oppression, such as those faced by women. In this positivist view, social change involved two steps, the primary step being the transition to socialism. Once private property was abolished, the argument went, the economic foundation for the oppression of women would disappear and women would become progressively liberated. Alterations in social attitudes and practices were only a matter of progressive economic change.

As Maria Meis summarized the positivist argument in *Patriarchy and Accumulation on a World Scale*, the integration of women into productive labour would be the foundation for the solution of all other problems facing women. The full employment of women outside the household would automatically bring about a change in the psychology and ideas of women and men. Women would become politically active, would demand equality in daily life and democracy in their marriages, and would be shown to be the social and intellectual equals of men. But these promises would be realized only after the socialist revolution. In the meantime, women must subordinate any of their particular demands and questions to the requirements of the class struggle in which proletarian women and men have the same anti-capitalist interests and must struggle together.

In the view of the German socialist and feminist, Clara Zetkin, for example, socialists should maintain a critical connection with the liberal women's movement, which included all women regardless of social class. While most of the issues facing women had arisen at some point or other in the women's movement, by the 1890s, in the main, the goals of the movement had been pared down to the demand for political rights. Zetkin realized this movement had no vision other than to make women politically equal to men and would not affect social class inequalities among women. Bourgeois women would be equal in law to bourgeois men; proletarian women would be formally equal to working class men. The bourgeois women's movement, then, was extremely limited in its goals but, Zetkin said, political rights constituted only one small step in ending the oppression of women. While women from all classes faced specific forms of oppression, she believed that working class women should have a distinct movement to express their interests. The key necessity was to integrate women fully into paid production outside the home. Once they were fully proletarianized, women would develop working class and, presumably, revolutionary consciousness.

It was in this sense that Marx had favoured women's employment, although not work that would physically cause harm – women, like children, being assumed in the nineteenth century to be more delicate than men (although Marx had speculated about the progressive side of integrating children into productive labour appropriate for their level of maturity). As Meis points out, however, from the time of Lassalle, reformists in Germany opposed women's employment. Many male industrial workers demanded that women be "free" from the abuse of performing productive labour in modern industry.

By the late nineteenth century, reformists in the German Social Democratic Party (SPD) had become explicitly anti-feminist. It was not just that they wanted to exclude women from "dangerous" or supposedly gender-inappropriate work; right-wing social democrats wanted to exclude women entirely. This exclusion was, first, because when women entered the workforce and competed for jobs, they lowered male wages, in fact providing relatively cheap labour for capital. Second, they echoed bourgeois claims that blamed the breakdown of the working-class family on the employment of women: the "proletarian family" was being undermined by women working outside the home. The largest socialist movement of the time adopted the position that married women should be primarily wives and mothers. If women stayed out of paid labour, they could maintain the family home while male workers should demand a "family wage" that would provide for their dependent wives and children. This stand reinforced the male working class monopoly of paid employment and meant that men controlled the finances of the working class family. It reproduced the bourgeois conception of the family in working class households.

Zetkin was critical of the reformists in the SPD and maintained ties with Luxemburg and Liebknecht. But she also stressed the important role working class women played as wives and mothers. In 1896, she argued that "new barriers need to be erected against the exploitation of the proletarian woman. Her rights as wife and mother need to be restored and permanently secured." Socialists should not "alienate the proletarian woman from her duties as mother and wife. On the contrary, she must be encouraged to carry out these tasks better than ever in the interests of the liberation of the proletariat."

The standard male-centred argument asserted that any struggles within the anti-capitalist movement that were aimed specifically at the oppression of women should wait until the revolution had succeeded. In the pre-revolutionary stage, the unity of the proletariat was all-important. Demands for the equal representation of women in the political party, for equality in the proletarian household (against patriarchal attitudes held by working class men, socialist or not), and for other women-centred issues would only divide the working class and weaken its struggle for socialism. Identifying men as the 'enemy,' for example, helped the bourgeoisie divide and control the proletariat. The struggle had to be singly focused on the bourgeoisie. Maintaining working class solidarity, including both men and women, was necessary for success.

Revolutionary Marxists realized that a crucial key to women's emancipation was their full integration into the labour force, but this was not the only issue that needed to be confronted. The argument that the specific nature of the oppression of women in capitalism should be ignored until some future time did not go over well with many socialist women or with some socialist men. They argued against any simple two-stage conception of revolution. Women could not be expected to put off their general emancipation until after the revolution. The condition for women's participation in the struggle for socialism was that women's issues would become part of the struggle, not be put off until sometime in the future. Without serious attention to these issues, women could not be expected to take part in the struggle for socialism. Since the full participation of women was necessary for the success of the revolution, a two-stage strategy was doomed to failure. As Marx's daughter, Eleanor Marx declared, the chief lesson of history was that no people are ever liberated by others but only by their own struggles. Women should create socialist women's organisations, which would be separate from men, to formulate, advance, and struggle for specifically women's issues within the socialist movement, and to ensure that their real and immediate needs were not sacrificed. Furthermore, women and men must fight for the liberation of women at the same time as they struggle against capitalism. Rather than wait for some promised future time, socialist men and women must create a new kind of mutual, free relationship based on equality and respect. Women must actively create the conditions for their own liberation within the socialist movement but also in all other areas of live including daily life where they and socialist men must confront male dominance. For socialists, while the liberation of all humanity could only occur through a socialist revolution, actually practicing equality in marriage was part of realizing this future.

For Lenin, full participation in productive labour was the fundamental condition for women's emancipation. Women worked in particularly harsh conditions, but the solution was workplace reform, not laws that banned their participation. Working in social production drew women out of the narrow circle of patriarchal isolation and dependence. The basic demand of many socialists was to integrate women fully into production. The main precondition for women's emancipation was financial independence and the opportunity to become fully involved in the social and political struggles at the level of the workplace. Economic integration would remove women from the private sphere of the household, bringing them into contact with other women, other workers, and the class struggle.

Beyond the overall argument that genuine liberation could occur only in a socialist society, the corollary was equally true: there could be no socialism without the liberation of women. It should not be assumed that so-called superstructural features of society (ideas, psychology) would be quickly and easily transformed after the socialist victory. A women's movement would still be necessary to identify women's interests and ensure that the proletarian state would actually create the conditions for women's full emancipation. Patriarchal attitudes would persist after the revolution and would have to be confronted individually and organisationally. The Russian Social Democratic Party had promised the political and economic emancipation of women in its 1902 programme, which included full equality for all regardless of sex, religion, or race. In its Party programme of 1917, the Bolsheviks included a brief, paid maternity leave of eight weeks before and eight weeks after childbirth, the establishment of nurseries in places of women's employment, and recesses for nursing mothers along with shortened working hours.

In *Women, Resistance and Revolution* Sheila Rowbotham said that women in the Bolshevik Party established an independent women's organization in 1919, but it was criticized by many Bolsheviks on the grounds it was too feminist. In the Soviet Union, women's faced traditional hostility from men everywhere – at work, at home, and in the Party. Deeply-rooted traditions worked against women's emancipation, particularly in the rural parts of Russia and in the eastern regions. Rowbotham noted that actually putting into practice a new code for family life proved an intractable problem in the chaos of civil war and during the NEP. With the emphasis on economic efficiency, short-term profitability took pride of place. Lenin criticized the passive attitude that existed among some male comrades, particularly in the "national sections," who did not realize the importance of creating "a mass movement of working women under communist leadership"; that is, the movement was independent but its leadership should be Bolshevik. Political work among women was equally the task of men and women in the Party; it was "as much as half of all the Party work," Lenin said. In the backward mentality of too many men, housework was defined solely as women's work, beneath a man's dignity: "The ancient rights of her husband, her lord and master, survive unnoticed.... We must root out the old slave-owner's point of view, both in the Party and among the masses."

In the countryside, Lenin wrote in 1918, one year after the Revolution, freedom of marriage "remains a dead letter" because "religious marriages still predominate." Changing religious views is a delicate struggle that must be carried out by propaganda and education because "lending too sharp an edge to the struggle" risks arousing resentment and divides what should be united. Women's status in the countryside is rooted in small peasant farms, and emancipation requires a movement to co-operative farming and the use of "collective methods to work the land." Furthermore, remaking legislation, such as abolishing the need for divorce procedures and eliminating the distinction between children born within or outside marriage, was merely clearing the ground; it was "not yet building.... Notwithstanding all the laws emancipating woman, she continues to be a *domestic slave*, because *petty housework* crushes, strangles, stultifies and degrades her, chains her to the kitchen and the nursery, and she wastes her labour on barbarously unproductive, petty, nerve-wracking, stultifying and crushing drudgery." The solution will come when the "*wholesale transformation* [of petty housekeeping] into a large-scale socialist economy begins." Institutions such as "Public catering establishments, nurseries, kindergartens" are the "everyday means ... which can *really emancipate women*, really lessen or abolish their inequality with men as regards their role in social production and public life." These are shoots of communism, Lenin suggests. Complete emancipation requires "housework to be socialized and for women to participate in common productive labour." This work, however, "will take us many, many years," and it will include "organisational work on the smallest scale." Furthermore, it was necessary for women to take an active part in the administration of socialised enterprises and the state. Lenin called for the election of more women to the Soviets, a tall order "because it involves the remoulding of the most deep-rooted, inveterate, hidebound and rigid 'order.'"

For Lenin, the "communist women's movement itself must be a mass movement, a part of the general mass movements; and not only of the proletarians, but of all the exploited and oppressed, of all victims of capitalism or of the dominant class.... [W]e have to win over the millions of working women in town and country for our struggle and, particularly, for the communist reconstruction of society." To rouse women as a group, bring them into contact with the Party, and "keep them under its influence," women in the Party should work within women's groups, committees, and sections to win them over to the class struggle and the leadership of the Party. For Lenin, practical, revolutionary expediency demanded "our own groups to work among the [masses of women], special methods of agitation, and special forms of organisation."

On the other hand, Lenin opposed the ultra-left argument, based on the "purity of principles," that women's equality required that no differentiation be made between women and men, women's and men's organizations, or the approach taken to men and women. Demands that are specific to the needs of women are not mere reforms meant to divert women from the revolutionary path. They arise from the "crying needs and disgraceful humiliations" faced by women in bourgeois and traditional societies. "We demonstrate thereby that we are aware of these needs and of the oppression of women, that we are conscious of the privileged position of men, and that we hate – yes, hate – and want to remove whatever oppresses and harasses the working woman, the wife of the worker, the peasant woman, the wife of the little man, and even in many respects the woman of the propertied classes." These demands do not stem from "patronizing reformism, but as the conditions necessary to bring women into revolutionary tasks and are advanced always in connection with the general interests of the proletariat and of revolution." It was necessary to "combine our appeal politically in the minds of the female masses with the sufferings, the needs and the wishes of the working women."

On divorce, for example, Lenin agreed that divorce legislation should be considered a national issue and must extend to all regions of the country, regardless of religious or customary practices that forbid divorce. He emphasized, however, that "recognition of the *freedom* to leave one's husband is not an *invitation* for all wives to do so!" In capitalist countries where women have the right to divorce, the right is "conditional, restricted, formal, narrow and extremely difficult of realisation." What is important in capitalist countries is less the winning of a right, and more the struggle that achieves it and exposes capitalism as the real limitation to the exercise of the right.

Lenin was equivocal about abortion. On the one hand, he demanded the "unconditional annulment of all laws against abortions or against the distribution of medical literature on contraceptive measures." But he opposed the ideology of neo-Malthusianism, which championed the use of contraceptives as a means of limiting the birth of children on the grounds that they faced a life of "unbearable oppression and suffering," injury, and desperation. In Lenin's view, the desire to be childless was characteristic of "unfeeling and egoistic petty-bourgeois couples" who wanted to keep their diminishing resources for their own pleasure. The working class, he said, need more children, more fighters.

In 1929, Rowbotham says, the independent women's organization was abolished as part of a serious retrenchment in the USSR of the legal gains made by women since the early 1920s. Legal abortions were abolished in 1936; divorce was made difficult and costly; homosexuality was made illegal in 1934. Traditional marriages reappeared, motherhood was emphasized, and the family was declared a socialist institution, contrary to all previous revolutionary theory and practice, a further indication of the solidification of revisionism in the Soviet Union at the time.

It is clear, following the experience of socialist societies in the twentieth century that full economic participation and equality of legal and political rights provide only a foundation for the equality of women. In the West, modern feminists are at least as likely to ask questions about the character of the personal relationships that socialist men formed with the women in their lives. In the 1960s and '70s, this question had revealed some of the hypocrisy of many male new leftists, whose personal politics reproduced some of the most patriarchal attitudes towards women. In the following section, we attempt to update what we consider a modern Marxist approach to the intransigent problem of female oppression and inequality.

Class, Capitalism, and the Terrorization of Women

THERE ARE TWO SIDES to the history and social situation of oppressed groups and social categories. One side of oppression, often hidden by the taken for granted institutional mechanisms of any society, involves the denial of rights granted to other groups or social categories or denial of rights, which could be granted with the more rational usage of technical apparatus. In the 'woman question' this type of oppression is reflected in the permanent income disparities in contemporary society between men and women workers or the segregation of women into "female jobs" or their double ghettoization into the demands of both paid and unpaid work. The second aspect of this type of oppression, which would indicate the limitations of the untapped potential of womanhood, demands a radical restructuring of our present political economy in ways which would affect almost the total working population. In such a restructuring, there would still be special needs of specifically oppressed groups to be met, their specificity being defined by the particular nature of their earlier conditions of deprivation.

The other side of oppression involves the more blatantly degrading treatment of specific groups and social categories. This is the repressive side of oppression, those modes of daily behaviour, the consequences of which are to keep certain people in their place. One of the progressive consequences of liberal capitalism has been a marked diminution of some of the traditionally repressive features of social life. Its emphasis on legal equality and the legal labour contract between those socially defined as equal has significantly decreased the arbitrary violence, degradation, and patronization, which were the daily features of pre-capitalist times. Much can be made of this change in the life situation of the ordinary citizen, while at the same time realizing that advanced technology and seeming legal-rational rule systems can also subject total populations to total annihilation, a form of repression specific to our own historical period. Thus, what may be called the increasing humanization of daily life has proceeded concomitantly with periodic examples of attempted genocide and with the threat of final human extinction.

Not all oppressed groups or social categories have shared equally in the attenuation of repressive treatment. The most notable exception undoubtedly involves the treatment of women. Here, again we have seen significant changes from the feudal or traditional period and from conditions faced by women right up to the present century. One only thinks of various institutionalized mechanisms of abuse of women at other times and in other societies such as foot-binding in China, the Indian suttee, concubinage, female slavery, and cliterodectomy in many places, female infanticide and normal wife-beating almost everywhere to realize the taken-for-granted nature of this abuse and the great strides that liberal capitalism and socialism have taken in extinguishing these practices. At the same time the continued acceptance of rape, prostitution, and women-beating as well as the more indirect but more intense phenomenon of pornography indicate that modern Western society is far from free of the problem of overt repression of women. The sustained existence of such activities, indeed often their institutionalization in male attitude and behaviour (and often in female outlooks as well), demonstrates that modern feminist arguments about the universality of sexism and its consequence have much evidence to support them. They also point to the probability that the degradation of women is a result of the partial autonomy of female inequality from other forms of inequality, most notably class inequality. The basic question for a theory of female oppression is how relative such autonomy is, how different forms may be affected by changes in other structures of inequality.

In her book *Against Our Will*, Susan Brownmiller argues that the psychological consequence of the existence of rape is to keep the female population in a permanent state of terror. This permanent fear is one of the more significant factors producing traits of dependency, insecurity, and even conservatism so common to much female character historically. Rape, however, is only one form of blatant repression of females and should not be seen in isolation from other forms. It is this tendency to isolate specific forms of repression and then to attempt to find their specific causes, which often gives the analysis of repressive forms its fragmented character. The salutary thrust of modern feminist analysis has resulted from its attempt to conflate the various forms of repressive behavior and repressive ideology toward women into a common institutional structure that it calls patriarchy. The common and uniform thread of oppression of women by men and its legitimation throughout history certainly warrants this theoretical conception of women's oppression.

If patriarchy refers to a relatively universal institutional structure of male domination of women, then the more repressive forms of this domination will consist of a relatively well-integrated body of repressive acts and legitimacy for such acts. Rape, for example, may then be considered one of the more extremely repressive activities of males near one end of a continuum of potentially less violently repressive activities. Activities such as pornography are forms of repression of women, which are less severe or in the case of pornography, less direct in their intimidating consequences than rape, yet they are both part of a sequence of such behavior. It is possible to postulate an abstract continuum or forms of female repression from least to most violent, which might look like the following:

MOST SEVERE
Murder
Sexual and Physical Assault (Rape)
Physical Assault
Prostitution
Pornography
Sexual harassment
Seduction with Objectification
LEAST SEVERE

In looking at the preceding model, it is probable that there will not be clear agreement on the degree of severity of some of these forms. Some might even argue that the process of seduction is not repressive at all while others consider prostitution a matter of simple commercial rights to services.[8] However, in the main, Marxists argue that these activities are repressive, and that they exist in bundles rather than in cultural isolation. On the other hand, they also do not always exist all at once with equal institutional emphasis or frequency in any particular culture. What is also significant is that, except for straight physical abuse of females, all of these activities include a manifest sexual component. Much has been made by feminism of the purely assaultive characteristics of rape, for example, and this is leading to some salutary changes in law, but the fact remains that rape is also a *sexual* assault. Why this is so and why female repression (compared say with racial repression), generally takes sexual forms is a significant question in a theory of women's inequality (although there are certainly sexual connotations to much racism).

By conceiving of the repressive side of female oppression as a constellation of potentially related acts of repressive severity and by seeing the way that this repression is different from that affecting other groups or social categories, certain other significant theoretical issues arise. For example, unlike the repression of racial, national, or ethnic groups so common in history, the systematic and often institutionalized abuse of females almost never takes the form of official state coercion (although mass rape has become an instrument of warfare). Examples like the holocaust or slavery or 'normal' warfare involve the use of politically sanctified violence against certain groups of people. Often the level of sanctity suffusing such violence is so high that social theory has not considered such violence repressive at all except for that stream of European theory including Marxism, which considers all state violence repressive. If this is so, why has political authority seldom been involved in the perpetration of violence against women? The state may look the other way thereby sanctioning men's private right to commit violence against women, but this violence has usually been a *private* right. Further, does this existence of 'private' violence against women have something to do with the more sexual nature of much of the abuse? Why does this sexual violence against women, common and more than tolerated, remain buried in the recesses of private social life, seldom being raised to the level of official, public abuse? If violence or its threat has social control as a major consequence, does the more surreptitious nature of violence against women lead to a different type of social control in the case of women? We will forward some tentative answers to these questions in concluding remarks, but first let us discuss the application of the model of degrees of severity of repression to concrete circumstances.

It may not be clear from this model that it represents a constellation of actions not common to all social systems. If we accept this as the case, the job of analysis involves the discovery and explanation of differential emphasis of repressive forms in social systems as well as an attempt to see if there has been an attenuation of some forms with historical evolution. Finally analysis would ask what kind of changes would be necessary for the extinction of all these forms of repression. The reason that this is not clear is because many thinkers use narrow definitions of some of these forms, definitions that would lead to a position claiming that certain of these forms have not existed at all in certain societies. For example, if pornography is defined with reference to only the most extremely degrading artistic representation and treatment of women, then it is probable that it does not exist in some societies. But when it is realized that even the 'normal' representation of women in the arts has a pornographic element (involving sexually demeaning representation), then pornography becomes far more universal than is usually conceived. Can it not be said that the representation of women in almost all modern advertising contains a pornographic element albeit less intensive than that found in hardcore magazines or films?

The same problem arises with prostitution. Western society, which has a central thrust toward economic activities, has tended to generate prostitution as an almost completely commercial venture. Lenin stated that one could sympathize with prostitutes as double victims of private property and "moral hypocrisy," but the correct way to deal with the question was to "Return the prostitute to productive work, find her a place in the social economy." The solution was not "to organise the prostitutes as a special revolutionary guild contingent and publish a trade union paper for them." The question, he said, still required "a great deal of effort" in the Soviet Union.

From a Western point of view, prostitution is defined as a contract involving the sale of sexual services with sexual consummation signifying the termination of the contract, a contract having a definite money price. Anyone taking a broader view of female prostitution to include social relations like the 'kept women' or the courtesan in nineteenth century France must realize that prostitution is not defined by its single commercial contract form. What appears to define a social relationship as prostituting is the obligation of the female to give sexual services in the context of her unequal social position vis-a-vis males.[9] This is why feminist analysis has often seen traditional marital relationships as potentially prostituting for women since they often involve the duty (often the legal compulsion) of women to provide sex with the implied threat by males of withdrawal of support, which may congeal in pure form in certain types of relationship (such as 'call girling') but which can suffuse other relationships as long as women's inferior social position is maintained.

Let us elaborate upon this issue with a concrete case. In China in 1949, when the revolutionary regime took power, one of its first acts was to ban prostitution, which had been rampant in old China. This legacy of the old society also included foot binding, female slavery, concubinage, and female infanticide all of which were banished by the new government. Moreover, this policy turned out to be more than mere rhetoric since foot binding, slavery, and concubinage have totally disappeared (infanticide diminished greatly at least until the recently-reversed emphasis on one-child families). The new regime also claimed that prostitution had been completely wiped out since it systematically eliminated the organized crime that maintained it while at the same time retraining existing prostitutes for more productive occupations. And this was a significant advance for women, but it by definition subsumes all prostitution into its commercial occupational form.

The case of women in modern societies initiated by revolutions is a very telling one. Is it in fact true that there was no prostitution in socialist China given the fact that they were never seen on the streets and there were no bawdy houses? Moreover, much of the economic basis for commercial prostitution was eliminated with women's universal involvement in the paid workforce, dispersed through the division of labour in a variety not found in traditional capitalist societies. What did not happen was the placement of women into positions of power in all the major economic/political structures. Major party, government, and managerial positions remained male (and old male at that). Here lies the seeds and the actuality of prostitution, albeit in non-commercial form. It is not uncommon for old males in positions of authority over female workers to use that authority to attain sexual favours. This exploitation occurs within the familiar context of fear of loss of job-related rights and possibilities if women refuse to grant such exploitation.[10] (The occasional use of sexuality by women for their own advancement is not an example of liberation, but occurs within a more general compliance to patriarchal power). The obligation by women to give sexual services under threat from male controllers of economic goods or services is at the core of prostitution, and the example given demonstrates that it may continue to exist even where strictly commercial forms have been extirpated.

The continued existence of repressive activities against women in post-revolutionary regimes, which have been seriously and systematically dedicated to the idea of sexual equality, has highlighted some of the major theoretical issues in the 'woman question.' These issues revolve around the nexus between class and gender inequality. Before the rebirth of feminism in the 1970s, it had been taken for granted by Marxist theory that women's inequality was centrally and inextricably linked to the class issue. As argued above, prevailing orthodoxy postulated that pre-class tribal societies were in a state of primitive communism where there was also equality between the sexes. Only with the rise of class systems and the rise of private property controlled by men were women reduced to reproducing appendages of male property owners. Capitalism, according to this theory, is the last class system maintaining women in subjection, and this subjection will disappear with the advent of socialism. When women have the independent economic security borne of productive work outside the home and when their special reproductive needs are met by state action, they will be living in full equality with men. It is on the basis of this received wisdom that post-revolutionary regimes claimed to have resolved the women's problem.

Two rather overwhelming sets of facts have shaken the older Marxist orthodoxy on this issue. One set deriving from a vast array of ethnographic data collected at first hand during the twentieth century demonstrates that the inferior status of women is extremely common in tribal societies. These societies that do not generate the economic surplus necessary for the existence of a propertied ruling class and which are often highly cooperative and egalitarian in economic activities still sometimes maintain women in various forms of subjection. Even when the sexual division of labour is roughly egalitarian in ambience and distributive consequence, other social, political, and religious activities are sometimes inegalitarian by gender. Thus, female inequality predates the class system. It must have entered historical societies with its own institutional basis and appears to maintain a definite autonomy from class exploitation.

The second set of facts derives from what we have previously discussed about post-revolutionary societies. There one finds the legal abolition of an ownership class and the introduction of a form of socialism without the abolition of female subjection. The most common form of indirect oppression of women found in modern capitalism – their double ghettoization in paid and unpaid work – is recapitulated often more intensely with the almost universal entrance of women into the paid workforce with little attendant engagement of men in domestic labour.

Many of the more repressive activities against women such as coerced prostitution, daily physical abuse, and a variety of forms of sexual degradation are definitely rescinded and abated in these kinds of societies, which is why the official claim made by them that women now have equal status with men can array a body of evidence, which does demonstrate a tremendous gain in women's social position over a very sorry past.[11] But in the same way that these supposedly classless societies still have classes, they sustain significant aspects of gender inequality.

The unequal position and treatment of women did not arise with class exploitation and they will probably not automatically disappear with the elimination of classes. To infer from this that class exploitation and gender oppression are completely independent processes would be too facile an inference, however. The changes in gender relations created by post-revolutionary societies do indicate that class and gender may involve interdependent as well as independent processes. There is a strong case to be made that the rise of private property and its control by a small stratum of male owners did reinforce the whole complex of attitudes and conduct, which is now called patriarchy. (Why class privilege was created by males is a so far unanswered question). It is with the creation of a ruling class that patrilineage takes on a central emphasis upon property and its protection in future generations. This new engagement with male inheritance leads to the seclusion of females into situations where their main obligation is the production of male heirs. In many cases, infertility is the responsibility of females and marriages can be dissolved if women do not reproduce. Also given that male status becomes connected to leisured control of property and of human labour as producer for property, wives of ruling class males become relatively useless appendages whose sole tasks include reproduction of male heirs in a cultural ambience of luxurious indolence.

The position of women as special property of property is a product of the class system. Since only women can reproduce continuity in the control of property for males, so they become pedestalized and sentimentalized if they meekly fulfill the obligations of loyal wifehood and faithful motherhood. They also remain under the protection of respectable males as long as they maintain the behaviour associated with such respectability. Protection, however, can go only so far as the power that protecting males possess vis-à-vis the potential depredations of other men. For competition between males is increased with competition for property, and females as special property are especially subject to their use for male aggrandizement. If women must be protected, this need is a real need since there is always the danger of male attack. Alongside this danger goes the ideology of the female as the eternal temptress and the demands upon women that they tempt men all the time, but not too much to damage their rights to respectable protection.

From this argument, it can be seen how the creation of social class must have exacerbated the repression of women. We must repeat that we are not here denying the existence of male domination in pre-class tribal systems. It existed in various forms and to various degrees across a whole range of tribal societies. But the uniformly lower status of females in such societies did not necessarily lead to the types and degree of repression found in more recent class systems. We are suggesting in this argument that the growth of a class-dominated society, by stripping women of indispensable economic activities and making them mere adjuncts of male property owners, also intensified and permanently institutionalized more blatant forms of female repression. The repression, which had been either relatively nonexistent or sporadic and local in tribal societies, became common and even normative in class societies. The social protection afforded women in extended family setups usually including sub communities of females performing obviously valued economic activities is eroded and destroyed by the rise of class systems. This is one of the main themes of Germaine Greer's provocative and highly original work called *Sex and Destiny*.

With class, women become instruments of the male need for reproductive purity and 'successful' women, that is, those married to propertied men, are defined and isolated in need of protection from other men (although not from their husband) and become luxuriating baby machines. The truism that the dominant ideology in a class system is the ideology of its ruling class bears bitter fruit in the treatment of women in dominated classes. Although the claims by some feminism that males and females are in fact social classes appears invalid, the implicit assumption of classical Marxist analysis that class is gender blind also appears invalid. Social class arises in history as a reflection of a mode of economic production and exploitation, but inclusive to this mode was the gender of its dominant economic controllers. And the 'normal' sexism of some prehistoric tribal societies took on the more virulent sexism associated with propertied male aggrandizement. The ruling ideology of class societies includes individual male or collective male controlled property, and concomitant with this control is the idea of women as 'special' reproductive property. This ideology was disseminated downward and became the popular outlook of all classes. Among males, even when they themselves are propertyless and severely exploited, it became and continues to enjoy a high degree of legitimacy. If anything, the repressive intensity of sexism is probably more institutionalized in working classes since the frustrations and hostility not vented toward ruling groups is most easily and tragically applied to women. Sexism and its attendant brutal forms become not just the bone thrown by rulers to the ruled, but is an ensconced set of beliefs and activities suffused throughout the social fabric.

The discussions of the significance of social class and women's oppression brings us to the central question of this chapter – the question of the intensity and variety of female repression in different types of societies. Do specific kinds of societies generate definite clusters of female repression? Is it true as suggested earlier that there has been progress for women with the development of modern capitalism, if by progress in this case has meant greater freedom from blatant repression?

These questions are difficult to answer with any definitiveness since the mitigation of some form of female repression may be accompanied by the increase in other forms. Moreover, what often appears to be an attenuation of repression in certain institutional areas often, on closer examination, turns up in other guises. For these reasons, it is understandable why some feminists have seen the history of women as simply one long, unending repression. Still, even if there appears no class society with full equality between the sexes, it does not follow that repression of women has been everywhere and always the same. The Chinese case again comes immediately to mind where it must be granted that the overthrow of traditional China and the introduction of a socialist society led to a great gain in the social position and social activities of women, and concomitantly to a clear diminution of repressive activities against them. This is certainly one of the reasons why the Revolution maintained legitimacy and why so many women in China asserted that the 'woman question' there had been basically solved.

In the case of contemporary capitalism when compared to early capitalism or earlier medieval society, delineating clear progress may be a difficult undertaking, yet it seems that enough is known to forward a number of tentative propositions. Insofar as the enormous productivity of advanced industrial capitalism has resulted in striking advances in longevity, in general health standards, and in living conditions, so women have shared in this overall change in the quality of life. Here the factors associated with the demographic transition to small families, more sophisticated reproductive technology, and fewer, healthier live births have fundamentally liberated women from certain traditional scourges (almost lifelong pregnancy, high maternal and infant mortality, enforced infanticide).

On the more strictly active repressive side, feudal society sustained features that also demonstrate the progress ushered in by modern capitalism. In a predominantly illiterate society, women were kept in almost total illiteracy. In this condition the subservience of the female first to father and then to husband was virtually complete. In a more static landed property system such as traditional China, this low status meant that females as mere agents for reproduction of male heirs suffused the treatment of women. Moreover, as potentially wayward agents, the presumed need for controlling mechanisms of fear, intimidation, and coercion was widespread and institutionalized. The distinction between the 'good woman' under the protection of strong males and the 'bad woman' with little protection at all was the common bifurcation of alternatives in this social system. In spite of their variation in so many cultural areas, societies as diverse as ancient China and India, the Arab world, and medieval Europe all maintained blatant institutionalized forms of female repression. Moreover, these forms were connected to the control and potential and actual coercion of women as reproductive instruments of male property. In the servile institutions sometimes found in these societies, the more manifestly reproductive qualities took on a commodity guise, and women were valued by their putative capacity to produce high quality slaves.

As examples of the repressive features of these feudal systems, a number of well-known social institutions including foot binding, the purdah, and 'normal' wife-beating have already been mentioned. Capitalism has seen the elimination of most of these forms and probably the decrease in frequency of many others, although probably not sexual and physical assault. Moreover, the legal equality of all citizens and their formal rights to state protection are notable advances over feudal rights of those in power to the arbitrary use of that power. It is for this reason that some of the 'traditional' abuses of women still persist in capitalist societies. These abuses are forced underground since the state is officially obliged to delegitimize arbitrary violence against all social categories. Women are allegedly protected from the gross assaults, which had been sanctified by tradition in feudal times. Some of the more successful results of feminist agitation have been made in the tightening of legal rules and protections, which exist in the ideological assumptions of modern law. The hiatus between state indifference to women's physical security and a male's private code to do with her what he wants is subject to critique and potential closure, but persists in all class societies. This hiatus can never be finally breached within capitalist legal systems since they are rooted in the idea of protection of *private* rights. Socialism is a necessary but insufficient condition for transcending these long-standing abusive practices.

As with the case of class exploitation where capitalism both plunders to a degree unknown and raises standards *at the same time*, so the question of women's repression is two-edged in the modern era. As Eli Zaretsky says in *Capitalism, the Family, and Personal Life*, capitalism expands the marketplace to a position of complete dominance over society while segregating reproductive and socialization activities into nuclear family units. These profound changes fundamentally affect the form and intensity of women's repression. The separation of the economy from domestic work has led to the creation of free wage labour for men and women, but the structure and meaning of work for money has been quite different for women. This difference has not been caused simply by a cultural lag or by some anachronistic body of discriminations to be overcome by reinforcing greater legal equality in the marketplace (although attempts to do this are necessary), but have been built into the very heart of the political economy of capitalism. The now well-known double ghettoization of women into lower paid defined 'women's jobs' and unpaid, reproductive domestic labour is a particularly capitalist (and post-capitalist, 'socialist') phenomenon.

This phenomenon, which describes women in their active productive phase of activities and the inequality built into it, represents what we called the restriction of recognized or potential rights in the system. But the mechanisms of active repression also have their specific features under capitalism. The overall commercialization of life, especially in the monopoly phase of capitalism where overproduction is endemic and selling is problematic, generates the greatest commercialization of sexuality in history. In this commercialization, both male and female sexuality tend to be commoditized, but the passed-down traditional, erotic objectification of women gives this aspect of commercialization a more central place. What was before the sexually protected male-dominated enclaves becomes the freely disseminated imagery of the marketplace. The bodies and manufactured allurements of females are huckstered in ways and in intensity which are unprecedented. This meretricious display of women in all the new and vast media of communications to a populace almost fully literate and in possession of a host of media receptors gives the issue of pornography a more massive scope. Capitalism more blatantly degrades women to the position of a sexually enticing object of male conquest than any other society, and basically this is what pornography is all about.

Much the same case can be made about prostitution under capitalism. Since capitalism is defined by its central institutional emphasis upon production for sale, the prostitution of women also takes on an almost completely commercial turn. Not only does the actual amount of sex for a price probably increase, but the colour and diversity of the expanding marketplace probably leads to an expansion of types of prostitution as well. The individuation of women as well as men leading to a free market in sexuality also results in a greater suffusion of prostituting elements in all aspects of interaction between the sexes. As long as women's overall social status puts them in a position of inequality where sexual exchange becomes an obligation under threat of loss of something necessary or desirable, prostituting possibilities become a central feature in much of most women's sexual life. Just like pornography becomes the representational aspect, so prostitution becomes a concrete behavioral aspect in the general treatment of women in capitalism.

If we look at one of the factors taken for granted as progressive in modern life, the right to free mate choice, we see the double-edged quality of progress for women. As opposed to the institution of arranged marriage, which was literally universal in pre-capitalist society, the right to court and marry who one pleases has always been considered an unequivocal social advance. But is it an advance for women? Isn't choice in the context of institutionalized inequality between the sexes fraught with problems for women? The open marketplace for mating, if anything, seems to increase the predatory features of male sexuality since the traditional protection of women in arranged marriage situations breaks down. Whether this free-range sexuality, for example, actually increases the amount of rape may be a question that is difficult to answer, but it is probable that the ideology of rapism becomes more widespread and intensified. As with pornography, the sophistication of attitudes, gestures, and symbols concomitant with highly developed means of communication add features to traditional sexist ideology resulting in greater receptiveness to degraded and apparently rapeable images of women.

The nuclear family unit, institutionalized by capitalism, and the expected consequences of free mate selection, also put women into new, specifically repressive situations. It is hard to tell whether the increase in wife battering is a real increase or whether it is a function of greater awareness of the problem, but it seems probable that living in isolation from all social ties except those to the husband is a highly charged atmosphere for women. The free right to fall in love and live in splendid insularity creates conditions whereby all the external pressures affecting men in capitalism can be channelized even into brutality toward his less powerful mate.

If we look at the panoply of repressive possibilities facing women, from incessant predatory seduction possibilities through to its most severe forms in murder and rape, there is reason to believe that female repression in a number of forms may intensify under capitalism. Women's greater formal rights and freedoms are contradicted by the actuality of greater actual repression and of more varied situations of intimidation and terror. At the same time capitalism breeds conditions for greater awareness of this repression. It is this awareness and the potential to organize to get rid of repression, which is by far the most progressive side of the modern experience.

The universality of the terrorization of women, especially when such terrorization is almost unique among oppressed groups (except perhaps for children), is still in need of explanation. Why is continual fear apparently necessary for the subjection of women when other than coercive forms work well in the oppression of other social groups? We think the answer may be in the nature of domination in conditions of presumed trust and intimacy. While we may not yet have an answer to this question, the analysis of the connection of class and the terrorization of women goes some way in understanding the social transformations that seem necessary to eradicate this terror. These include the full and equal participation of women in productive work leading to complete equality between women and men in economic life. For this, nothing less than destruction of the present contemporary capitalist class system would be necessary. Concomitant with class transformation, however, must be major changes in ideological and legal realms, which empower women and their rights against male sexism and its attendant terror. Change in economic power without changes in women's power seems destined to help partially in the diminution of male terror over women. But this is not enough. The growth of specifically women's power over ideological forms like heterosexism and homophobia as well as predictable legal responses to all forms of intimidation and coercion of women is also a necessary part of any progressive movement toward real female freedom. In short, the battle for women's equality must include changes in both class conditions and patriarchal conditions of existence. The problem of gender inequality must be central and not peripheral to any programme of socialist transformation.

CHAPTER NINE

Conclusion

We hope that this book will help to navigate the minefield that is political Marxism. Knowledge of the history and present status of these various political strands is necessary as a basis for deciding how to act and what to do in the especially crisis-ridden time in which we live. Without theoretical knowledge, one is acting in the dark, often committing old mistakes and even engaging in opportunism without even knowing that one is doing it. This truism is certainly not to assert that theoretical knowledge is enough, for there is no substitute for active political engagement. And while theory is often black and white, active engagement can come in many colors.

So what have we learned from this summary of the various forms and the various famous and infamous personnel involved in revolutionary Marxism, and its close cousin anarchism, since the founders of Marxism in the nineteenth century? In the first instance, we have discovered that this is a very complex subject fraught with almost insurmountable difficulties, difficulties intrinsic to the very historical newness of the problem of socialist transformation. We also have had over two centuries of a particular and historically unique experience of industrial capitalism and liberal democracy, presumed by established opinion to be an integrated and unified duality. Marx's original attack on capitalism demonstrated both its productive advance for humanity and its darker exploitative and destructive side. Out of this attack came a powerful theory of capitalist development, which pinpointed the general characteristics of the new capitalist economy and predicted the historical trajectory of this system – a system of relentless capital accumulation generated by freely exploitable labour leading to the centralization and concentration of capital along with crisis-ridden contradictions. All this was expected by Marx's original formulation, and all this has come to pass. He was, however, optimistic about the probability that the new industrial working class produced by capitalist development would become conscious of the source of its exploitation and overthrow its capitalist masters ushering in a society possessing the technical advancement produced by industrialization and using it to realize a classless and abundant future. It was in this latter political dimension where Marx and Engels left little in their voluminous writings. They did mention some of the political necessities of the transition to socialism in their later response to the Paris Commune experience, but presented even less about the kind of leadership necessary to institute and maintain the transition.

Two fundamental attitudes toward state power emerged out of the bourgeois revolutionary tradition. They include an antipathy toward and mistrust of state power. Along with these attitudes was an emphasis on individual economic activity free from state limitations and an emphasis, overall, on individuality. This tradition, unlike those in all preceding class systems, meant to separate the political from the economic spheres. The major political ideologies stemming from this tradition, liberalism and Marxism, reflect these attitudes by seeing social progress as coterminous with greatly reducing state power to the point that Marxism and left-wing anarchism mean to do away with it entirely. When dealing with anarchism in ideological terms, however, it is only its left wing that talks about the destruction of the state. Anarchism has many wings, many of which articulate other ideological formats, combine various formats, or even seem to be devoid of clearly articulated ideas. These outlooks can be so diverse in their expression that it is often difficult to perceive where anarchist attitudes can be delimited from more consolidated anarchist and individualist ideologies. In order to try to explain and ultimately respond to this conundrum, we think that we must turn to other aspects of the bourgeois tradition.

Also unique to the bourgeois tradition is a commitment to rationality either in the form of wealth production with the use of the most efficient tools available or in the development of science as a mode of understanding and as assistance in the production of wealth. The emphasis on wealth for secular happiness as well as the debunking of religious and metaphysical thought is also unique to this Western experience. All this was to occur as a consequence of the activity of individual thinkers and producers working rationally and free from the stultifying ignorance of medievalism. It must be remembered that feudal Europe conceived of society as a static, organic entity with people in it playing pre-ordained roles. Conflict could only exist as the evil behavior or evil thoughts of those who worked against natural harmony. In the anti-feudal world, conflict and competition between individuals freed from restraints of superstition and irrationality made the very concept of society subject to suspicion. If there is social harmony, it is the invisible hand of competing individuals producing a mutual prosperity. It was in this sense that Margaret Thatcher was glorifying a nineteenth century conception of the world when she proclaimed that there was no such thing as a society.

The fact that the twin ideas of rebellion against public authority and the dedication to competitive individualism could not possibly lead to social harmony was recognized quite early in the history of the modern world. The beginning of capitalist industrialization produced such a mélange of urban pollution, mass poverty, and mass misery that the ideas themselves began to take transmogrified forms. Rebellion against public authority often evolves into a rejection of all authority, and competitive individualism often expands into a wondrous display of colorful distractions. In these consequences, one can see how the problem of anarchism cannot be encompassed in an easy formulation. It has been common in Marxism to see the roots of anarchism in the petty bourgeois tradition of small business, suggesting that the growth of large enterprise would generate other forms of political behavior. We are, however, suggesting something slightly different; that individualism, especially in its rebellion against authority, is common in many sections and classes. In a moment of hyperbole, one can even say that anarchistic tendencies are the stuff of the whole capitalist epoch. And when these tendencies articulate into more solid ideologies, they often shift and modify themselves according to diverse individual actors and circumstances. Moreover, given that the crises and injustices of capitalism are in the nature of the beast, rebellions often take left-wing forms, obliging us to pay attention to anarchism as it has embraced these rebellions. The underlying individualistic rebellion of anarchism, however, can take right-wing forms as well; for example, look at something so ostensibly diverse as the popularity of Ayn Rand in right-wing circles as well as the fascist tendencies in these same circles. In both cases, there is the glorification of individuals who rebel, not in the name of justice, but in the name of their special, even charismatic qualities when compared to the sheep-like backwardness of everyone else.

It is certainly understandable that no blueprint could exist for the socialist society of the future; in fact, Marx disavowed the possibility of delineating such a blueprint. This absence did result, however, in much variation and much conflict in all those post-Marx situations where socialist transformation appeared to be on the historic agenda. It is the similarities and especially the differences in the political positions that have occurred under the rubric of Marxism, which this work has attempted to analyze. It is sad to report that there have been far more failures than successes at socialist transformation, and even successes have been short lived. So while Marx's economic analysis of capitalism has proved the test of time, its political side has produced much *sturm und drang* about the appropriate ways to transcend the capitalist juggernaut. Capitalism has reached its predictable dead end of misery, wretchedness, and planetary degradation without producing very precise means of overcoming its obvious shortcomings. We have attempted to wade through the major Marxist political responses to this situation and to evaluate the still hopeful aspects of its various strands.

While the advance of capitalist industrialization has clearly proven its technical genius, the liberal optimism of its nineteenth century origins have been much frayed by the crises, wars, and planetary ruination displayed in its later, more monopolistic phase. Moreover, its supposed commitment to human betterment and democracy has been strongly undermined by the human misery created by the universalization of the capitalist mode of production and its very cynical and manipulative control of the electoral process, which it nevertheless trumpets throughout the world. The apogee of this cynicism is demonstrated by capitalism embracing fascism when facing economic crises of its own making and by initiating and supporting any and every corrupt dictatorship as long as that dictatorship shores up the needs of capital accumulation. Into the breach has arisen the popular recognition that only socialist transformation can resolve the intractable problems generated by capitalism. Indeed Marx's famous remark that the spectre of socialism haunts capitalism strikes a prophetic chord to the point that the very idea of socialism is still seen by those in power as perhaps the single worst abomination. The media mills, in the United States and elsewhere, seldom any longer feel it necessary to spew out explicitly how wonderful is capitalism (often called the free market) and how impossible and awful is the socialist alternative, although these ideas are not far from the surface. On the other hand, in many parts of the world, the idea of socialism still has a positive ring, although the word has been commonly used to refer to systems that bear little resemblance to anything approaching socialism – witness, for example, movements that called themselves Arab or African socialism. In fact, neo-liberalism in the West has largely succeeded in labeling 'socialist' any restrictions on the freedom of corporate capitalism to plunder the world.

It is not to these often fringe socialist movements with which this work is dealing. Rather, it addresses another phenomenon: the development and growth of political movements, which derive their legitimacy from the original works of Marx and Engels (or in the case of anarchism, from opposition to some of their fundamental ideas) and are committed to a root and branch transformation of capitalism into socialism. That is, they often consider themselves revolutionary movements. At the same time, they are often at odds with each other on many political issues with regard to the manner by which such transformation should occur and to the contours of what the beginnings of socialism should look like. We have attempted to analyze these different movements in terms of both their essential theoretical and practical characteristics and their similarities and differences with the other movements. We have also attempted to evaluate their actual or potential possibilities as revolutionary movements toward socialism.

Two major positions with reference to revolutionary political theory were articulated and often repeated by Lenin. The first proclaims that there can be no revolution without revolutionary theory. It was articulated in opposition to what he considered the opportunist direction of revisionist Marxism – that Marxism which rejected the need for general political goals in the name of immediate practical possibilities. This revision of Marxism has led inexorably to a reformist politics ultimately embracing capitalism and denying the very need or possibility of socialism. The second position by Lenin states that revolutionary transformation is not possible without a "concrete analysis of concrete conditions." Although presented in various situations, we think that the critique implied by this demand applies most cogently to those on the left who misread and act upon conditions in ways that presume progressive forces and directions which do not accord with reality – something most common to ultra-leftism. This book has suggested that these still valid propositions have contradictory consequences, often because they imply outlooks taken for granted in original Marxism, outlooks changed by contemporary thought and contemporary conditions.

What must be remembered, it seems to us, is that the postulates of revolutionary theory were first delineated late in Marx's life in his analysis of the Paris Commune after its defeat and dissolution in 1871. In the resurrection of these postulates later by Lenin, in a book written just before an unexpected (except by Lenin) Bolshevik Revolution, he could not discover them anywhere else in the whole corpus of Marx and Engels' work since they are in fact not found there. *State and Revolution* was written as both a very general prescription for revolutionary transformation and as a polemical critique of the pragmatic and reformist Marxism, which denied the validity and the need for this prescription. In the latter sense, it was a frontal attack on what passed for Marxism on the European continent. Lenin did not recognize that these postulates have their own contextual relevance, one that applied specifically to 1871 Paris and to Russian events. In this book, we have defended the need for recognizing and applying the basic tenets of revolutionary theory articulated by Lenin. These include the necessity for a professional revolutionary party as a means to successful socialist transformation, for a period of political dictatorship by the working classes in the socialist transition, and for party members and other high officials to be obliged to live a modest existence. All but the Cuban revolution adhered to these demands in the whole process of taking power, and in the Cuban case, they were applied soon after the revolutionary forces took power. What we think must be realized in the evaluation of political organizations professing to be socialist is the significance of denying these precepts. Except in specific circumstances where socialist regimes initially take power by standard democratic means, we think that overt denial is a clear index of opportunism.

After saying this we must proclaim that these precepts of revolutionary theory do not have universal application and demonstrate their validity in specified historical circumstances. Lenin admits this specificity in other of his writings when he suggests that there is such a thing as a revolutionary situation, one where the possibility of taking power is at its highest. This situation, says Lenin, includes the working class being at a state of strength and consciousness in which it is capable of taking power and the ruling class being in a state of disarray and weakness, making it less capable of maintaining power. The fact of the matter, it seems to us, is that such an historical situation is quite unusual and does not present itself very often. Most concrete situations are so different from this scenario that the theoretical components of revolutionary theory do not precisely apply. This is certainly the overwhelming case for the present conditions in advanced capitalism.

At the center of the conflict within Marxist politics is the difference between reform and revolutionary Marxism recognizing that, at its origins and even later, reform Marxism still considered itself part of a revolutionary project. At this late date when political Marxism remains riven by divisions and acrimonious conflict, it should be remembered that, by the late nineteenth century, Marxism almost completely dominated the left-wing revolutionary environment. Moreover, it was accompanied in European countries by a large and relatively unified political movement consciously recognized by a growing industrial working class. The central principles of revolutionary unity, derived from Marx, were fairly clear and direct. They stated that classes and class conflict were endemic to capitalist development and that the working class in the course of this development would discover through its own conflict with capital the necessity for its revolutionary overthrow. It was, however, recognized by the likes of Lenin, Trotsky, Luxembourg and many others that the unity was fragile and based on unspoken and often unrecognized fundamental differences. Rosa Luxembourg, at that time a leading member of the very formidable German Social Democratic Party (synonymous with revolutionary Marxism) recognized and detailed in her *Junius* Pamphlet what she considered a growing trend toward rejecting the revolutionary side of Marxism. While she considered it dangerous, she also considered that the growing strength and consciousness of the working class would clearly overcome these temporary tendencies toward reformism.

Instead of reform Marxism becoming a footnote in the overwhelming surge of revolutionary Marxist success, history has presented us with a quite different scenario. Not only did reformism become a steady and institutionalized part of the historical process, but even the more revolutionary side of Marxism has taken unexpected turns. Political Marxism has fragmented and splintered to the point that dissensus and conflict have become fairly standard in the Marxist world. And we often find that there has been little attempt within Marxism itself to survey and attempt to evaluate the political significance of these various trends. We have also found that there has been little engagement with the problem of opportunism in contemporary Marxism, especially in its academic guise where Marxism has had some revival, steadily in Europe and since the 1970s in North America. It is this absence which led us to survey the various strands of revolutionary thought bringing the problem of opportunism to the fore again.

The demonstration of right opportunism has been much the easiest to validate in the development and denouement of social democracy. On this issue, the knotty problem of distinguishing mistakes from opportunism, of distinguishing necessary from unnecessary compromise has been less difficult since the result of the early reformism criticized by Luxembourg and Lenin has transmogrified into a complete legitimation of the very capitalist system it was supposed to resist. One has only to look at contemporary labour or social democratic parties to see the results of earlier opportunism. This is so much the case that we would contend that it seems analytically advisable to use the term opportunism only for this steady and relentless brand of political falsification. Ultimately, opportunism is applicable only when a rightest movement presents itself as Marxist; now that social democracy has abandoned any pretense to Marxism, it is 'opportunist' only in the most common and banal terms consistent with bourgeois politics in general. In advanced capitalism especially, where the overwhelming wealth of the system allows for the potential buying off of significant parts of still exploited working people, a fertile ground is prepared for the wedding of opportunist ideas with material betterment. What Lenin called a temporary, miniscule labour aristocracy has become less temporary and much less miniscule.

We have also attempted to demonstrate how important is the problem of delineating the positive contours of political Marxism, if only because political economy or the most economic aspects of Marxism tend to dominate the intellectual scene. This is perfectly understandable given the more scientific validity of political economy and the fact that no viable political activity is possible without a firm grounding in the more objective direction of events, what Lenin called analyzing concrete conditions. Moreover, direct political activity is more open-ended, difficult, more demanding, and often more dangerous to career and life itself. There is always a connection between analysis of the world and actions to attempt to change it. These two aspects are separated in Marxism only to the detriment of the very ends being sought by this outlook. We have only emphasized the political side because we think it has been denied by much of contemporary Marxism, or if not denied, it has allowed the easy play of various problematic political trends.

We would also contend that political theory and attendant action present difficulties not found in political economy. Political economy presents the general direction of capitalist society; it cannot predict the highly variable contingencies that exist in concrete conditions. No historical theory can predict the contingent and variable direction of specific capitalisms or specific historical conditions. And it is these factors which are often the stuff of immediate political action. It is for these reasons that Marxist political theory, what we have of it, can be no more than general guidelines for action, guidelines that often demand new interpretations with changing conditions. In the face of Marxist falsifications or misuse of the very guidelines, the guiding principles are significant more in telling what should not be done rather than what should be done.

What are the major guidelines of Marxist political action? It is useful in discussing these guidelines to distinguish two different moments in the revolutionary process, the first dealing with the problem of taking socialist power and the second with the issue of sustaining socialism after the accession to power. The distinction has special relevance when it is recognized that there has basically been no success in attaining socialist power in advanced capitalist societies, making this problem appear almost overwhelming there, whereas accession to power has occurred in many technically backward societies where the sustaining of socialism has become especially problematic. As to the taking of socialist power, the idea of a fairly quick insurrection by a highly conscious and well-organized urban working class held strong sway over the Marxist imagination up to and beyond the Russian Revolution, a revolution which seemed to validate this viewpoint. This was so much the case that Chinese revolutionaries faced much opposition from this viewpoint when it rejected the urban insurrectionary project and introduced the idea that socialism could take power by a slow accretion of rural liberated peasant areas leading to a final taking of national power in the cities. After the Chinese success along with a number of similar other such successes, notably in Cuba and Vietnam, this liberation from the countryside tended to dominate the revolutionary scene culminating with Che Guevara's famous cry in the 1960s that what is needed for world revolution was "many Vietnams." Sometimes called 'focoism,' this political direction, presented at the time as a fundamental principle in the underdevelopment world, can at the present time be seen as rooted in passing circumstances. The depopulation and fragmented wretchedness in the third world generated by advanced imperialism has led to a wave of rural migration to the cities, cities with huge and ever-growing slums. These cities are often the loci of new electoral movements for socialist transformation, as for example seen in Latin America in the late twentieth and early twenty-first centuries. With this development and with the diminution of the possibility of rural insurrection, all that may be said of a definitive nature by revolutionary Marxism is the necessity that state power must be taken by socialist forces as a first step in class transformation, but how it should be done has become more problematic than has been thought in the past.

Foremost among political guidelines at both stages of transformation is the revolutionary viewpoint regarding the nature of the state and the problems of state organization during the process of socialist transformation. While it is almost axiomatic to Marxism that the mode of production is the dominant feature that defines the contours and direction of any class society, and defines them in fairly predictable fashion in capitalist society, the actual transformation of a society demands primary attention to the concentration of political power within the state. Put most baldly, the primary focus of economic transformation is indeed the control of the means of production, but the primary aim of such control is determined by control over the levers of state power. And unlike reform Marxism, revolutionary Marxism sees the state as much more than the politically governing power alone. It includes an aggregate of institutions including the police, the army, education, the judiciary, the civil service, as well as the official government. Control of the government alone by a socialist power is of course always necessary for socialist transformation, but a belief that socialism can be instituted by the election of a socialist government without clear control of all these other institutions is a recipe for disaster. We have witnessed the tragic results of such an outlook in the Allende government in Chile. There, the belief, for example, that a seemingly neutral professional army would sit by and watch a government institute a socialist programme without that army ultimately showing its essential connection to capitalist power ultimately led that army to overthrow the socialist government (with the assistance of US imperialism). It also led to a long period of overt fascist tyranny destroying popular progressive leadership and institutions. On the basis of this experience and many others, the central plank of any socialist programme must be the recognition that socialism can never construct a strong foundation without the complete destruction of the whole older state apparatus and the initiation of a completely new socialist state form. And this destruction, according to received nineteenth century ideas, can occur only if socialism comes to power in a wave of violent insurrection.

To state this fundamental political guideline must, however, raise significant questions in more specific historical conditions, conditions which face societies in the present time. For example, there are many societies in Latin America today in which governments have been elected under standard democratic procedures forwarding themselves as openly socialist in programme and direction. It has always been asserted by revolutionary Marxism that the capitalist ruling class will never relinquish power without violent overthrow since it will protect its interests, when threatened, in any way possible. This point seems to us essentially true, but the categorical division between peaceful and non-peaceful avenues to power, often associated with this point, cannot be asserted in simplistic terms. Looking at these present Latin American conditions, for example, the possibility, indeed the necessity, of socialists taking immediate, if fragile, government power has been presented concretely on the continent. An almost unspoken assumption for revolutionary Marxism is that it can never refuse power even if it is only given in the normal democratic process; that is, the absence of insurrectionary possibilities is never a reason to reject the need to use whatever is available within existing capitalism to forward socialist objectives. Thus, socialists, and we have every reason to believe that these socialists are not ordinary bourgeois politicians parading as socialists, have seen the democratic path to power and have taken it. But, if our view of the state retains its validity, such access is full of many pitfalls. The significance of other state institutions remain overwhelming roadblocks to almost every socialist policy forwarded by the new socialist government. Since the government in power derives its legitimacy from an existing legal and constitutional structure within which it was elected, it is saddled with this same structure at every stage of necessary reform. This means that everything necessary takes time at the same time that the pre-existing bourgeois class remains untouched with its hands on a multitude of political and economic levers. One of the most important levers involves the media of communications, which are still privately owned. They continue to spew forth "news" and interpretations which oppose all that the new government desires and stands for. In the Venezuelan case, for example, what has been called the Bolivarian Revolution has had access to and uses state broadcasting facilities to educate the populace for the socialist cause, but the magnitude of state broadcasting pales in comparison with the private broadcasting apparatus. In addition to blatant anti-government propaganda, the same old bourgeois 'entertainment' and schlock dominates the airwaves, and it is the stuff from which much of the populace has gotten its ideas, and which it has sadly learned to like.

But this is only the beginning of the problem. As was mentioned before in the now tragic Chilean case, the socialist government accepted the idea that the army would remain professional and neutral with the implementation of socialist policies. The upper echelons of the army, however, retain in a myriad of ways – materially, educationally, socially, and so on – connections to the older ruling class. With the rank and file of the army remaining cowed, this officer class ultimately showed its true colors by violent overthrow of the socialist government. This state of affairs always remains true as shown by the army's kidnapping of Hugo Chavez in a palace coup attempt. It failed not only because of popular opposition to the coup but, more significantly for the present argument, because Chavez himself came from middle echelons of the army, which remained loyal to him and which assisted the popular uprising with armed support. What these examples clearly demonstrate is that an elected socialist government remains very insecure without the transformation of the military into a new people's army. Similar arguments can be made for other elements of the pre-existing state apparatus. The judiciary, the school system, the civil service, all must be transformed into new institutions opposing the old system and supporting the new one. It is on this basis that Lenin's stricture that the old government must be smashed becomes a guiding principle for the initial stage of revolutionary transformation.

Even with the acceptance of this principle, we are still left with the fact that socialist governments are now coming to power with the rest of the state apparatus left intact. Moreover, they take power on the basis of a legitimacy which stands in the way of revolutionary change – the legitimacy of bourgeois elections, of bourgeois parliaments, of adjusting popular demands for change to the timetable of 'legitimate' procedures. By way of difference, we might mention what occurred in the Cuban case. When the Cuban guerillas took power in Havana in 1959, they indicated that they were more than willing to institute progressive and anti-imperialist programmes. This inclination, as would be expected, elicited immediate opposition from the privileged elements in Cuba, and the privately-controlled media voiced strong criticism against such programmes. In this revolutionary situation where much of the working population was prepared for radical change, there was also immediate demands for socialization of large private enterprise. A focal point of this class conflict was the press where the anti-progressive outpourings of the newspapers caused the working staff of the papers to take over the papers in order to correct what it considered false presentation of events. The owners of the press appealed to traditional legitimacy of bourgeois ownership of property, but in this kind of revolutionary situation, the workers were appealing to what is considered "revolutionary legitimacy" and the newspapers were transformed immediately into new and progressive organs of information and interpretation of events. Had the guerilla government accepted the call of the bourgeois owners to return the newspapers to them and put the workers in their place, there would have been great frustration and disillusionment among the workers. In the Chilean case where similar events transpired, the elected government was appealed to in order to uphold the legitimacy of the rules that elected it, and the workers were forced to give up their occupation of the press and told to wait until the legislative process would give them the right to public ownership and control. And, of course, the latter process becomes another time-consuming and problematic process, only increasing frustration and dampening revolutionary fervor.

Clearly, a revolutionary situation is a very unusual and very time-bound event. It is a time when great things are demanded and great things seem possible. Any continued existence of the traditional way things have been done in the face of these new demands become roadblocks to the solidification of revolutionary power. Significantly, the old ruling class retains control of all these traditional roadblocks in state institutions and in control of media of communications. The longer these institutions remain untouched, the more the demands for revolutionary change become undermined. These are exactly the problems faced by a government elected to power under the rubric of standard parliamentary rule. By the next election, so many problems have been thrown in the way of revolutionary change that more standard bourgeois parties may be returned to power in a wave of popular disillusionment with the socialist government, as happened in the Nicaraguan situation and in Venezuela. In cases where this electoral defeat does not occur, there is always recourse to the military solution to the socialist threat. This is the final trump card in the bourgeois arsenal. It is for this reason that the transformation of the military power is a most central guideline for sustaining a socialist direction.

It should be clear from this discussion that the problems faced by contemporary attempts at socialist transformation have their roots in much earlier divisions that arose at the inception of major Marxist political activity in the late nineteenth and the beginning of the twentieth century. With the shift of revolutionary activity to the underdeveloped world, the earlier engagement with the problem, seen at that time in the advanced capitalist context, seems to have disappeared, or at least is little discussed. It is because the problem of opportunism and revisionism has not only not been resolved, but reappears in all modern attempts for revolutionary change that we think we have to discuss anew the minimal guidelines for such change.

A central feature with regard to revolutionary guidelines involves the problem of reform as it affects Marxist politics. Here a fundamental distinction must be made between reform and reformism. While it is not difficult to make this distinction theoretically, the distinction becomes much knottier in its application to concrete circumstances. Marxism recognizes the need for commitment to the betterment of economic and social conditions of oppressed classes in whatever way possible in existing capitalist conditions. To reject such possibilities of betterment in the name of putatively higher revolutionary principle simply isolates Marxism from the exploited and oppressed people that it is supposed to represent. This rejection is the centerpiece of ultra-leftism and certain varieties of anarchism. This understanding still leaves intact the major problem of reformism, especially in those countries living under the auspices of manifestly democratic regimes where the avenues of reform are, or appear, open. In that context, ultra-leftism still represents a formidable obstacle since ultra-leftism helps the regime to paint Marxism and socialism in a deleterious light.

Left social democracy, on the other hand, implicitly rejects Leninist Marxism while idealizing all non-Leninist attempts at revolutionary change. What defines such social democracy as left is its continuing engagement with Marxist political economy while rejecting or remaining silent about the Leninist contribution to Marxism. In its engagement with activism, it tends to inflate whatever new militancy may be occurring, or if not occurring, it predicts that militancy will inevitably happen, a form of 'left' positivism. Presently, left social democracy is the most radical wing of the social democratic phenomena. Found often in university faculty circles, it supports the need for full socialist transformation and maintains a solid class struggle analysis of contemporary monopoly capitalism. This approach to left politics often has much that is valid to say about how capitalism operates and what kind of working-class actions are necessary for a socialist transformation. Spontaneous people's movements with often local and temporary leadership are common, particularly in times of crisis: Arab Springs, factory occupations, co-operative movements, identity-based social movements, progressive NGOs, for example. Left social democracy celebrates these radical events but does not theorize beyond them to the need for common and centralized organization to sustain them and lead them in a more permanent, socialist direction.

Furthermore, left social democracy has given strong support to the Cuban Revolution and to measures necessary to maintain it in the face of continuing American pressure, from boycott and sabotage to the new dangers in recognition and economic intervention. On almost all major international issues, it supports progressive causes including the recent attempts in Latin America to introduce socialist programmes in Venezuela and Ecuador. Perhaps because of its rootedness in academic conditions, left social democracy tends to develop political positions that are not based in every day activism. Instead, its analysis often seems to be made from a lofty position waiting for outside forces to spring it into action. One of its main political activities involves periodic attempts to radicalize existing social democratic parties by boring from within. Left social democrats tend to think that the major problem in still existing social democracy is that it is not socialist enough and that the influx of radical ideas alone can resolve that problem. This is because left social democrats are silent and implicitly anti-Leninist in their outlook on party organization. They almost never mention the work of Lenin on party formation, and only bootleg their antipathy to it by calling all such parties Stalinist, therefore hopelessly tyrannical and undemocratic. The problem during non-revolutionary times is not engagement with social democratic parties that are rooted in progressive causes in order to further social reforms or counter right-wing power, especially if politics is taken outside parliamentary politics; rather, it is failing to see the limitations of this engagement. In this way they end up supporting the standard 'democratic' road to socialism, a central plank in the right opportunist outlook. Along the way, for example, all the recent attempts in Latin America to introduce socialism through the ballot box are embraced uncritically and are often given new names for what left social democrats consider totally innovative revolutions. In the past they have shown strong uncritical support for other attempted socialist revolutions, for example, the Nicaraguan one, as long as they were not led by Leninist parties. Left social democracy gives support for Cuban socialism without mentioning the significance of the leadership of a communist party. Finally, the right opportunism of left social democracy is demonstrated by its avoidance of other major guidelines to revolutionary success, such as the need for overthrowing the old state apparatus and constructing a new type of state or the need for a people's army rather than a professional one.

To add even more difficulty to this recalcitrant problem, capitalist power in the neo-liberal era of globalization has been so successful in undermining reform that progressive forces are obliged to fight battles to re-instate reforms that had been won and have now been taken away. This is most noticeable in the trade union movement, which has been reduced to a shadow of its former self, and seemingly victorious battles have to be fought all over again. Social democrats glorify the electoral process and only gear up their constituency at election times. In more recent times it is hard to even call social democracy 'social' since it has erased socialism from its constitutions (fearful that someone might find out) and has embraced the measures of budget balancing and austerity (for everyone except the bourgeoisie). At best, these parties have become the liberal wing in the panoply of pro-capitalist parties. On top of these monumental defeats is the new recognition that capitalism is destroying, or has already destroyed, the natural environment that sustains human and other organic life. We now face the unprecedented conundrum that socialism may be the only means of escaping environmental disaster while less relevant reform represents the only avenue for successful progressive reform.

What reforms, then, are to be forwarded and how sure can one be when revolution is such a distant hope that many reforms may not be worth the effort? If we accept the view that all policies, which better the life and working conditions of ordinary people or which defend the democratic rights of oppressed groups such as women, minorities, and other vulnerable people, are worth pursuing, then it can be concluded that all progressive reform must be within the purview of revolutionary Marxism. This was essentially Lenin's argument when he opposed the position of what he called narrow economism in his early forays against Menshevism and proclaimed the need for revolutionaries to publish a national newspaper to discuss the problems and needs of all oppressed groups rather than working-class issues alone. This is what he meant when asserting that revolutionaries must become "tribunes of the people." We agree with this position, but the pressing of reform and how it is to be done still depends very much upon context.

The identification of reformism is fairly simple, however, when dealing with political actors who reject in principle some of the obvious guidelines of revolutionary Marxism. If, for example, groups or individuals assert that they are against a revolutionary road to socialism, or extol the parliamentary path as the only path, or deny the need for class struggle, then we are in the company of obvious opportunism. In saying this we recognize that the shouting of revolutionary principles from the rooftops is equally not the best thing to do, but even if the forwarding of these principles demands nuanced silence in certain contexts, they cannot be renounced. The same can be said for other revolutionary principles like the need for a professional carefully selected party or the need for total overthrow of the bourgeois state. We also recognize that it may be extremely difficult to maintain revolutionary guidelines while living in an atmosphere where reform appears to be the only possible road, but theoretical recognition of their importance is a first and necessary safeguard against opportunism and attendant reformism.

We have, in this book, spent much of our time on the fundamental political features of Marxism that have developed since its founders. Special emphasis has been given to the opportunist distortions that have characterized contemporary left-wing politics. In addition, it is important to discuss one other aspect of revolutionary politics: the specific personal characteristics demanded by this kind of activity. In the first instance, the Marxist revolutionary is supposed to engage in a lifetime of unselfish commitment to the betterment of humanity. This means that any activity tinctured by the ordinary corruption of everyday politics or sullied by scandal can and will be used to undermine his/her reputation. Often the bourgeois media will lie about or distort a revolutionary life in order to debunk the ideas for which that life stands. We are certainly aware that many of the most revolutionary leaders can be reproached for their failings in everyday life. Also the demands of revolutionary commitment are not easily handled in the circumstances of comfortable career or domestic routine. It is no accident that almost all successful revolutionary leaders until they take power have been males who have burned all their bridges to an ordinary family and working life. If one thinks, for example, of the life of Che Guevara, it is clear that this quintessential revolutionary owes his success as a revolutionary by standards that cannot be measured by the usual indexes of worldly success. Mao once claimed that a revolutionary activity is an example of romantic realism, a combination of long-range commitment to a very risky ideal along with the recognition of a slogging grind of day-to-day activities in the here and now.

All the great virtues that come down through history – selflessness, generosity, loyalty to high principles, courage, honesty with oneself and others, material simplicity as well as the more unusual combination of being disciplined and demanding along with being tolerant and understanding – are expected of the Marxist revolutionary. It is a tall order. Many who make such a commitment in the romanticism of youth fall by the wayside in the later demands of such a life. For those who stay, it can also be imagined that they find the demands too much for them but are so ensconced in such a life that they cannot get out or cannot give up the lofty imagery associated with remaining in a revolutionary movement. After a movement takes power, many others flock to the revolution for self-interested reasons and this becomes another breeding ground for opportunism. These situations demonstrate that opportunism is a very complex and difficult issue not completely covered by the historic devolution of social democracy since the latter has involved a movement already successfully integrated into the bourgeois scheme of things, and therefore already corrupted by its success.

As we see it, opportunism is not only a matter of character, but of context perhaps more so. And as with all things, these are subject to change in biographical and historic conditions. In everyday language the meaning of opportunism is fairly simple and straightforward. It refers to the capacity to take advantage of opportunities. And other than the perennial question about the means and ends of these opportunities, there is little pejorative about this usage. In the political arena, however, opportunism is a much more complex subject. For Marxism, it is only used to refer to people engaged in progressive practice who apply ideas or commit actions that do the opposite of what people think they are doing. Marxists do not apply the word to other than progressive people and ideas because Marxism assumes that hypocrisy is the natural bedfellow of classes in power. All such power always presents itself as acting upon the highest ideals while its actions demonstrate routine examples of exploitation and oppression of other classes and groups. This is why the well-known definition of hypocrisy as the tribute that vice pays to virtue is so appropriate for the activities of ruling classes. Among Marxists and other progressives, however, the commitment to honesty and clarity about exactly what they are doing is considered the very essence of their activities. After all, to liberate the wretched and downtrodden from their oppression is supposed to, in the first instance, rely on truth. It is often a commitment to truth and honesty that makes the issue of opportunism so difficult to evaluate in concrete cases. Of course, honesty is always specific to time, place, and circumstances. Honesty and self-criticism are essential within the democratic centralist organization; but not all truths can be presented outside that organization in an unvarnished form. Furthermore, truth does not have an absolute character. We have seen that, in well-functioning parties, internal discussion and analysis lead to decisions about practice in specific circumstances. But the effectiveness of any policy must be measured by two mechanisms: is it consistent with the principles of socialist transformation, and in its implementation does the practice effectively promote this transformation?

We come, then, to perhaps the most difficult and often the most controversial guideline for revolutionary action. This is the need for a tightly organized, Marxist-educated political party. As said before, this need was not clearly articulated by Marx and Engels and is the defining characteristic of Lenin's contribution to Marxist political theory. It is for this reason that this kind of party is usually called, by its friends and its enemies, a Leninist party. Except for the Cuban case where a radical guerrilla group took revolutionary power and only instituted a party later, no socialist revolution has succeeded to power without the leadership of a Leninist party. And all of these parties called themselves Communist Parties, an unfortunate appellation since the term 'communism' in the Marxist lexicon has always been attached to the end result of a successful socialist transition. The confusion over this terminology has led hostile observers to call societies led by communist parties "communist societies" when in fact they are not communist societies. This confusion also leads to the perception that problems and failures of such societies can then be seen as intrinsic to the very nature of such societies rather than to the nature of their leadership. And communist parties are seen as the inherently flawed leaders of such societies. The defense of this kind of party really resides, we think, in its critical response to traditional political parties.

Typical bourgeois parties, while attendant to the trappings of democracy, are far from democratic institutions. The ideologies that unite them are usually so amorphous that membership in them is tenuous and often transient. Moreover, the significance of money and stark careerism make ordinary opportunism the central feature of all such parties. By this, we mean that the gap between what the party putatively stands for and what it actually does is, as the saying goes, wide enough to drive a truck through. The emphasis on elections makes for a tremendous burst of energy at election time with almost no connection of party members to the party between elections. The process of choosing leadership involves decisions made only by insiders, and leadership conventions have a circus-like atmosphere with little sense of serious people discussing serious issues. Perhaps nowhere does Michel's iron law of oligarchy have greater validity than in the operation of bourgeois parties in a bourgeois society. It is strange to Marxists that these parties are seen by conventional opinion as the ideal vehicles of democracy, and Lenin, in attempting to forward another political vehicle, was quite aware of their shortcomings. Membership in his party is not frivolous or easy since he recognizes that commitment to Marxist principles must be a serious commitment. Therefore, there must exist at least some significant understanding of fundamental Marxist ideas to become a party member. And intellectual understanding is not enough since there must also be concrete proof in practice that one can live up to party principles. For this reason, one cannot become a member without a probationary period of actually working within the party. It is strange and ironic that in large economic institutions in capitalist societies, procedures of this type are common while they are strongly condemned in the political sphere where inexperience or sloppiness is considered the epitome of democratic openness.

Another aspect of Lenin's attempt to overcome the superficiality of standard parties is almost willfully misunderstood by the standard critiques of this type of party. Here we refer to the concept of democratic centralism, which is seen by Lenin as the normal process of getting things done in a new way. It is seen again as a way of ensuring full membership commitment but also as a way of avoiding bureaucratization by integrating legislation of policy with its implementation. Democratic centralism simply means that all members of the Party must openly forward their views at all decision-making assemblies. Debate and difference are assumed to be a normal part of this process as would be expected in any open discussion about important matters. At the end of debate an open vote is expected after which all members are expected to follow the dictates of the majority and may not oppose party decisions until the next meeting. This is what is meant by the centralization of decision making, the expectation that party members will unify behind the decisions of the party, even to the point of willingly initiating policy with which they may have initially disagreed.

It seems to us that, at the theoretical level, the idea of democratic centralism is a real progressive development in its attempt to overcome the shortcomings and failings of normal bourgeois parties. Unlike the latter, this idea makes no attempt to act above class divisions, an attempt which exposes the fundamental hypocrisy of bourgeois parties. Democratic centralism is seen as a necessary process in a revolutionary situation where powerful bourgeois opposition still exists and where party activities must demonstrate their clear-cut partisan dedication to the needs of the working class and other formerly oppressed groups. We must recognize that actual practice of these revolutionary parties has had a very spotty record, leaving much of a hiatus between theory and practice. Baldly stated, Leninist parties, in those cases where they have taken power in a manifestly revolutionary way, devolved over time into organizations with little democracy and much centralism. Party decision-making often became lockstep agreement by party members to the decisions of higher unquestioned leaders. One cannot avoid these facts, forcing us to ask the obvious question: Is the whole theory of a professional political party run on the principle of democratic centralism so fundamentally flawed that it must be rejected as an instrument for socialist transformation? This is certainly the overwhelming opinion of almost all Western intellectual thought from the right to the social democratic left. Or is the failure of such parties a result of overwhelming objective obstacles, which have not been fully understood, an understanding necessary to lead future parties to fulfillment of their revolutionary goals? Or are the contradictions that lead to failure built into the party model as a potential outcome, and it is necessary to develop new practices to deal with these problems within the Party, as well as new institutional arrangements among the people and between the people and their leaders? To try to answer these questions is central to the future of revolutionary Marxism, but can only be answered by future Marxists through political practice. We would contend that the necessity of leadership and of organizing it in a new way remains a central axiom of revolutionary Marxism, and at the present time, the Leninist attempt to develop such leadership has been and continues to be the indispensable guide in forging such leadership. We also admit that this political advance is in need of honest appraisal and change in the face of obvious shortcomings.

We also recognize in this work the significance of the famous aphorism that denying the mistakes of the past inevitably leads to their recapitulation. We indicated that clear-cut evaluation of such mistakes, taking into account the interweaving of context and personality in the analysis of political action, is often extremely difficult. It has led us to categorically reject reformist and social democratic Marxism as hopelessly opportunist with regard to socialist transition. Regardless of the apparent revolutionary rhetoric often heard by its practitioners, the political trajectory of such Marxism inevitably leads to full-fledged collaboration with capitalism. This problem has been the most pressing problem for Marxism since it is often most appealing to popular classes, demanding little of them while promising everything. This rightward form of socialist activity is so common and widespread that we have reserved the concept opportunism for this form alone.

Our analysis of anarchism demonstrates that it is really in a place of its own, especially with regard to the problem of opportunism and ultra-leftism. In the first place, anarchism is not a Marxist point of view. It is so varied in its manifestations that some forms of anarchism can take a clearly leftward as well as rightward direction. Sometimes anarchist practice takes a terrorist form against almost any established power, sometimes it postures as violent rebellion in circumstances that alienate most potential allies, and sometimes it is worker syndicalist refusing involvement with any reform activities. And sometimes it is strictly libertarian with contempt for the conditions of ordinary people. It can include such varied people as Bakunin, Kropotkin, Emma Goldman, Noam Chomsky, and as we have contended, someone as right wing as Ayn Rand. So much of anarchist activity has been considered progressive and so much has often contended and even collaborated with Marxist activity that we thought it necessary to deal with it in this volume. Our general conclusion with regard to anarchism is that it normally suffers from ultra-left idealism. It tends to romanticize oppressed groups in any time and place as the agents of revolutionary change. It also tends to reject all forms of reform, which it perceives as collaboration with the hated state. Finally, and most importantly, anarchism rejects and openly opposes the need for revolutionary leadership and a revolutionary state to the point of actively and violently attempting to overthrow such states. For all these reasons, we see anarchism as a major obstacle in any attempt to overthrow capital and to build a socialist society. In making this conclusion, we must reiterate that this in no way denies that it may be necessary to work with anarchists in specific situations, work which can only be decided in any specific political context.

In the history of Marxist political theory, the understanding of opportunist and ultra-left currents is extremely difficult, but in most cases such currents demonstrate definite theoretical postulates, and these postulates allow a fairly precise judgment of their opportunism; that is, wrongheaded theory is a good predictor of retrograde practice. Anarchism, however, presents the political activists with uniquely difficult problems. The roots of anarchism in individualist rebellion are widespread in a capitalist culture that sanctions rebellion against authority as part of the very lifeblood of that culture. Consolidated anarchism gives some theoretical coherence to this all-too-typical predisposition, yet often the essence of anarchist theory is the absence of theory, or more precisely a theory that no theory is necessary. In this case, along with the fact that left-wing anarchism is often displayed with a high degree of exciting militancy, the actions of anarchists are often highly attractive, especially to people in their first engagement with progressive politics. Moreover, under conditions of great crisis, anarchists are often first in the field, and depending upon historical context, they are the militants who act as positive stimulants for progressive action. This combination of the absence of theoretical direction and the presence of adventurous militancy within anarchism makes the question of context most important for tactical decisions facing Marxist politics.

Considering the issue of context, the question of Stalin should not be understood simply as a cult of personality or as a manifestation of Asiatic despotism. In light of the universal condemnation of the Soviet Union by the dominant capitalist world and the threat posed by US imperialism to the existence of the USSR, we have concentrated primarily on the consolidation of revisionism in the CPSU under Stalin. In our analysis, we are faced with a new form of revisionism that emerges under conditions of socialist transition as, first, a potential, which then congeals into a semi-permanent structure. In the Soviet case, we trace revisionism back to Stalin (with the potential contradictions already apparent in the very Leninist party that makes successful revolution possible). Revisionism was increasingly apparent in the degeneration of inner-party democracy and was made manifest in the Lenin recruitment. It is perhaps ironic that the CPSU was taking what Mao later called a "productivist" road through the period of collectivization, which was a necessary aspect of rapid industrialization. Revisionism became permanent in the 1930s, highlighted by the 1936 Constitution that proclaimed the USSR to be classless. At that point, it was no longer possible for the CPSU to again move 'left' towards a socialist transition. What grew instead under a form of revisionist capitalism was the groundwork for the development of a new bourgeois class in embryo leading to the final turn back to capitalism and, indeed, imperialism in Russia. There was a long period, during and after Stalin, when key economic structures of socialism remained in place in the USSR, so that it still represented an alternative economic and social form vis-s-vis global capitalism. But revisionism is and proved to be a temporary alternative. The final reversion to capitalism was, by and large, a peaceful transition in which the leading figures in control of the economic and political heights converted public to private ownership. Simultaneously, the political system was changed in its form to multi-party and the new bourgeois class was fully realized in all its dimensions as a ruling class.

As to Trotsky, here we must face the issue of contingency in its starkest form. Because of the nature of his personality and the specific historical conditions in which he lived, we have presented a nuanced view of his contributions and political short-comings. Since Trotsky himself died before the doctrine that bears his name became a continuing part of the Marxist scene, we have separated our evaluation of Trotsky's political career from that of the Trotskyism which emanated from his life. With Trotsky's life we see a political person of staunch revolutionary conviction and great leadership and intellectual qualities from an early age. When very young, he was a leading light in the first revolutionary upsurge in Russia in 1905. At that time, he opposed Lenin's conception of a Marxist political party while attempting to bring about a rapprochement between the Mensheviks and the Bolsheviks. While this was a hopeless venture, nobody, including Lenin and the whole of the revolutionary left would have considered it an unacceptable attempt at that time. That is, if Trotsky made mistakes along this path, it seems to us quite wrong-headed to condemn someone in hindsight for actions that any revolutionary could have taken. Moreover, on the question of the two most important events during the First World War, the necessary response by the proletariat to the war and the need for revolutionary insurrection in the October Revolution, Trotsky's actions are above reproach. Moreover, from the beginning of Soviet power until Lenin's death, Trotsky's contributions to the Revolution put him in the front rank of leadership second only to Lenin in world and Soviet recognition. Accordingly, and in opposition to many pro-Soviet Marxists at the time and to some Marxists today, we can find nothing fundamentally wrong with Trotsky's actions during this whole period.

After Lenin's death, however, things get a bit murkier in Trotsky's politics. The major political conflict in the Bolshevik Party up to and after Lenin's death was the problem of factionalism. The existence of differences within the Party, differences which, it seems to us, are inevitable, came up against the question: what differences from party consensus are considered acceptable and which ones represent the development of harmful factions? Given the crisis-ridden nature of the Soviet situation and the continued existence of reactionary classes and reactionary ideas, this problem has taken on special significance in all modern revolutions. Also given the revolutionary direction of the society, factional rebellion commonly manifests itself as more revolutionary than the party majority; that is, if wrong-headed, it will be an ultra-left manifestation. This was the case in the first great revolution, and Trotsky, over time, became the foremost representative of the ultra-left rebellion against the Party. In the usual evaluation of this activity from the left, it is common to attempt to distinguish the progressive from the retrogressive aspects of the Bolshevik Party from those of the left opposition (to which Trotsky first reluctantly and lately willingly belonged). The results of this kind of evaluation are a balance sheet, which supposedly indicates the side that was more correct than the other. We think that such an evaluation is only possible when a broader historical context is taken into consideration. The question is complicated because the Soviet Union under Stalin, as noted above, was moving towards revisionism. In part, the left opposition responded to the erosion of inner party democracy and the over-centralization of power. But it had a history stretching back to Brest-Litovsk, the commandism of war communism, and opposition to the NEP. It is not whether Trotsky was right or wrong in a particular policy decision, but the overall significance of his activities over a longer historical period, and they represent primarily an ultra-left turn in revolutionary history. Moreover, it is not decisions alone but the theoretical interpretations he gave to justify his decisions, justifications which became the central features in the ongoing political outlook that bears his name.

From what he considered the true Marxist perspective as opposed to the falsity of Soviet positions at the time, Trotsky considered that the October Revolution had been betrayed by the Soviet Party, saving his more pointed barbs for Stalin, often seen as the almost sole instigator of this betrayal. As a Marxist, he of course could not maintain an only personalist interpretation so he forwarded a theory that was more social and historical. He characterized the Soviet Union as a workers' state betrayed by a bureaucratic elite sitting atop a still revolutionary base. And, he surmised, the bureaucratic elite was a result of the continuation of Russia's feudal past expressed in the activities of the elite. Stalin then becomes a conniving, intriguing medieval monster who has taken over the reins of power. What was necessary was that the masses made revolutionary by the Soviet experience, and still powerful in this "workers' state," must simply overthrow this tiny elite. Whatever else this interpretation might be, it is not a Marxist interpretation. It is not a class analysis since it does not perceive of a socialist society as one still possessing classes. Only by avoiding a class analysis could Trotsky fully condemn Soviet leadership as tyrannical while upholding the idea of working-class control of the society. How Trotsky could maintain such a contradiction is partially explained and even justified by the fact that the clear-cut realization of the continuing class nature of a post-revolutionary socialist society was not articulated until the later development of this idea by Mao. Trotskyism, however, in its fixed notion that even later revolutions suffer from the horror of 'Stalinism' has always considered that it has special sensitivity and special theory to deserve to be the critic of such societies "from the left." For this reason, post-Soviet revolutions, which have all occurred in the third world and which perhaps have more sympathy with the difficulties faced by the Soviet experience, have been treated essentially as further manifestations of 'Stalinism.'

In the advanced capitalist world, Trotskyism has had great staying power. In an earlier chapter we have even mentioned that Trotskyists are often the only groups that articulate some of the central ideas of revolutionary Marxism. The problem of evaluating this phenomenon takes on special difficulty because there are such a variety of Trotskyist groups, often at odds with one other. We think that, in the present context, it would be too doctrinaire to condemn all of it with the same brush as was done in the earlier storm of 1930s politics. Trotskyist groups have sometimes done progressive work and are also, as has been suggested, often the only groups that rhetorically at least defend the idea of a Leninist party. In the recent past, however, this has been little more than rhetorical since Trotskyists in general seem to make easy alliance with the antics of all-pervasive anarchism. On these grounds and on the grounds of its facile theorizing, we have thus considered Trotskyism to be an ultra-left tendency in contemporary Marxist politics.

Finally, we considered the significance of Mao Zedong's contribution to Marxist political theory. It is our opinion that Mao has made major contributions to political Marxism, so much so that his ideas and actions often represent the most important advance over those attributed to Lenin. We have already mentioned the engagement with rural liberation rather than urban insurrection as a major revolutionary tactic by Mao. However, we do not consider this idea as unique to him because other later twentieth century revolutions, with little reference to Mao, have taken the rural revolutionary route. What distinguishes Mao's work is his central focus upon class and class ideology in the transitional period. In so doing, he is the first Marxist to recognize that the problem of class conflict is so embedded in this transitional period that this period must be seen as just that – transitional and therefore vulnerable to falling back into capitalism if the issue of class conflict is not addressed properly. Lenin's epigram that socialism can be defined as soviet power plus electrification now can be seen as still embedded in positivist assumptions. The socialist transition is not a smooth movement in which revolutionary control of the state assists in the building of an industrial society as the basis for an inevitable movement to classless communism. Instead it must be seen as a tumultuous period suffused with class conflict and facing dangers of counter-revolution both from within and without. This is especially the case where revolutionary change is occurring in underdeveloped, poor societies, which must go through the rigors of industrialization at the same time that an advanced capitalist world fears its example and wishes to destroy it.

We owe this new and advanced conception to Mao, a conception that is more in line with the most revolutionary assumptions of Marxism. Mao implemented numerous attempts to counter the solidification of bourgeois attitudes and actions with, among other tactics, mass ideological movements. These movements targeted these problems both within the population at large and, most significantly, in the top echelons of the Party. His realization that the top leaders were ready and willing to take "the capitalist road" led to his final attempt to meet what he considered this central problem in the transition period. He instituted a Cultural Revolution where top leaders faced criticism and where they and many intellectuals and cadres were sent to the countryside where, by working with ordinary people, they were supposed to be cleansed of backward attitudes and behavior. After ten years, this Revolution failed in its goal, and with Mao's death, the criticized leaders took power and initiated capitalism in China. It appears to us that Mao's analysis of the problem of potential bourgeois class restoration under socialism is probably a sound one. His method of dealing with it was obviously full of mistakes, the proof of which stands fully before us in a capitalist and potentially imperialist China. The lack of appropriate response to this problem represents a fundamental crisis in Marxist political theory, one which future revolutionaries must resolve since without its resolution, political theory has reached a dead end in the sustaining of revolutionary change.

Typical and more normal opportunism tends to glorify and often idealize successful practice while denying revolutionary theory. With ultra-leftism, the tenets of revolutionary theory become the programme and slogans of every day practice regardless of the context. While paying obeisance to the need to analyze context, ultra-leftists always overblow and inflate both themselves and the revolutionary possibilities in whatever context they happen to be acting. During the ultra-left upsurge in what was called the new communist movement in the 1970s, for example, the numerous sects in Canada proclaimed that the Canadian working class at that time demonstrated militancy and consciousness similar to the Russian working class at the beginning of the twentieth century. They also demanded of its members that only revolutionary calls for an overthrow of the bourgeois state and a dictatorship of proletariat, and soon, be made to the working class, and condemned as economist any attempts on picket lines to support better wages or working conditions. These sects inflated and idealized both contexts and themselves announcing literally out of nowhere that they were communist parties. As over-excited adventurers, they did not and do not last long, but they cause a great deal of trouble by attacking progressive activities; they also make Marxism look ridiculous while confirming the typical lies that are conventionally made about left-wing revolutionaries.

To be specific, let us look at the great anarchist upsurge during the Vietnam War period. Opposition to imperialist invasion and occupation of Vietnam increased greatly concomitant with expansion of American military involvement and intensive bombing of that small country. The American policy of drafting all males of a certain age – particularly African-Americans – was the centerpiece of youthful opposition, especially in the United States. A number of side issues involving university governance and cultural rebellion has led some to perceive that a major revolutionary possibility had developed during that period. There is little question that the underlying ideological atmosphere of what is still conceived as a new left was anarchist. What distinguished the anarchism of the new left from earlier anarchism is that its most articulate spokespersons conceived that they were renewing Marxism, quite different from the totally anti-Marxism of much of earlier anarchism. More to the point, the constituency that followed the new left, mainly rebellious youth and students, made forays within and without a highly raucous and highly amorphous movement. When the dust had settled, the repeal of the draft had been won, much counter-cultural *bric-à-brac* had been added to the color of bourgeois society and, more pointedly, the new left had burned out with a small minority moving to individual terrorism and later into ultra-left Marxism, or into comfortable professional or academic careers. Strangely this period was accepted uncritically by the Marxism of the time and is still treated rather romantically by much nostalgic writing about that period. Given that the whole movement was suffused with ultra-leftist practices, that other progressive voices had been silenced or were inactive, what could Marxism have done besides supporting the progressive parts of the movement, its anti-war and anti-draft content while doing what it could to discover some part of the movement, which might move beyond ultra-leftism? What is meant by critical support is all that was possible, for here was a case where there were little else but anarchists to support.

Spontaneous and often creatively militant outbursts of anarchist rebellion can often be a catalyst for progressive action. Witness the whirlwind of rebellious action by the IWW (International Workers of the World) in the early twentieth century, action not condemned by Lenin since it represented spontaneous working class militancy. This is why the problem of tactical support of individualized rebellion becomes extremely tricky, especially with the recent upsurge of the Occupy movement, a movement that possesses a strong anarchist current but includes many inexperienced youth in a far more precarious economic future than the original new left, and existing in the context of an unprecedented environmental crisis. The fact that the Marxist left and even working class militants have largely remained on the sidelines of the environmental movement demands that Marxism must take a fresh look at the necessity for tactical engagement with rebellious youth involved in the global warming catastrophe. The issues and the historical context have now changed, but the substructure of individualized rebellion defended on much of the old anarchist ground is as strong as ever. But that change, it seems to US, demands an even greater tactical flexibility than demanded before.

To put the matter more generally, the valid postulates of Marxist revolutionary theory are a general guide for successful revolutionary practice. As such, they tell very little about what should be done in any particular context. In fact, it has occurred that great revolutionary leaders in conditions unexpected by prevailing theory have broken with such theory resulting in the need to revise theory, making its ideas more relevant for a repetition of such circumstances. This has certainly been the case in the actions of Lenin in the Russian Revolution, Mao Zedong in the Chinese Revolution, and to a degree in Cuba. Under prevailing Marxist orthodoxy in Lenin's time revolution was supposed to occur first in societies whose productive system had reached full fruition When Lenin declared that the time was ripe for socialist insurrection, only his status and argumentation won the day; the arguments he presented, as we are suggesting here, were based on what he considered changed circumstances. The success in implementing these arguments resulted in new developments in revolutionary theory itself. The same kind of point can be made with regard to Mao Zedong's rejection of Soviet advice in the 1920s that China follow the Soviet urban proletarian insurrectionary model, resulting in a new political emphasis on creating rural liberated base areas depending upon the peasantry as the leading revolutionary force. And his theory of the capitalist road as representing the concrete manifestation of a form of opportunism within a Leninist party is also a major contribution to Marxist theory.

What has faced advanced capitalism has been the continued crises and depredations predicted by Marxist political economy, but without the revolutionary situations within which revolutionary guidelines become appropriate. We also know that those political organizations on the left of the political spectrum, which in principal reject the need for revolutionary transformation, are mired in defense of bourgeois democracy as the only means to change things for the better; that is, they suffer from what may be called electoral fetishism. All this means that revolutionary Marxism really possesses little in the way of a political theory to deal with non-revolutionary circumstances. With such difficulties, the best that

Marxists can do is attempt to be tribunes of the people, to support all those progressive causes that continue to infuse capitalist reality. This may still be all to the good but it makes all-important the problem of specific historical context, especially when anarchist forces are a significant part of the fray.

What we are here calling political theory represents the guidelines for actions necessary for the transformation of capitalism into socialism as well as some lessons for problems in the predictable transitional periods. As guidelines, they confront political action with problems somewhat different from the usual problems faced by political economy. First of all revolutionary guidelines are typically guidelines for revolutionary action, and therefore are significant for revolutionary situations. Almost all of contemporary Western history has been noticeably without revolutionary situations. Except perhaps for the short periods early in the twentieth century, after the world wars in some places, and in the great depression in the 1930s, there have not been periods when revolutionary guidelines would dictate political strategy and tactics. Even the events of 1968 in France, which have often been presented by new left activists as potentially revolutionary and therefore in need of revolutionary action, seem, in hindsight at least, to be dubious in their potential, not least because the trade union movement and the French Communist Party settled early and easily for the limited goal of new elections.

We reiterate that there is nothing new for Marxism to make great compromises in the face of difficult concrete conditions. Along with Lenin's dictum about revolutionary theory was his recognition of the need for a "concrete analysis of concrete conditions." And concrete conditions often demand practical compromises divergent from the abstract guidelines of socialist transformation. In Lenin's case, for example, the Bolshevik battle cry before its access to power in 1917 was "bread, peace, and land," hardly anything close to a socialist programme. What makes this tactical compromise revolutionary was that Lenin, while making it, never loses sight of the need for real socialist policy as soon as it becomes a possibility. In this way the seemingly contradictory demands for a revolutionary theory divergent from immediate compromise are not a compromise at all. This is quite different from the compromise made by social democracy; it rejects in principle the very tenets of revolutionary theory and in principle embraces bourgeois democracy as the only means for progressive social change.

The historical context in contemporary North America, and Europe as well, presents, if possible, even greater problems in the relation between theory and practice. First of all, there has never been a successful socialist transformation in any advanced industrial country, which means that there is no historical model to turn to as a baseline for action. Second, and more importantly, the working class as a potential leading agent of revolutionary change has become moribund. Not only is its present stage of union membership at its lowest level in the modern era; the leadership of the class is at best totally involved in day-to-day economic issues and at worst merely treading water. This has put the onus of progressive action on youth and student activism where immediate rebellion is the order of the day. It explains the rather overwhelming presence of the anarchist animus in most recent militant activity. Marxism is either extremely weak or found mostly in academic surroundings, demonstrating a definite academic style. When Marxism has erupted in practice as in the 1970s, it has been ultra-left Marxism, an ultra-leftism that not only accords well with anarchism, but has even been initiated by former new left activists looking for newer playing fields. In both cases, burnout was the fairly inevitable outcome.

Mao has often been quoted as saying that revolution is not a dinner party. We believe that this aphorism is more profound than it sounds. Part of the legacy of prior revolutionary experience involves images of large popular explosions, which overthrow all forms of entrenched tyranny, much like the images so well presented in Victor Hugo's *Les Miserable*. This insurrectionary phase is clearly no dinner party, but we think that Mao was suggesting something even more difficult in the process of socialist transformation. The time after successful insurrection, the time of socialist transition, seems to present unforeseen and heretofore insoluble problems. The regime is not assured of automatic success and the transition is just that, a transition that may take a long time and can go backwards as well as forwards. Indeed, it can, as we have seen, be aborted and produce new forms of capitalism. It is to Mao then that we owe the idea that classes continue to exist throughout the transition with the most backward attitudes and ideologies existing in the leadership of the revolution itself. Classes have to be defined by more than simply the ownership of productive property. Beyond attitudes, a potential new ruling class in embryo emerges in control of the Party bureaucracy and in dominant and powerful economic positions. The move to fully-defined classes occurs after the infrastructure of a new bourgeois class is already in place, a process Mao termed the "capitalist road" and, we argue, reflects revisionism within the Party. A revolutionary regime cannot simply take power and assume that the future is secure and certain. Any regime must look for stability, but stability in a revolutionary transition is a contradiction in terms. It is because of our own sense of the difficulty of this situation that we can say little about how to solve problems that arise in the great transition. We can only offer the optimism that future revolutions, which we think must occur, will find the way. Part of this way, we think, however, is to learn the few lessons still important from the past.

Poor agricultural nations are forced to meet what Engels called the tyranny of mechanized production for the time it takes to develop a level of industrialized that took capitalism over a hundred years. How can this be done without the carrot of unequal payment and the stick of insecure employment, for this is the way of capitalism and it is this way that must be done away with? We do now know that almost all existing socialist revolutions have returned to the capitalist path to industrialization, and we now think that they became examples, when proclaiming themselves Marxist, of a somewhat hybrid society, which we have called revisionist capitalism, a societal form that we consider tenuous and short term. Future Marxist activists facing similar problems are the only ones to resolve these problems. It is our contention that Marxism will not even reach the stage of confronting these problems unless it understands and applies the lessons we have tried to articulate in this book.

Climate Change

THE GUIDELINES and pitfalls we have presented may have little strategic relevance in the present for rather unique and unexpected reasons. The first has to do with the fact that the capitalist class in the advanced capitalist countries is at the present time in almost complete command over the working classes and the working classes are not an organizational counterweight to this command; the latter have even seen almost all their former gains systematically taken from them. In short, there is nothing resembling real working class opposition to capitalism. As for a socialist movement, it is pretty much disconnected from the class it is supposed to represent. Second, an overriding issue has arisen, which has changed the trajectory traditionally connected to historical Marxism. That issue is global warming and climate change caused mainly by the extraction and burning of fossil fuels, which continue to provide the energy for the process of modern industrialization. The destructive effects of capitalist industrialization upon the very planet on which we live have put in jeopardy the future of humanity as we know it.

According even to the most optimistic scientific predictions, the tipping point in climate change, that point in which runaway change cannot be stopped, is very close to occurring (some claim that it is already upon us). While we are still sure as Marxists that if capitalism follows it normal trajectory it will continue to generate crises and that, soon or later, socialism will become the only solution to the horrors of this system, the present unprecedented crisis gives us no time for this kind of optimism. Climate change is intimately connected with industrialization (whether capitalist or revisionist) and we do not doubt that socialism would be the best way for humanity to deal with this crisis. Presently, however, genuine socialism is hardly on the historical agenda, and this agenda is seriously foreshortened by the impending ecological crisis.

Climate change imprints a completely new quality on the present historical context. Combined with the political absence of working class militancy (and the attendant strength of the ruling capitalist class) is a crisis facing the very sustainability of the human species. The global warming generated by capitalist industrialization has created the possibility, in fact the probability, of environmental catastrophe. Moreover, the only social force responding to this crisis has been indigenous people with little power and youth often more inexperienced politically than the youth in the earlier new left but still suffused with a similar type of rebellion. Yet, with working class and traditional progressive forces mainly muted on the environmental front, what else follows from these quarters but a clearly compromising response? And who but the kind of youth found in the recent Occupy movement can be expected to initiate rebellion?

The destruction of sustainability of the earth's resources by capitalism was clearly indicated in the work of Marx and Engels. But they understandably expected the problems associated with capitalism's destructiveness, by its drive for profit at all costs, to be transcended with the overthrow of capitalism and the onset of socialism before such a catastrophe could occur. Even with the great disappointment they faced with failed revolutions in Europe in 1848 and with the destruction of the short-lived Paris Commune in 1871, they could not imagine that a powerful world-wide capitalism would be thriving, more or less, into the twenty-first century.

Moreover, the socialist revolutions, which were expected to occur in the advanced capitalist countries, have occurred in poor underdevelopment countries where the difficulties due to underdevelopment and the threats and actual military interventions by rich imperialist countries have generated insoluble problems often leading to the end of socialism and the restoration of capitalism in these countries. In the rich nations, the weakness of the working class has left it fighting to maintain the few gains it made in the post-Second World War period; in North America the vast majority of workers is without even the protection of union membership. The condition of atomization and weakness of the organized working class has left it palpably absent from the fight against climate change.

The threat of environmental catastrophe is serious enough, but to happen in contemporary circumstances presents Marxism with an extremely difficult dilemma. Even with great mistakes and great failures, Marxism could always remain optimistic since time was on our side. It seemed almost inevitable that capitalist irrationality and crises, and the class struggle engendered by them, would lead to a socialist victory and a transition, even with more failures, to a classless future. Now this future might be even farther removed and more difficult to reach because there are not enough socialist forces to counter the looming end of human sustainability. It is interesting that China, which most pundits and scholars in the West now claim has little to do with socialism, has a better record in confronting climate change than the United States or Canada.

Marxists have never been reluctant to look hell in the face, but we have never confronted exactly this kind of planetary catastrophe. The guidelines for Marxist revolution presented in this book still retain their long-term validity, and they are of particular significance in those places where revolutionary movements have the greatest potential, such as in Latin America. They remain significant guidelines if we can get safely through the environmental crisis. Some Marxists, recognizing the crisis and seeing its cause in the inherent destructiveness of capitalism, proclaim the need for nothing less than socialist transformation to counter it. While having fundamental validity, such proclamations have almost no political force behind them and, as such, do nothing but leave us fiddling while Rome burns. Undoubtedly, the devastating consequences of climate change on some of the poorest people and regions will lead spontaneously to widespread social rebellions. In the present conjuncture, given the absence of progressive, not to say Leninist leadership, these rebellions will likely degenerate into ultra-nationalist or other forms of fundamentalism.

Bluntly, the environmental crisis is upon us and there is no realistic left-wing programme to do anything about it. The concrete conditions for such a programme are not auspicious. They may even demand a kind of compromise with capitalism, at least in certain of its forms, that has always been anathema to Marxist practice.

We certainly would be utopian to believe that capitalism would limit its hunger for profit by embracing fully green investment. But there are sprouts of a wide multi-class movement to control climate change, and even parts of the ruling class see the necessity for green investment and for limiting carbon emissions. The revisionist capitalism of China with its greater mechanism of centralized decision making as well as China's overwhelming urban pollution (created by the demands of early capitalist industrialization) has been forced into the forefront of a greener capitalism. It is probable that this is the direction that Marxist practice should take in the present and for the foreseeable time.

There is an environmental movement and while recently it has added climate justice to its policy directives, it suffers from its connection to capital itself and is implicitly and often explicitly aligned with some capitalists as potentially green and even others connected to the capitalist sources of the problem. This movement is, in most places, all we have at the moment, and it is incumbent on Marxists to make the necessary compromises and join the fray. At its most effective, the movement locates the fossil fuel industry as the culprits who must be fought and, in this sense, Marxism can imagine common strategy and policy. Green capitalism may be anathema to Marxist analysis, but at the present moment it is tactically important to support, among other more collective actions, potential cleavages within the ruling class as they are now beginning to display themselves. Appealing to the conscience of capitalists is necessary, but what is most useful in this context is a mass international people's movement prepared to be militant and demanding private and public action on climate change. We are not abandoning Marxism by making this claim, which advocates reforms and, in our view, is not reformist. We are simply realizing that this great threat to our species demands a different set of tactical guidelines in the present and immediate future, given the very limited options for socialist politics. And it means continuing to locate the fundamental problem behind our ecological crisis in capitalist industrialization itself. That is, like any new programme demanded by concrete circumstances, participation and even leadership of the environmental movement does not negate the principles of socialist transition that have been discussed and enunciated in this book. Tactical alliances are meant to come to an end, and that part of the future must continue to be theorized and sustained ideologically.

In concluding our review of the history and results of over a century of politically-active Marxism, we wish we could assert with some certainty what has and what must be done to liberate humankind from the depredations and stark injustices generated by industrializing and industrialized capitalism. Sadly this does not appear to be the case. Instead, we think we have left the reader with a sense of failure and mistakes, of opportunism and ultra-leftism parading as Marxism, of what *not to do* rather than what *to do*. We do think, however, engagement with revolutionary work demands knowledge of those fundamental mis-steps and wrong avenues, since the absence of such knowledge very simply leads to their repetition. Moreover, the demarcation of positive guidelines to political action, though only guidelines in a labyrinth of inevitable concrete difficulties and contingencies, are still fundamental in the way forward.

If revolutionary activists do not know the contours and limits of social democracy, Trotskyism, anarchism, and ultra-leftism, then it is fairly certain that one or another of these false siren calls may draw them into what history has proven to be dangerous and counter-productive. In making this claim, we must repeat that a critique of these historical dead ends does not mean that Marxist must never unite with all and sundry individuals and groups in the progressive demands of contingency and circumstance since this unity is the stuff of everyday political work, especially in the face of climate change and impending ecological catastrophe. It does mean that awareness of these problems is a fundamental preparation for obstacles and dangers that these false outlooks and activities will present, especially in crisis situations where they must be dealt with in forceful and straightforward ways.

APPENDIX

Details of Lineage and Political Connections in Ma Village

Brigade Head Ma Jin-you

MA JIN-YOU had five sons and four daughters, and five of them married within the village. Second son Ma Shi-guo married Ma Yu-ying, first daughter Ma Pei-ying married Li Hong-xiang, third son Ma Shi-sui married Ma Xiu-shan, fifth son Ma Shi-ye married Ma Zong-teng, and third daughter Ma Chun-ying married Ma Shi-yuan.

Bridgade Mediator Ma Yu-shan

MA YU-SHAN had five children and three of them married in the village. First son married Jiang, first daughter married Li Zhan-lin, the party secretary's third son, and second son married Ma Xiu-mei.

Some of the families seemingly had no direct connections, but they often were connected indirectly. For example, Ma Jin-you and Ma Yu-shan had no direct connection. But Ma Jin-you's fifth daughter-in-law Ma Zong-teng, her uncle Ma Xian-zen's second daughter Ma Zong-qin married Ma Xian-gui, and Ma Xian-gui's brother was Ma Xian-sui, whose daughter Ma Xiu-mei married Ma Yu-shan's second son.

Table 3 Connection Diagram of Party Members

Team 1	Team 2		Team 3	Team 4
Li Xuehua	Ma Suifa	Zhao Yuxi	Huang Shumin	Ma Xiangbo
Li Zhanyou	Yang Zhie	Ma Junming	Ma Xuemin	Ma Xiangbin
Li Xuetai	Ma Jingju	Ma Yingzeng	Ma Shiyi	Ma Caisan
Li Guanting	Ma Jinxi	Ma Guozeng	Ma Jinyou	Ma Xianggui
Wang Honghua	Ma Jinsheng	Ma Guangshan	Ma Xinzeng	Li Hongjian
Wang Meiguang	Ma Xueqi	Wang Peie	Ma Xuegu	Ma Xueliang
Wang Shuqin	Ma Junyao			
Li Hongfu	Ma Youshan			
Ma Yushan	Zhao Yutian			

Appendix

The following are relations that are interwoven:

Primary Relations	Secondary Relations
In-laws	Wang Honghua's sister married Ma Junyao's third uncle
Ma Yushan's first daughter married Li Hongjian's third son	Wang Honghua's wife is Ma Yushan's niece
Ma Jinyou's third daughter married Ma Xueliang's fourth son	Ma Guozeng's father is Ma Junyao's grandfather's third brother
Ma Junyao's father-in-law is Li Xuehua	Ma Suifa's father is Ma Yushan's third uncle
Ma Xiangbo's father-in-law is Zhao Yuxi	Yang Zhie's father-in-law is Ma Yushan's third uncle
Family	Ma Jinyou's third daughter-in-law is the brother of Ma Jingju's son-in-law
Ma Xueqi is Wang Peie's husband	Ma Jinyou's eldest son-in-law is Li Hongfu's fourth brother
Ma Suifa is sister-in-law is Yang Zhie	*Same Clan*
Ma Yingzeng is Ma Junming's first son	Ma Guangshan, Ma Youshan, Ma Yushan
Ma Jinxi is Ma Jingju's third son	Ma Jingju is Ma Jinyou's uncle within five generations
Ma Jingsheng is Ma Jingju's second son	Li Xuehua, Lu Xuetai
	Ma Xueqi, Ma Xueliang, Ma Xuemin, Ma Xuegu
Ma Youshan is Ma Guozeng's fifth uncle	Ma Xiangbo, Ma Xianggui, Ma Xiangbin
Ma Youshan's eldest brother is Ma Junyao's grandfather	Zhao Yutian, Zhao Yuxi
Huang Shumin is Ma Xinzeng's third uncle's wife	Ma Yingzeng, Ma Xinzeng, Ma Guozeng

- 349 -

ENDNOTES

1 All the data on Ma village come from the following two books: Ma Zhanbin, *The Empty Village: A Quantitative Analysis of Ma Village in East Shandong from Early Ming to the present,* Changchun: Jilin University Press, 2013, Chinese Edition and Ma Zhanbin, *Kinship and Marriage: Intra and Inter-Ma Village Transformations in Rural Shandong (1886-2012),* Guilin: Guangxi Normal University Press, 2014, Chinese Edition.

2 For example, Ma Tai-shan's son Ma Ji had a daughter but no son, so a male from a relative in another village was adopted, Ma Tong-fa, to carry on the family line. For those families with only daughters, usually a son-in-law would be married in from other villages and he would assume the role of a son; thus future generation would still carry the maternal family line. Sometimes, if the family no longer had male offspring (dead or moved), then children of a married daughter would be brought in to look after their maternal grandparents; the Zhao's in Ma village, having continued for eight generations, is an example. Or if the daughter was married out, a related family usually within five generations upon mutual agreement would look after the elderly, then the house and land would be bestowed upon the related family. Like Rui-wu and his wife who had no children, they for example, were looked after jointly by two of Lai-feng's grandsons Xian-zeng and Shu-zeng,

Endnotes

and Xiang-wu's grandson Shao-zeng. The three divided the land and the house. Ma Chuan-jing had one daughter married to a man from Upper Yang Village and this couple was looked after by Ma Pi-qin, son of Ma Cheng-jiu.

3 Jiang-feng (silver dollar 5 *yuan*, copper coins 37 *qianwen*), Xue-wu (silver dollar 40 *yuan*), Chun-fang (copper coins 40 *qianwen*), Lai-feng (silver dollar 20 *yuan* , copper coins 5.6 *qianwen)*, Zhu-feng (silver dollar 25 *yuan*), Tong-xian (silver dollar 10 *yuan*, copper coins 7.5 *qianwen*), Xi-jing (copper coins 15.4 *qianwen*), Dian-wu (silver dollar 15 *yuan*), Bi-feng (silver dollar 15 *yuan*), Fu-jing (silver dollar 15 *yuan*), Xun-feng (silver dollar 14 *yuan*).

4 Ma Xu-zeng (Jun-fu's first son, and Jun-fu is Jiang-feng's first son), Ma Jin-zeng (Jun-fu's third son); Ma Guang-rong (Jun-lu's only son, and Jun-lu is Jiang-feng's second son). Ma Guang-rong, Ma Xu-zeng and Ma Jin-zeng were all long-time major peasant families, and Jun-qi, Jiang-feng's third son, did not live in the village. Ma Jun-yong (other name Ma Jin-tang), first son of Ma Xue-wu; Ma Jun-shou (Xue-wu's second son, Jun-shou has two sons Fu-zeng and Xiao-zen, and one daughter Shu-lan); Ma Xue-min (Xue-wu's third son), had three sons and one daughter. All of them lived in the village and were considered of rich peasant background.

5 Ma Xun-feng, Ma Bi-feng and Ma Zhu-feng were three sons of Ma Hong-xiang. Ma Xun-feng immigrated to Qingdao, Shandong's most commercialized coastal city. His descendants all live in Qingdao. Ma Bi-feng (with wife Feng Wei-zhi) had a first daughter named Jun-ci, only son Jun-you, and a second daughter Jun-lian. Jun-you married Wang Hong-sheng, resulting in no children. Jun-you was doing business in the Northeast and married a Japanese woman, Yasu Shi. They had three sons Chun-yi, Chun-zhong and Chun-ji, and one daughter Chun-ying. Ma Fu-qian, Ma Fu-shou, Ma Fu-zhong, and Ma Fu-hou were four sons of Ma Tong-xian. Ma Fu-qian and Ma Tong-lun went to the Northeast working for Ma Bao-jing, and later on his own doing business

in Manchuria. The family back home was then able to purchase more land. Descendants of Fu-qian and Fu-shou did not live in the village, and Fuzhong's daughter married out to Liu village and his wife remarried after Fuzhong's death and left Ma village. Fu-zhong, Fu-hou and son Xiang-guo were all rich peasant families. The family whose past generations did not donate, yet were still classified as a rich peasant family, was Ma Jun-long, whose father Ma Kui-wu had three sons, Ma Jun-cai, Ma Jun-ye (living in Tianjin), and Ma Jun-long. Ma Kui-wu somehow missed the opportunity to make the donation. Ma Jun-ye joined Ma Bao-jing and pursued business in Harbin, and sent home money to purchase land.

6 Zhu-feng was also a businessman in the Northeast and passed away when his daughter was three. Zhu-feng's wife Huang Ti-zhi bought a cow for her daughter and son-in-law with her gold ring and also gave five mu of land to the new couple as presents. Huang was not classified as a rich peasant, yet Jun-you and his son were both considered as rich peasants.

7 For instance, sub-plots #57-60 formed a bigger plot of only 11.2 *mu*, were owned by four different brigades, they were #57 Yang Brigade (3.4 *mu*), #58 Zhang Brigade (1.2 *mu*), #59 Zhang Brigade (1.0 *mu*), #60 Li (1.8 *mu*), and Ma Brigade (3.8 *mu*). After exchanging and consolidating, plots #57 and #59 were allocated to Team One of Ma Brigade, and the rest to Team Two of Ma Brigade. Apparently these four plots were owned by at least four families (as there were two sub-plots from Zhang village) from four different villages before land reform.

8 These positions seem dubious since prostitution almost always takes place in a context of *unequal* exchange while seduction is also suffused with a repressive ambience, as long as social conditions generally engender higher status males having sexual *rights* to lower status women.

Endnotes

9 Seen in this way male prostitution becomes possible, and occurs, but with less frequency given the generally higher social position of men. For this reason also, it is probably common in the male homosexual community.

10 This information was gleaned during one of the author's one-year stays in China in 1979-80 and in 1986-87.

11 It must be granted that these poor and less developed societies have made important strides in securing greater economic independence and equality for women while providing more public service to alleviate some traditional female burdens (for example, expanding daycare facilities, maternity leaves, etcetera).

REFERENCES

Engels, Friedrich *The Peasant Question in France and Germany,* Volume 3, Marx and Engels *Selected Works.*

Freedman, Maurice *Chinese Lineage and Society: Fukien and Kwangtung,* London: Athlone Press, 1966.

Hinton, William Review of Robert Weil's *Red Cat, White Cat, Monthly Review,* New York, 1996.

Lee, Ching Kwan *Against the Law: Labour Protests in China's Rustbelt and Sunbelt,* Berkeley: University of California Press, 2007.

Liang, Xiao-min "The Root Cause of China's Tyranny for Two Millennia," *Dongfang Daily Book Review,* Shanghai, 8 August 2010.

Liu, Chang *Peasants and Revolution in Rural China: Rural Political Change in the North China Plain and the Yangzi Delta, 1850-1949,* London and New York: Routledge, 2007.

Lu, Huilin "Model and Transformation of Social Stratification in Rural China," *Zhongguoxiangcunyanjiu* [Rural Chinese Studies], Beijing: Commercial Press, 2003, Chinese Edition.

References

Mao, Zedong "Analysis of the Classes in Chinese Society," *Selected Works of Mao Zedong,* Beijing: People's Press, 2005, Chinese Edition.

Qin, Hui *Tian Yuan Shi Yu Kuang, Xiang Qu (Eclogue and Rhapsody),* Beijing: Yu Wen Press, 2010.

Qin, Hui *Peasantry and Chinese Rural Society,* Lecture 2012, Qinhua University.

Skinner, G. William "Marketing and Social Structure in Rural China, Part I," *Journal of Asian Studies* 24, 1 (Nov. 1964).

Szonyi, Michael A. *Practicing Kinship: Lineage and Descent in Late Imperial China.* Stanford: Stanford University Press, 2002.

Wang, Jia-fan *The General History of China,* Shanghai: East China Normal University Press, 2000.

Wei Sen "Fiscal and Taxation Reform and China's Economic Growth," *Southern Metropolis Daily (*Nan Fang Du Shi Bao), April 6, 2014.

Wen Jia-bao *Government's Work Report,* 2011, http://www.china.com.cn/policy/txt/ 2011-03/16/content_22150608.htm.

Wen Tie-jun *Why Can't Our Country Implement Private Land Ownership in the Rural Areas,* http://www.aisixiang.com/data/24349.html, Jan.18, 2009.

Xie Wei-yang *Early Chinese State,* Hangzhou: Zhejiang People's Press, 1995.

Zhu Xue-qin "China in the Past 30 Years – Two Reforms," preface to *The Chinese Media Storms,* Hong Kong: Cosmo Book, 2008.